G

HIGHLIGHT

3

Cornelsen

English G · Highlight · Band 3

Im Auftrag des Verlages herausgegeben von
Frank Donoghue, Nenagh, Irland

Konzepterarbeitung von
Susan Abbey, Nenagh, Irland
Wolfgang Biederstädt, Köln
Frank Donoghue, Nenagh, Irland

Erarbeitet von
Sydney Thorne, York
Susan Abbey, Nenagh, Irland
Frank Donoghue, Nenagh, Irland

in Zusammenarbeit mit der Englischredaktion
Susanne Döpper (Projektleitung), Silvia Wiedemann (koordinierende Redakteurin), Britta Bensmann, Eva Baumgart (Bildredaktion) sowie Jenny Dames, Michael Dunkel, Sandhya Gupta, Annegret Hauser, Anne Linder, Karin Wedepohl

Vokabelanhang
Ingrid Raspe, Düsseldorf

Beratende Mitwirkung
Armin Düpmeier, Warendorf; Petra Klein, Villmar; Christa Lüdemann, Hannover; Tobias Pfeifer, Dossenheim; Stefan Royl, Lörrach; Dagmar Wengh, Ankum; Ellen Wiegard-Kaiser, Bielefeld sowie Herbert Willms, Herford

Layoutkonzept und technische Umsetzung
Klein & Halm Grafikdesign, Berlin

Umschlaggestaltung
Cornelsen Verlag Design unter Verwendung der Entwürfe von Klein & Halm Grafikdesign, Berlin und kleiner & bold, Berlin

www.cornelsen.de

1. Auflage, 2. Druck 2016

Alle Drucke dieser Auflage sind inhaltlich unverändert und können im Unterricht nebeneinander verwendet werden.

Druck: Mohn Media Mohndruck, Gütersloh

ISBN 978-3-06-032758-4 – broschiert
ISBN 978-3-06-032759-1 – gebunden

PEFC
PEFC/04-31-1033

PEFC zertifiziert
Dieses Produkt stammt aus nachhaltig bewirtschafteten Wäldern und kontrollierten Quellen.

www.pefc.de

Dein Englischbuch enthält folgende Teile:

Unit 1 bis 4	Die vier Kapitel des Buches
In Ireland	Ein fakultatives, kurzes Kapitel zum Abschluss
Diff-Bank	Weitere Aufgaben – unterschiedlich schwer
Wordbank	Zusätzliche Wörter zu bestimmten Themen
Text file TF	Interessante Texte, passend zu den Units
Skills file SF	Beschreibung wichtiger Lern- und Arbeitstechniken
Language file LF	Zusammenfassung wichtiger Sprachregeln
Vocabulary	Wörterverzeichnis zum Lernen der neuen Wörter
Dictionary	Alphabetisches Wörterverzeichnis zum Nachschlagen (*English-German* und *German-English*)

Die Units bestehen aus diesen Teilen:

Lead-in	Einstieg in die neue Unit
Theme 1 / Theme 2	Neue Themen mit vielen Aktivitäten und Übungen
Story	Eine Geschichte zum Lesen
Skills training	Hören | Listening (L) – Lesen | Reading (R) – Sprechen | Speaking (S) – Schreiben | Writing (W) – Sprachmittlung | Mediation (M) – Hör-Sehverstehen | Viewing (V)
Focus on language	Texte und Aufgaben zum Entdecken von Regeln und Üben wichtiger Strukturen
STOP! CHECK! GO!	Üben, Vertiefen, Lernfortschritt feststellen

In den Units findest du diese Symbole:

	Partnerarbeit / Gruppenarbeit
	Nur auf CD / Auf CD und im Schülerbuch
	Filme auf der DVD
○	Leichtere Übungen
●	Schwierigere Übungen
○ //●	Bei dieser Aufgabe gibt es eine leichte Variante in der Unit und eine schwierigere in der Diff-Bank.
More help p. 125	Hilfen zu einer Aufgabe in der Diff-Bank
More practice 1 p. 123	Weitere Übungen in der Diff-Bank

INHALT

	Lerninhalte	Your task (Lernaufgabe)	Texte
Unit 1 I love London 	· etwas über London erzählen · seine Meinung zu Mode äußern · Zustimmung und Ablehnung ausdrücken · sagen, was man tun muss, kann oder soll	**London plans** Ein Poster zum Thema *A Great Day in London* gestalten (S. 13) 	**Quiz** *What do you know about London?* (S. 8) **Magazine** *What's special about London?* (S. 10) **Advert** *London adverts* (S. 12) **Story** *Clever Sherlock!* (S. 14–15)
***Revision** (simple past)			
Unit 2 Country life 	· über das Leben auf dem Land und in der Stadt sprechen · sagen wie etwas geschah · einen Kommentar verfassen · ein Bild beschreiben · sagen, dass man etwas schon einmal oder noch nie gemacht hat	**Find out about students in your class** Eine Umfrage durchführen (S. 41) 	**Picture story** *This isn't a park!* (S. 31) **Article** *Well done, Molly!* (S. 32) **Story** *The country detectives* (S. 34–35) **Internet forum** *My ideal place* (S. 37)
***Revision** (will-future)			
Unit 3 Liverpool – the world in one city 	· Liverpool und seine Geschichte kennen lernen · sich mit Problemen in der Schule auseinander setzen · über Essen sprechen · seine persönliche Meinung ausdrücken · sagen, was passiert, wenn ... · Vergleiche anstellen	**Are you good at business?** Einen Geschäftsplan entwickeln und vorstellen (S. 53) 	**Letter** *A letter from school* (S. 51) **Dialogue** *What's wrong?* (S. 52) **Story** *Something special* (S. 54–55) **Article** *Liverpool girls want to be like Tasha!* (S. 56)
***Revision** (simple present)			

	Kompetenzen	Sprache	Seite
	Listening and Speaking | Hören und Sprechen Seine persönliche Meinung äußern (S. 18) An einer Diskussion teilnehmen (S. 18) **Writing course 1 | Schreiben** Ideen sammeln: Listen, *networks*, Vorlagen nutzen (S. 16) **Viewing | Hör-Sehverstehen** *A London tour* (S. 9); *The funny ringtone* (S. 19) **Study skills | Methodentraining** Wortbildungsregeln (S. 17)	**Wortschatz** *London sights, my neighbourhood, agreeing and disagreeing, word building* **Strukturen** *have to, can, should* (S. 20) ***Stop! Check! Go!** Üben und vertiefen	8
			26
	Listening | Hören *Radio programme* (S. 28); *dialogue* (S. 30); *picture story* (S. 31); *telephone conversation* (S. 33) **Speaking | Sprechen** Ein Bild beschreiben (S. 36); telefonieren (S. 33) **Writing course 2 | Schreiben** *Linkers and time phrases* (S. 37) **Reading and Mediation | Lesen und Sprachmittlung** Authentische Kurztexte (S. 38) **Viewing | Hör-Sehverstehen** *Cotswold Cycle tours* (S. 29); *Chill in the country* (S. 39) **Study skills | Methodentraining** Notizen anfertigen (S. 33)	**Wortschatz** *town and country words, informal language, talking on the phone* **Strukturen** *present perfect* (S. 40) *adverbs* (S. 32, 37) ***Stop! Check! Go!** Üben und vertiefen	28
			46
	Listening | Hören *picture story* (S. 50, 55); *dialogue* (S. 58) **Reading | Lesen** Wesentliche Informationen mithilfe von Notizen erfassen (S. 56) **Writing course 3 | Schreiben** Einen Kommentar gliedern (S. 57) **Mediation | Sprachmittlung** Verschiedene Ausdrucksmöglichkeiten nutzen; Höflichkeitsformen wahren (S. 58) **Viewing | Hör-Sehverstehen** *The Beatles* (S. 49); A *competition* (S. 59)	**Wortschatz** *food and drinks, polite phrases, countries, business words, money* **Strukturen** *if-sentences I* (S. 60) *comparisons* (S. 63) ***Stop! Check! Go!** Üben und vertiefen	48
			66

INHALT

	Lerninhalte	Your task (Lernaufgabe)	Texte
Unit 4 Scotland is different 	· Fotos beschreiben · sich mit drohender Arbeitslosigkeit auseinander setzen · ein Zimmer buchen · Personen oder Dinge näher beschreiben	**Find out about Scotland** Informationen selbstständig erarbeiten (S. 69) 	**Article** *Another Inverness shop closes* (S. 70) **Dialogue** *Hard times* (S. 71) **Website** *Bed and breakfast next to Loch Ness* (S. 72) **Jigsaw** *Ghosts don't exist* (S. 74–75) **Song** *Amy Macdonald, Pride (S. 77)*
***In Ireland** 	· Erfahrungen bei einem Schüleraustausch austauschen · Dublins Sehenswürdigkeiten entdecken		**Story** *A German student in Dublin* (S. 86–88)

PARTNER-B-Seiten	90
DIFF-BANK	93
***TEXT FILE**	
London facts (Unit 1)	116
Dick Whittington – a Christmas pantomime	118
Liverpool and the Titanic (Unit 3)	121
Scotland facts (Unit 4)	122
SKILLS FILE	
Vokabeln lernen	124
Unbekannte Wörter verstehen	125
Im Wörterbuch nachschlagen	126
Texte markieren	127
Prüfungen und Klassenarbeiten	128
Texte besser verstehen	130
Hören und Notizen machen	131
Eigene Texte schreiben und korrigieren	132
Bilder beschreiben	135
Einen Kurzvortrag halten	136
Mediation	137
LANGUAGE FILE	138
***WORDBANK**	
My neighbourhood	146
City and country	147
Food	148
Useful words for tourists	149
VOCABULARY	150

Kompetenzen	Sprache	Seite
Listening | Hören *Conversations* (S. 70, 72); *Radio programme* (S. 77); *Song* (S. 77) **Reading | Lesen** *Jigsaw* (S. 74); *Skimming* (S. 78) **Speaking | Sprechen** Eine Reservierung telefonisch bestätigen (S. 73) Unbekannte Wörter umschreiben (S. 81) **Writing course 4 | Schreiben** Eine Geschichte strukturieren (S. 76) **Viewing | Hör-Sehverstehen** *Welcome to Scotland* (S. 73); *Tally's video diary* (S. 79) **Study skills | Methodentraining** Sprachliche Regelmäßigkeiten entdecken (S. 71, 80)	**Wortschatz** *useful words for tourists, paraphrasing* **Strukturen** *relative clauses* (S. 80) *reflexive pronouns* (S. 71) ***Stop! Check! Go!** Üben und vertiefen	68
Reading | Lesen Einen längeren Lesetext verstehen (S. 86–88) **Writing | Schreiben** Einen Blog schreiben (S. 88) **Viewing | Hör-Sehverstehen** *A tour of Dublin* (S. 89)		86

Dictionary (English–German)	166
Dictionary (German–English)	183
List of names	197
Quellen	198
Irregular Verbs	200

Die Angebote des Schülerbuches sind nicht obligatorisch abzuarbeiten. Die Auswahl der Übungen und Übungsteile richtet sich nach den Schwerpunkten des schulinternen Curriculums.

*** fakultativ**

Unit 1

I love London

1 **What do you know about London?**
Do this quiz with a partner. Pick A, B or C.
If you don't know the answer, just guess. Then check on pages 116–117.

THE LONDON QUIZ

1 Who lives at Buckingham Palace?
A The King. B The Queen. C The President.

2 On the Tube you can travel by ...
A bus.
B train.
C car.

3 In books and films Sherlock Holmes is a famous London ...
A detective.
B film star.
C singer.

4 The name of the bell in this famous clock is ...
A Big Tom. B Big Bill. C Big Ben.

5 What's the name of this famous football stadium?
A Westminster. B Wimbledon. C Wembley.

6 Tourists are on the London Eye for ...
A five minutes. B thirty minutes.
C two hours.

7 London buses are red. But London taxis are ...
A red. B yellow. C black.

▸ Workbook 1, p. 3 ▸ Text file 1, pages 116–117

2 PEOPLE AND PLACES A London tour

a) Watch the film and enjoy the tour.
b) Then watch the film again and follow the tour on the map.

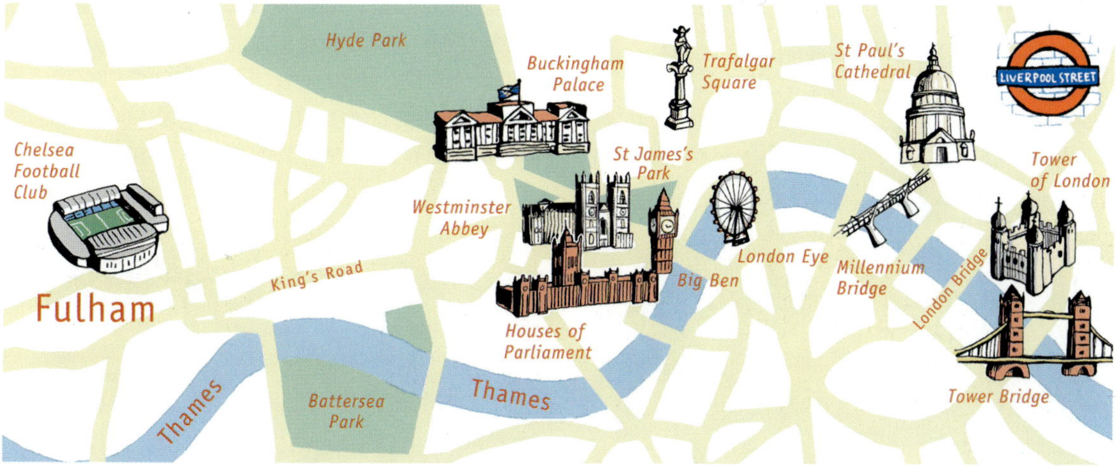

c) Watch the film a third time. What's the right information?

1 The best bus for tourists is number 11 / 21.
2 Buses are free for London children under 14 / 16.
3 Tower Bridge can open for big boats / buses.
4 You can feed birds / sheep in St James's Park.
5 The London Eye is 35 / 135 metres high.
6 Buckingham Palace has 775 windows / rooms.

d) What do you think? Talk to a partner.

I think	London the film	is looks	boring • cool • exciting • fun • funny • great • interesting • OK

I agree.

I don't agree. I think ...

Young Londoners

1 What's special about London?

a) Read about four young Londoners. Who would you like to meet? Why?

I'd like to meet ... because he / she is ... / looks ... / ... likes ... / says ...

buzz a magazine for Fulham and Hammersmith

Why do we ♥ London?

by our young reporter, Sam Holmes

Find out what young Londoners really think of their city.

Sam Holmes

I live in London and I love it here! I've lived here all my life. But what's so special about London? And what's the downside of London?
I asked some of my friends.

Ruby Philips

I love fashion, and in London you can see the hottest clothes before they're in the magazines. I also really like London's shopping centres and markets. The markets are cheaper – and they're really cool ☺. I like Camden Market best. I'm allowed to go there with my friends sometimes.

Tally O'Connor

I love the different cultures in London. My mum's family is Greek. (My real name is Talia – that's Greek.) My dad is Irish and Scottish. With so many different cultures the food in London is amazing.
And it's a great place for music and concerts. There's only one problem. I'm only allowed to go to concerts with mum or dad ☹.

Alfie Harper

There's one good thing about London: Londoners are very friendly. I made friends very quickly when we came here from Plymouth two years ago. But the best thing about London is the football. There are two big football clubs near where I live – Chelsea and Fulham. I'm a big Chelsea fan. (My friend Tally is a Fulham fan, but nobody is perfect!) The downside is that London is noisy and very expensive.

b) Match the headings A–E with Sam, Ruby, Tally and Alfie's texts. Careful! One sentence doesn't fit.

A London isn't cheap.

B I've never lived in a different town.

C You can see great new clothes in London.

D Arsenal is the best London football club.

E London is great because lots of different people live there.

c) True or false?

1 Sam doesn't like London very much.
2 Sam is a reporter for **buzz**.
3 Ruby says that London is special for clothes.
4 Ruby thinks that shopping centres are better than markets.
5 Tally likes the food of different cultures.
6 Tally goes to concerts alone.
7 Alfie says that Londoners aren't friendly.
8 Alfie thinks that London has no downsides.

2 What do you know about London now?

Pick a) or b).

a) ○ Copy and complete the sentences. All the information is on pages 8–11.

1 Wembley is famous for its football ...
2 Sherlock Holmes is a London ...
3 London buses are free for ...
4 Camden has a famous ...
5 Chelsea and Fulham are London football ...
6 Buckingham Palace is the home of ...
7 Big Ben is the name of a big ...
8 The London Eye is ... metres high.

b) ● What information about London was new for you? Write a list.

London has many different cultures. ...

Partner check: Compare your list with a partner. Did he/she write the same things?

Camden Market

▸ Workbook 3–5, pp. 4–5

Amazing London – for teens

1 London adverts

Which adverts (A–G) are about music, shopping, sport or transport?

A

B

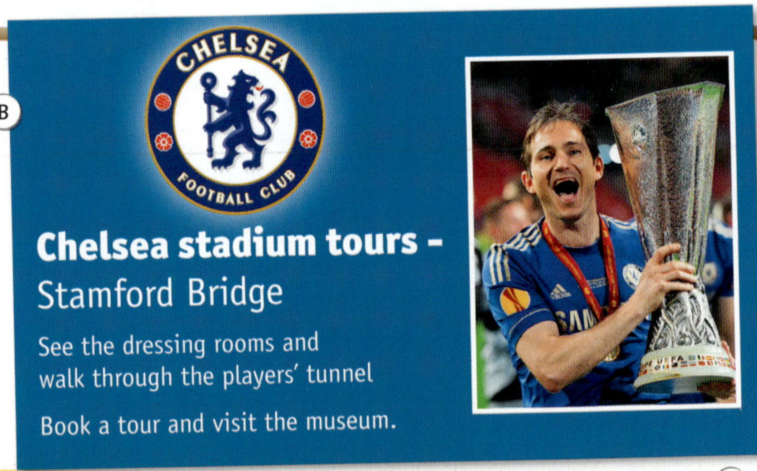

C

D

E

F

G

More practice 1 p. 93

2 YOUR TASK London plans

You are going to give young people tips for a great day in London. First you'll work alone, then in a group. You'll also make a poster. Follow steps 1–5.

Step 1: Find ideas: What can tourists in London do? Where can they go?
Work alone. Look at pages 8–12 and 116–117. Write two or more good ideas:
Young tourists can ...
They can also ...

Step 2: Agree with partners in a group.
Work in a group. Talk to your partners and agree on three (or more) ideas. Write them down.

Write why it's a good idea.

More help p.93

Step 3: Find out more.
Work with your partners. Go to www.cornelsen.de/highlight and put in the webcode: *High-3-13*. Make notes, for example:
- When does it open/start?
- How much are the tickets?
- How can you get there?

Step 4: Make your poster.
Write your London tips on a poster.
- Put information on the poster.
- Get photos on the internet.
- Draw some pictures.
- Write captions.

Step 5: Reading circle
Put your poster on the classroom wall.
Then look at the other posters.
Put a smiley ☺ on the best poster.

1 Before you read

Look at the pictures. Where do the friends go? What do they do?

They go to the Tube. | They go to a ... | They play ...

Clever Sherlock!

About me

My name is Sam Holmes. But everybody calls me Sherlock. Like Sherlock Holmes – the great detective!

Everybody calls me a geek because I like things like books, history, museums. My friends like normal things – shopping, music, football. But I don't like normal things. They're too ... normal!

geeky things

normal things

Saturday plans

So when I met my friends (Ruby, Alfie and Tally) last Saturday, I wanted to go to the

I love the dinosaurs there. But of course my friends laughed. They said: "BORING!"

My friend Ruby wanted to go shopping. I said "BORING", but the others said, "OK". I said: "We have no money, so we can't go shopping." "Very clever, Sherlock," Ruby answered.

Disaster on the Tube

We went to the Tube station in Fulham. We ran down to our train, but Alfie was too slow. The train left and poor Alfie was still on the platform.

We tried to phone Alfie, but our mobiles didn't work on the Tube.

Then I had an idea. "We'll get out at the next station and wait for the next train." And that's what we did. Ten minutes later the next train came and Alfie was on it. He was happy to see us. "That was very clever, Sherlock," Tally said. So I was happy too.

Shopping disaster

So our shopping adventure began. But we didn't go to a normal shop! No, we went to the most famous shop in London!

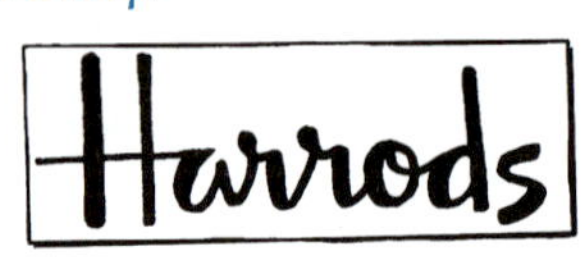

When we went through the door, Ruby said, "We have to go in quickly. They don't like groups of kids here."

This was a very expensive shop!

Alfie had a rucksack with a football in it . And that was the next disaster. The security man came and said, "You aren't allowed to have a rucksack in Harrods. And if you're under 15, you aren't allowed in the shop without an adult."

Then I had an idea. I saw a woman in the shop and I shouted, "MUM, we're here." The woman looked surprised. The security man looked surprised too. We left the shop quickly.

"Very clever, Sherlock!" Tally said to me.

Disaster in Hyde Park

So next we went to Hyde Park. We played football, but we didn't see the teenagers behind a tree. They drank something ...

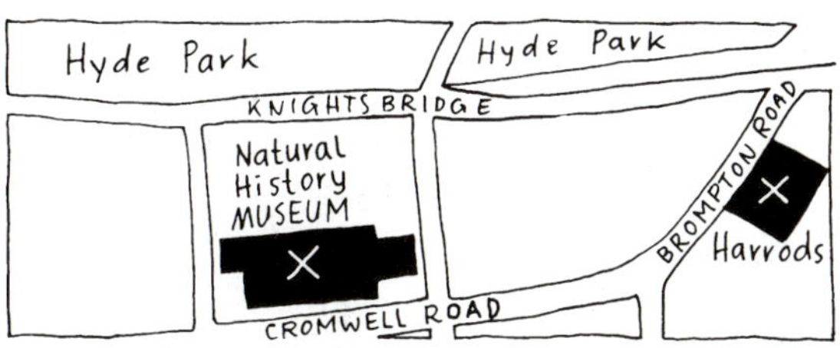

Then Alfie kicked the football into their picnic. "Hey, you idiot!" a big boy shouted. "We're keeping your football!"

Then I had an idea. I went behind a tree and took out my mobile. A LOUD noise came from it – like the noise of a police car. The teenagers heard it, ran away – and left the football!.

"Very clever again, Sherlock," Tally said. I felt like a million dollars!

In the museum, at last

So we were in Hyde Park with NO money and NO more ideas. "Erm ...," I said. "The Natural History Museum is near here – and it's free."

So we went there. First we went to see the dinosaurs – and my friends loved them.

And they all loved the earthquake room too. You can really feel the earthquake there! It's amazing and everybody loved it. And now everybody loves the museum – especially Tally. So I think that I am a VERY clever Sherlock!

2 What places are in the story?

1 a Tube station 2 a hospital 3 a shop
4 a park 5 a post office 6 a museum

3 Who thought this in the story?

Alfie, Tally, Ruby, Sherlock – or all of them?

1 I want to see the dinosaurs.
2 I want to go shopping.
3 I can get the next train!
4 Sherlock was very clever in Harrods.
5 Thanks, Sherlock. I have my football back.
6 The earthquake room is great!

More practice 2 p. 93

4 Why and what? More help p. 94

Copy and complete the sentences.

1 Sam's friends call him *a geek* because ...
2 His friends said "BORING!" when ...
3 Alfie missed the Tube train because ...
4 They had a problem at Harrods because ...
5 The teens in the park ran away when ...
6 They went to the museum because ...

More practice 3 p. 94 More practice 4 p. 95

► *Workbook 6–8, p. 6*

Collect ideas before you write

> Before you write, collect ideas from texts in your English book.
> ▸ Skills file 8, p. 133

1 Ideas for a text about your neighbourhood

a) First collect ideas from texts in your book.
For example read this text: Who likes Fulham and why? *... likes Fulham because ...*

Is Fulham a great place for young people? Tell buzz what you think!

The best thing about Fulham is the river. Also, there's an amazing market near our house and there are lots of nice cafes here too.
Darren

I don't like Fulham much. We live near a busy road. And we aren't far from Heathrow Airport, so we hear the planes too.
Livvy

I think Fulham is great! You can go shopping in the Westfield shopping centre. And you can watch great football at Fulham Stadium.
Ruby

We live next to a big hospital. There aren't any parks near us and our nearest Tube station is 15 minutes away. I think it's boring here.
Josh

b) WORDS Work with a partner. Collect words for your neighbourhood from the buzz texts. Make lists or a network:

My neighbourhood

transport	shopping	sport	other
...	market	...	river
...	...	...	...

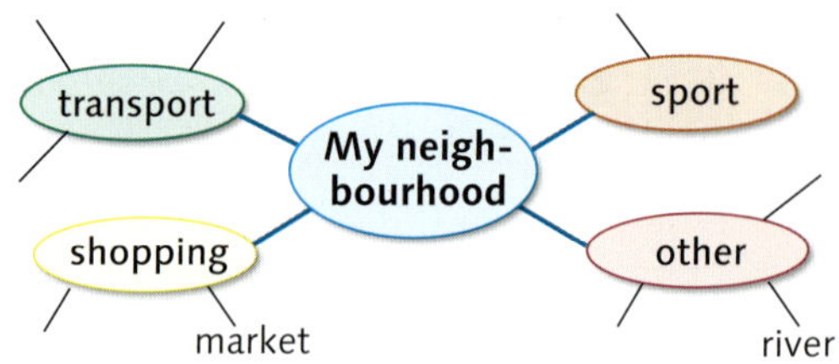

Write as many words as you can. More help p. 95 ▸ Wordbank 1, p. 146
School, post office, ...

c) Collect sentences for your text.
Read these sentences from the buzz texts. Then change the words in orange and write about **your** neighbourhood.

1 The best thing about Fulham is the river. → *The best thing about my town is the park.*
2 There's an amazing market near our house. → *There's ...*
3 There are lots of nice cafes here.
4 You can go shopping in the shopping centre.
5 There aren't any parks near us.
6 Our nearest Tube station is 15 minutes away.

2 NOW YOU More help p. 95

Now tell Ruby or Darren from buzz about your neighbourhood.
Write about 40 words (● 60 words).
Put your text in your DOSSIER.

> Make your text more interesting
> – with words from 1b),
> – with sentences from 1c).

 ▸ Workbook 9, p. 7

Understanding new words

> Sometimes words that you know can help you to understand new words.
> For example you know *work*. So *worker* = *work* + *-er* is someone who works *(Arbeiter/in)*. That's easy!
> ▸ *Skills file 2, p. 125*

1 Word building

a) Look at the words in black.
Match each word with a photo A–D.

Madame Tussauds LONDON

nearest Tube station: Baker Street

Come and meet the world's most famous singers, runners, footballers and divers at Madame Tussauds!

A

B

C

D

b) What could these new words mean?
Talk to a partner and write your ideas. Then check in a dictionary.

1 driver
2 reader
3 listener
4 walker
5 writer
6 skiver
7 dancer
8 talker

> Driver: I think it comes from *drive*.

> So in German it's ...

c) Look at these examples: **sun ➜ sunny, cloud ➜ cloudy, rain ➜ rainy.**
The red words below are like these words. What do they mean in German?

> The walkers started early, so they were a bit sleepy.

> Hampstead, in the north of London, is hilly and has a big park.

d) Some words have two parts. Look at these examples:
bus stop = bus *(Bus)* + stop *(anhalten)* → *Bushaltestelle*
postcard = post *(Post)* + card *(Karte)* → *Postkarte, Ansichtskarte*
What's a *bus driver*? And what's a *postman* or a *postwoman*?

2 From the newspaper

What do these red words mean?
Partner check: Compare with a partner.

More practice 5 p. 96

> Young swimmers and divers from all parts of Britain were at the Olympic swimming pool yesterday. One winner was John Burns. He said in a TV interview, "I was ill yesterday. It was a long car trip and I was travelsick. But today I'm OK."

1 Is fashion important?

a) Serena and Andy are talking about shopping and fashion. Listen to them. Do you agree with Andy or Serena?

More help p.96

Serena

b) Work with a partner. Take roles. Listen to Serena and Andy again. Repeat the sentences in the speech bubbles with as much feeling as you can.

More practice 6 p.97

2 PLACEMAT What things are most important for teenagers?

Step 1: Work in groups of four. Every student writes three ideas in one corner of the placemat.

Step 2: Read out your ideas to the group.

Step 3: Talk about the ideas. Agree on three things that most students in your group think are important. Write them in the middle of your placemat.

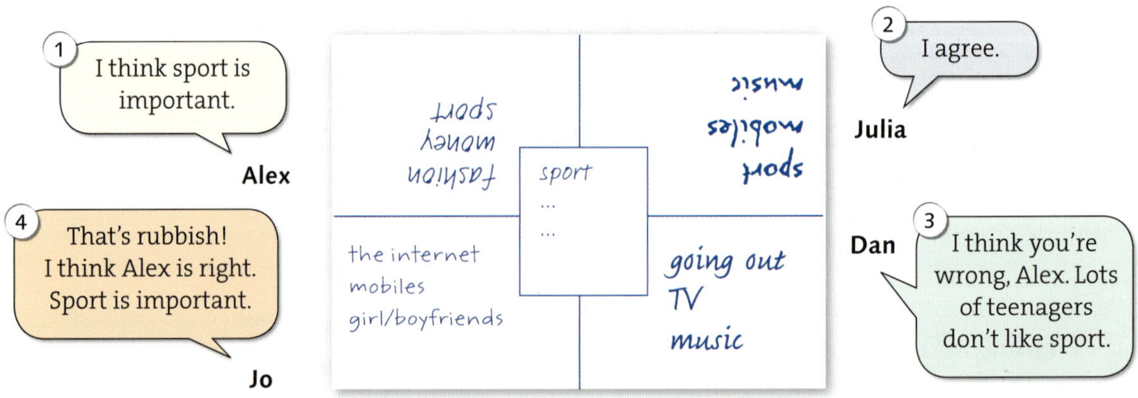

Step 4: Tell the class about your group's ideas. Do the rest of the class have the same ideas? What are the most popular ideas in your class?

We think that the most important thing for teenagers is ... Number two on our list is ...

▸ Workbook 11–12, p.9

1 Before you watch

a) Look at the photos from the new DVD in exercise 2.

Think about these questions:

1 Is the DVD in Plymouth or London? How do you know?
2 Who is in the film?
3 Where will the people go in the film? (to a shop, cafe, park, market, stadium, ...?)
4 What will happen?

b) Pair: Talk about the questions in a) with a partner.

c) Share: Tell the class what you and your partner think.

I think the film is in ...

Yes, you're right. And ...

We think that the people will go to ...

2 The funny ringtone

a) Watch the film. Then put the photos in the right order.

b) Watch the film a second time. Then answer these questions:
Who goes to the cafe? What do they drink? Where do they go then? Who has a problem?

c) Now watch the film again and check your answers.

3 What can you remember?

Ask your partner three questions about the film.
Can he/she answer them?

Who	lives in London SW6? gives Ruby her phone? has a smoothie / cup of tea? buys clothes at Camden Market? puts on a hat? loses something? ...?

1 Tips for visitors to London

a) Match the parts of the brochure (1–3) with the pictures (A–C).

Stay safe in the city!

Like in all cities, you have to be careful when you're in London. But London is a very safe place, so you don't have to be nervous.

1 Crossing the road: When you cross the road, you have to look right, then left, then right again. You should use the subways, so you don't have to cross busy roads.

2 Pickpockets: Sometimes there are pickpockets in shops or on buses and trains. Please be very careful if you have to open your bag or use your mobile.

3 On the Tube: Please stand on the right on the escalators. Then other people can walk past you on the left.

A

B

C

b) Look again at these sentences from the text and complete the FOCUS-box.

1 You have to be careful.
2 You have to look right, then left.
3 You don't have to be nervous.
4 You don't have to cross busy roads.

FOCUS

- Mit ... sagst du, was jemand tun muss.
- Mit ... sagst du, was jemand nicht zu tun braucht.

▸ Language file 7, p. 143

2 School rules

Alfie is talking about his old school and his new school in London.

a) Listen. Which school is stricter – Alfie's old school or his new school in London?

b) Listen again and take notes.

	old school	new school
wear a tie	✓	✗
wear a blazer		
wear normal shoes		
stay at school all day		

c) Use your notes and complete the sentences.

At Alfie's old school the students have to ..., but at his new school they don't ...

▸ Workbook 13, p. 10

3 *Can*, *should* or *have to*?

a) Match the sentences on the left with the speech bubbles.

FOCUS

1	Du willst sagen, was jemand tun kann oder darf.
2	Du willst jemandem raten, etwas zu tun.
3	Du willst sagen, dass jemand etwas tun muss.
4	Du willst sagen, dass jemand etwas nicht tun muss.

a) You have to do it.

b) You don't have to do it.

c) You can do it.

d) You should do it.

▸ *Language file 7, p. 143*

b) Now look again at the tips for visitors on page 20.
Tell your partner these tips in German.

1 You have to be careful in London.
2 You should use the subways.
3 You don't have to be nervous.
4 You have to look right, then left.
5 Stand on the right on the escalators, then people can go past you on the left.

4 A letter to buzz

a) Complete the letter with the correct form of the verb. //● p. 97

Dear buzz
My friend often visits me in the evening, but then she has to / doesn't have to (1) walk home alone. Her mum and dad can't pick her up because they have to / don't have to (2) work in the evenings. The problem is that she has to / doesn't have to (3) walk along dark streets. She says that I have to / don't have to (4) worry about her, but I worry a lot. I have to / don't have to (5) be sure that she's OK, so I phone her on her mobile.
A nervous friend

b) Complete with *should / shouldn't*.

Dear nervous friend
Your friend really ... (1) walk along dark streets. She ... (2) walk on busier streets. If someone says something unfriendly to her, she ... (3) answer. She ... (4) say nothing and walk away quickly. If she's very scared, she ... (5) ask for help.
buzz

5 Tips for visitors in Germany

Copy and complete these tips for British visitors to Germany.

A

You ... wait when the man is red.

B

You ... cross when the man is green.

C

Currywurst is popular – you ... try it!

D

It's 7 pm. You ... pay.

More practice 7 p. 97

Ein Lösungsblatt für die Aufgaben 1–4 und 6 kannst du von deiner Lehrerin/deinem Lehrer erhalten. Den Hörtext (S. 23) findest du auch auf der Audio-CD im Workbook.

1 REVISION My class trip

A German student is on a class trip to London. She wrote an email to her cousin in Canada. Write the verbs in the simple past.

Example: *We arrived in London …*

Hello Pinar

We … (1 arrive) in London three days ago. My English family … (2 be) at Heathrow airport. They're really nice – especially Kate. At first I … (3 have) problems because they all … (4 talk) so fast. I … (5 not understand) anything! But it's OK now.

On the first day I … (6 not see) the German students in my class. I … (7 go) with Kate to her friend's house and we … (8 play) computer games.

Yesterday I … (9 meet) the other German students at the Tower of London. It was really cool.
… you … (10 visit) the Tower when you were in London last year? … you … (11 like) it?

See you soon
Sandra xx

► Language file 3, p. 140

2 WORDS Travel in London

a) Copy this table. Then write the words from the box in it.

transport	*people*	*places*
boat	*adult*	*bus stop*
…	…	…

adult • bike • *boat* • bridge • bus • bus driver • *bus stop* • car • child • detective • drive • escalator • football fan • ferry • harbour • hill • king • market • plane • platform • queen • river • ride • road • sea • security man • shopping centre • stadium • street • taxi • ticket • traffic lights • train • train station • tourist • travel • Tube

b) Find one word to complete all three phrases.

1 Cross the … Walk along the … Go to the end of the … and turn left.
2 Go by … to town. Wait for the … on the platform. The … is leaving the station.
3 Buy a … from the bus driver. A … to London, please. You can get a … at the station.
4 The cars must stop at the … Turn left at the … The … are red.
5 Sit on the … The best … for tourists is number 11 … Wait at the … stop.
6 See boats on the … See fish in the … Cross the … on a bridge.

c) Write sentences about you and travel – as many as you can. Some ideas:

I often travel by … to … *I get on the … at …* *When it's raining I …*
Sometimes I go to town by … *For our summer holidays we …* *Yesterday I …*

3 LISTENING Travelling in London

A

B

C

a) Listen to the three scenes and match them with the photos. The sounds can help you.

b) Listen again and answer the questions.

1 a) When is the train going to leave? A 11.00 B 11.40 C 3 pm
b) Which station is Waterloo? A the first station B the second station C the third station.

2 a) The woman can take the bus number 9 to A the Strand B Covent Garden C Harrods.
b) How often does the number 9 bus come? Every A 2 or 3 minutes B every 4 or 5 minutes C every 6 or 7 minutes .

3 a) Where do the people want to go? A to the Tower B to Big Ben C to Baker Street.
b) Why do they want to be there by 2.30? A to see the Queen B to meet their children C to buy a ticket.

4 MEDIATION Staying with a family

Während eurer Klassenfahrt nach London bist du in einer englischen Gastfamilie. Hilf deinem Freund Paul, die Hinweise der Gastmutter Mrs Green zu verstehen.

Mrs Green — Welcome to our home. We hope you'll enjoy your stay in London. We usually have dinner at 7.30, so you should be here at around 7.

Paul — Was war das mit dem Abendessen?

You — Abendessen ist gewöhnlich um halb acht, deshalb ... (1)

Mrs Green — You don't have to walk home after your activities. Just phone me when you're ready and I'll pick you up in the car.

Paul — Was war das mit anrufen?

You — Nach unseren Ausflügen ... (2) laufen. Wir sollen Mrs Green anrufen und sie ... (3)

Mrs Green — After dinner you aren't allowed to go out again alone. You have to stay at home.

Paul — Dürfen wir nach dem Abendessen ausgehen?

You — Nein, ... (4)

Mrs Green — There isn't a TV in your bedroom. But of course, you are allowed to watch TV in the living room with us.

Paul — Was ist mit Fernsehen?

You — Wir ... (5)

Mrs Green — We only have one bathroom, so nobody should stay in there too long.

Paul — Ich habe leider nur *bathroom* verstanden – worum ging es genau?

You — Da es nur ein Bad gibt, ... (6)

5 WRITING My day in London

Look at the pictures. These young people spent a day in London.

Molly

Anna

Luke

a) Molly, the girl in the first picture, wrote about her day. Read her text.

On Saturday I went to London. I went with my friend Andy. We travelled by bus. I was hungry when we arrived, so we went to a cafe, had breakfast and chatted.
After breakfast we looked at the shops in Oxford Street. I felt especially happy because I found a T-shirt for Andy's birthday.

In the afternoon we had a ride on the London Eye. The weather was perfect and we saw the river, the bridges, Big Ben ... It was great!

After that we felt a bit tired, so we went to Covent Garden. We bought a sandwich and a drink, and sat and listened to a guitarist. And then it was time to take the bus back home.

Molly

I really liked the London Eye!

b) Now imagine you're Anna or Luke. You're going to write about your day. Decide who you are and collect ideas about the day in London. Look at Molly's text for help.

- Who was with you?
- What was the weather like?
- What did you see?
- What did you do?
- What did you buy?
- How did you feel?

c) Can you use Molly's sentences for your text too?
Example: I went with my friend Andy. => *I went with my friend Kate.*

1 I was hungry when we arrived, so ...
2 I felt especially happy because ...
3 The weather was ... and we ...
4 We bought ... and ..., and sat and ...

d) Now write your text. Write as many sentences as you can.

e) Partner check: Read and correct your partner's text. He/She corrects your text.

► Skills file 8, pp. 132–134

6 READING Tally's blog

Tally.blog.com

July 17th

We're staying at home this summer. My mum wants to visit The Tower of London tomorrow – with me :-((The Tower of London – how boring! We learned all about it in Year 4 at school …, but who is interested in all that history? And we have to get up at 7 am tomorrow – in the holidays! That's unfair! But the good thing is that my friend Marty can come with us.

14 comments share

July 18th, 9 pm

I had a great day at the Tower of London! And I learned a lot of new things. I knew the stories about the big black birds here (the legend says that England and the Tower will fall if the birds leave). But I was surprised that many years ago there was a zoo inside The Tower: lions, bears, elephants, tigers and kangaroos. In the Brick Tower we played computer games and found out about all the animals: we could even smell them.

25 comments share

July 19th, 8 am

I got up at 7 in the morning to play the *Tower Mystery* game on my phone. I love it. You learn a lot about the history of London – and the sounds are really funny. Mum says we're going to The Tower again when my cousins visit in August. I think it'll be great!

2 comments share

a) Match three of these sentences with the parts of Tally's blog (17th, 18th or 19th):

1 I didn't know about the wild animals!
2 Tower of London? No, thanks!
3 Do I want to go again? Yes, please!
4 Tower of London? Never again!

b) Pick the correct answer.

1 On July 17th Tally is happy because (A) she likes visiting the Tower of London. (B) she can sleep late. (C) her friend Marty is going to be with her.
2 The Tower of London legend says the big black birds (A) are bad for England and the Tower. (B) are good for England and the Tower. (C) must leave the Tower.
3 On July 19th Tally (A) plays the *Tower Mystery* game in the Brick Tower. (B) doesn't want to go to The Tower of London again. (C) doesn't sleep late.

7 My learner log

Copy and complete your learner log. You can put it in your DOSSIER.

My learner log for Unit 1

Now I can ...
- talk about the good and bad things where I live: ...
- take ideas from a text when I write: 😀 😐 😟
- talk about things I can, should and have to do: ...
- talk about things I don't have to do: ...
- say if I agree or don't agree with somebody: ...

After Unit 1:
- I know a lot of city words, for example ...
- Some places I want to visit in London are ...
- These pages in the Unit were easy: ...
- These pages in the Unit were difficult: ...

My progress in English is: GREAT! / OK / NOT VERY GOOD

► Workbook (Portfolio), p. 13 ► Workbook (Revision), p. 14

A visit to a city – using the simple past

Emily lives in Leeds. Three days ago she came to London to stay with her friend Ruby.

1 Emily's postcard from London

a) Read the postcard. Do you think Emily liked London? Why (not)?

Hi!
I arrived here in London three days ago. On the first day Ruby and I visited all the famous places. They were great! We walked for miles and miles! So we were tired and we didn't do very much in the evening.
On the second day we went shopping in Oxford Street. Did you go there last year? I bought some cool presents. (One for you – surprise!)
In the evening we saw some famous bands at a free concert in Hyde park. It was fantastic!
See you soon! Emily

LONDON-Postcards © kleinundhalm.de

b) The simple past

Regelmäßige Verben enden auf ***-ed***.

1 Copy three examples from the postcard.

Unregelmäßige Verben enden **nicht** auf ***-ed***.

2 Copy four examples from the postcard:
were, …

Verneinungen verwenden das Wort ***didn't***.

3 Copy one example from the postcard.

Fragen beginnen mit dem Wort ***Did …?***

4 Copy one example from the postcard.

► *Language file 3, p. 140*

2 Emily and Ruby

a) Emily is telling a friend about her time in London. Pick the right verbs 1–8 from the box.

came • had • made • played • told • wanted • went • wore

Last week I visited my friend Ruby. Ruby is really nice and she … (1) a cake when I arrived in London! One day we … (2) to a park. We … (3) badminton and then we bought ice creams. Ruby … (4) me lots of funny stories and I laughed a lot! On the last day Ruby's mum took us to a concert. I … (5) my new dress. We … (6) to come home by Tube, but Ruby checked the time and it was too late. So we drove home in a London taxi!
I … (7) a great time with Ruby and I was really sad when I left London and … (8) home.

b) Now find the simple past forms of these verbs. They're all in the speech bubble.

1 visit *visited*
2 arrive
3 laugh
4 check
5 buy *bought*
6 take
7 drive
8 leave

3 Emily's photos

Now Emily is showing photos of her trip to London.
Copy and complete the sentences. Use the right verb forms.

1 I didn't travel into London by bus because it was quicker by Tube.

> I **travelled** by bus.
> I **didn't travel** by train. *(no -ed)*
> I **went** to London.
> I **didn't go** to Paris.

1 I ... (not travel) into London by bus because it was quicker by Tube.

2 I took photos of Buckingham Palace, but I ... (not see) the Queen.

3 I was at Big Ben at 18.20, so I ... (not hear) the famous bell.

4 I ... (not visit) the Tower of London because the tickets were expensive.

5 We went to the zoo, but we ... (not see) the tigers.

6 We ... (not go) on a boat trip on the river because we ... (not have) time.

4 NOW YOU

a) Write an email to Emily about a visit to a city. Write as many sentences as you can.

Hi!
I hope you're OK.
Last week I was in Berlin/Hamburg/...
I stayed with a friend/in a hotel/...
On the first day ...
On the second day ...
On the last day ...

> You can use some sentences in exercises 1, 2 and 3 and change them for your text:
> On the first day Ruby and I visited all the famous places.
> => On the first day I visited the Brandenburger Tor.

b) **Partner check:** Show your email to a partner and check your partner's email.

5 An elephant's trip to London

a) Copy and complete the rhyme.

Elephant, elephant, where did you go?
I went to London two hours ago.
Elephant, elephant, what ... you ...? (see?)
I ... lots of people, but they ... me! (saw, not like)
Elephant, elephant, what happened then?
I ... a young woman the way to Big Ben. (ask)
Elephant, elephant, then what ... you ...? (do?)
I ... the wrong Tube and ... back at the zoo.
(take, arrive)

b) Say the rhyme with a partner.

Unit 2

Country life

Hills, fields and trees in the Cotswolds

Small towns like Chipping Campden have nice old houses.

The village of Mickleton

1 Young Lives

a) Listen to the radio programme *Young Lives*. Pick the right answer.

1 Molly talks about ...
- A her family.
- B where she lives.

2 Molly ...
- A likes living in the country.
- B wants to leave her farm.

b) Copy the notes. Then listen again and complete them with the words in the green box.

About Molly
1 lives on ...
2 goes to school in ...
3 goes to school by ...
4 goes shopping in ...
5 best friend's name: ...
6 dog's name: ...

A Alex
B a farm
C Stratford
D Chipping Campden
E Missy
F bus

c) Now check your notes with a partner: *Molly lives ... She goes ... Her dog's name is ...*

It's a great place for dogs!

The Cotswolds are famous for sheep.

2 PEOPLE AND PLACES *Cotswolds Cycle Tours*

a) Look at these pictures. Which of the ten things can you see in the map and photos?

a crossroads

a church

a block of flats

an old market

a high street

a gate

a wood

a pub

a hill

a farm

b) Now watch the film. Which of the ten things was *not* in the film?

c) Look at the map of Chipping Campden.
Which route (red, green or blue) did Becky take? Watch the film again and check.

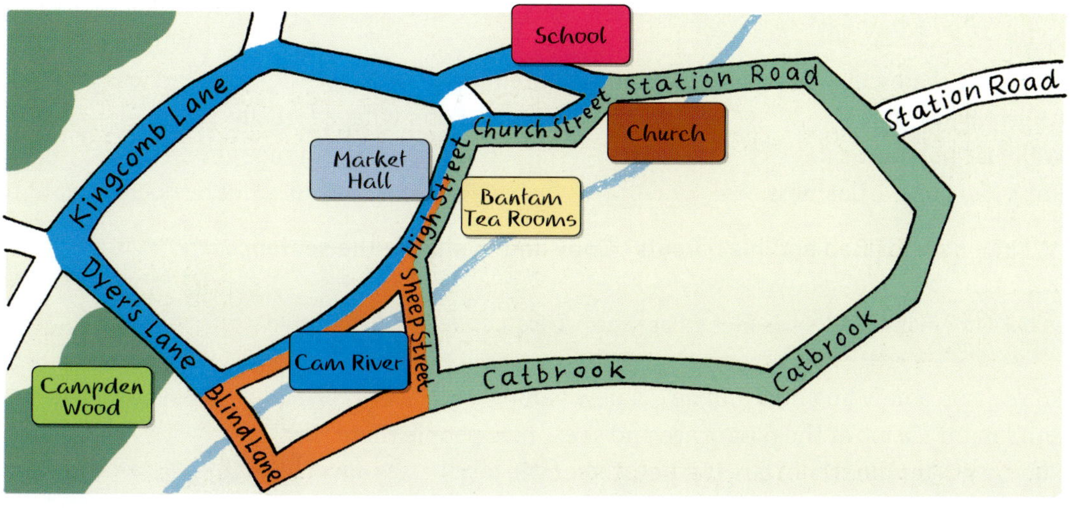

► Workbook 1–2, p. 15

A new life

Rob Blake

Alfie Harper

1 In the country

a) Rob Blake is from London. He's new in the Cotswolds. One day he phones his friend Alfie. Is Rob happy in the country? Why (not)?

Rob — Hey Alfie. How are things in London?
Alfie — Hi Rob. All's good here. How are you? Are you busy?
Rob — You're joking! There's nothing to do here. This is the country.
Alfie — Oh come on! I like the country – remember!
Rob — Well ... we've bought a dog. His name is Wally. He's great.
Alfie — Cool!
Rob — And dad has started a new CCTV business. He has bought a new van. So he's happy.
Alfie — That's cool.
Rob — Mum is happy because she has found a job in the post office. And she has met nice people there.
Alfie — That's good. But you don't like your new life?
Rob — No – it sucks! The village is **really** small. There's **one** shop, the post office ... and that's all! No cinema, nothing! But school is OK.
Alfie — And have you met some nice girls???
Rob — No. Well ... No.
Alfie — I don't believe you!
Rob — Well, there's a girl on the school bus. She's a neighbour ... well, from the next farm. I've seen her, but I haven't spoken to her – yet!
Alfie — Sounds good!
Rob — Hey, I must go and cut the grass! What a pain!

It sucks! and *What a pain!* are teenager talk.

b) Read the dialogue again and finish these sentences.

1 Alfie still lives in ...
2 Wally is Rob's new ...
3 Rob's dad has a ... business.
4 Rob's village is really ...
5 Rob has seen a nice girl on ...
6 Rob now has to ..., but he doesn't want to!

c) What's new for Rob and his parents? Copy and complete the sentences.

has bought • has found • has met • has seen • hasn't spoken • has started

1 Rob's dad ... a new business and he ... a new van.
2 Rob's mum ... a job at the post office and she ... nice people there.
3 Rob ... a girl on the school bus, but he ... to her yet.

More practice 1 p. 98

2 This isn't a park!

a) Look at the pictures. Then listen to **part 1** of the story and put pictures A–E in the right order.

A

B

C

D

E

b) Now listen to **part 1 and part 2** of the story. Choose the correct answer.

1 Rob and Wally are — A in a park B in a garden C on a track D at a zoo.
2 Wally is running after — A a cat B a dog C a sheep D a rabbit.
3 The girl in the car is — A a friend B a neighbour C a sister D a postwoman.
4 In the end the girl is — A friendlier B worried C scared D angry.
5 The girl can drive — A on the farm B on the road C in the village D in the city.
6 They'll meet again — A in town B at school C on the bus D on the farm.

c) Who asks these questions – Rob or Molly?

1 Is that your car?
2 How old are you?
3 Can you drive?
4 Where are you from?
5 Do you like it here in Mickleton?

Listen to **part 2** of the story again and check your answers.

d) Find the right answers for the five questions in c). Say more than one word.

More help p.99

▸ Workbook 3–4, p. 16

Molly and the sheep

1 Molly is in the newspaper

a) Before you read: Look at the photo and the headline.
Who is the article about? Is it a happy or a sad story?

COTSWOLD POST

Well done Molly!

Last Wednesday Molly Taylor went to check her family's sheep near the village of Mickleton – but she found three of them in the river. Molly, 14, saw that she had to save them. First she quickly phoned home. But she couldn't wait for help. So brave Molly calmly walked into the water to help the sheep.

Later Molly said, "It wasn't dangerous for me because the water wasn't deep. But it was deep for the sheep. The sheep were really heavy because they were so wet. So I had to work hard."

Molly's father, John Taylor, spoke proudly about his daughter. "Molly did so well," he said.

Farmer's daughter, Molly Taylor, saved three sheep.

"She saved the sheep. We've never had an accident like this before."

The police think that dogs ran after the sheep and have asked people for help.

Police officer Dave Butler said: "Dogs often behave dangerously in fields where there are animals. Please tell us if you have seen dogs near the Taylors' farm."

b) Who was it? Match the people and animals (1–3) with actions from the green box.

1 Molly Taylor ...
2 Molly's dad ...
3 Dogs ...

behave dangerously. • did well. • quickly phoned home. • spoke proudly about his daughter. • worked hard.

More practice 2 p. 99
More practice 3 p. 100
▸ *Language file 9, p. 144*

c) You saw a dog in the fields near Mickleton! Pick dog A or B.
Then tell the police about the dog. Your partner takes the role of the police.

Police — What's your name?
You — *(give your name)*
Police — Can you spell that, please?
You — *(spell your name)*
Police — What's your address in Germany?
You — *(give your address)*
Police — Thanks. Can you describe the dog, please?
You — Yes. The dog was ... It had ...

A

B

black / white / brown long / short leg / tail / ears

▸ *Workbook 5–6, p. 17*

2 Can I take a message?

Rob wants to phone Molly.

a) Read and listen to the dialogue. Can he speak to her?

Mr Taylor — Hello.
Rob — Oh, hello. Is that the Taylors?
Mr Taylor — Yes, it is. Who's speaking?
Rob — This is Rob Blake. Can I talk to Molly please?
Mr Taylor — I'm sorry, Rob, Molly can't come to the phone right now. Can I take a message?
Rob — Oh yes, yes please. I read about Molly in the paper. I wanted to ask if she's OK. And I wanted to say "Well done."
Mr Taylor — That's very nice of you, Rob. I'll give her your message. She's fine now. I think she'll be at school tomorrow.
Rob — Great, I'll see her on the bus then. Thank you. Goodbye.
Mr Taylor — You're welcome. Bye.

b) Listen again. Then copy and complete the Taylors' notepad.

Messages

Who phoned?: ....

Wanted to speak to: ....

Message: *Asked if Molly is ...*

3 ROLE-PLAY Talking on the phone

a) How can you say these things in English on the phone? Write your answers. Look at exercise 2 for help.

1 Du bist am Telefon. Frage, mit wem du sprichst.
2 Sage, wer du bist.
3 Sage, dass du mit deinem Freund Adam sprechen möchtest.
4 Sage, dass er gerade nicht zum Telefon kommen kann.
5 Frage, ob du etwas ausrichten kannst.
6 Sage, dass du die Nachricht weitergeben wirst.

b) **Partner B:** Go to page 90.

Partner A: You're in England. You phone your host mother, Mrs Smith, because you won't be home at 4 pm. You're going on a trip and you'll be back at 8 pm.

First practise what you want to say:

Hello. This is ... Can I ... to Mrs Smith, please?
I won't ... at 4 o' clock.
I'm going ... trip. I'll be ... at 8 o'clock.
Thank ...

Now phone partner B.

c) Copy the notepad. Then swap roles. Now you're the babysitter for the Smiths. Listen to your partner.

- Say Mr Smith can't come to the phone right now.
- Ask if you can take a message.
- Make notes on your notepad.

Messages

Who phoned? ________

Wanted to speak to: ________

Message: ________

____

____

▸ Workbook 7, p. 18

1 I need help

Listen to the phone call. Are these sentences true or false?

1 Molly says she needs help.
2 Molly's dad is feeling well.
3 Rob can come now.
4 Rob is unhappy.

The country detectives

The country girl

Rob and Wally ran along the track and met Molly in her car. Then they all drove across the fields. Rob opened the gate when they came to a field with lots of sheep. The sheep ran into the next field and Molly and her dog Missy came behind them.

"You're very good with the sheep, Molly," Rob said. Molly smiled. And Rob smiled too. He really liked her.

Bags in the bushes

Suddenly Wally put his nose into some bushes. "What is it, Wally?" Rob asked. Then he saw lots of big bags in the bushes. And they were full of rubbish.

"Molly, look at this," Rob shouted.

"Lots of people leave their rubbish here," she said angrily. "And the police can't catch them because they do it at night."

"I have an idea," Rob answered. "Dad could put CCTV cameras on your farm. Then you could catch the stupid people! What a great advert for dad's business!"

Lights at night

Rob's dad was interested and the Taylors agreed happily. On Saturday Rob and his dad put CCTV cameras in different places on the farm and a monitor in the farm office.

In the evening Molly's dad still didn't feel well, so he had to stay in bed. Molly and Rob watched a DVD and then they checked the CCTV monitor. First there was nothing, but suddenly they saw a fox.

"Wow!" Rob said. "I've never seen a fox before."

"It has one of our chickens in its mouth!" Molly shouted. "Come on!" They ran quickly to the chickens – but then they suddenly saw car lights!

A clever trick

"Rob," Molly said quietly, "you drive my car. Park at the end of the track, in front of the gate, so they can't drive away. I'll stay here and write down the car number."

Rob was a bit nervous. "Erm, Molly, last week I told you I can drive ..., but I can't really drive!"

"Oh Rob!" she said. "OK, I'll park the car. You stay here and write down the number. Here's a pen."

Rob went nearer the lights. He wrote down the number of the big black car. Then he went back to the farm and waited for Molly.

Not so clever really

Later two police officers were at the Taylors' door. They spoke with Molly's mother.

"Good evening. Do you have a car, number P399 DOJ?"

"That's my daughter's car," Mrs Taylor said. "Is there a problem?"

"Well, yes. We're trying to catch people who leave rubbish on your farm. She parked her car at the end of the track and we can't go home."

That week there was an article in the Cotswolds paper:

New business helps farmers

A new business in Mickleton has put CCTV cameras on a farm to catch people who leave their rubbish there. Lots of other farmers are interested.

"It's a good idea," police officer Butler said. "But if people see something, they should phone the

And Rob chatted on the internet with Alfie:

Rob:	Molly and I are good friends now.
Alfie:	Only good friends?
Rob:	Well ...
Alfie:	And what about life in the country?
Rob:	It's great! I really like it now ☺.

2 ○ **You're a reporter!** //● p.100

Put sentences A-H in the right order and tell the story for a newspaper.

A Rob ran to Molly's field with his dog.
B Molly phoned Rob.
C The two police officers couldn't drive home.
D The police said the CCTV was a good idea.
E Rob wrote the number of the car.
F Rob and Molly saw lights of a car at night.
G Rob's dad put CCTV cameras on the farm.
H Rob's dog, Wally, found some rubbish.

More practice 4 p.100

3 NOW YOU What do *you* think?

a) Read the sentences. Pick A or B, or write your own idea C.

1 Molly phoned Rob because A she needed help B she wanted to see Rob again C ...
2 Molly's idea to park the car at the end of the track was A brave B stupid C ...
3 Rob now likes life in the country because A he has a dog B he likes Molly C ...

b) Compare with other students in your class. Did you have the same answers?

More practice 5 p.101

▸ *Workbook 8, p. 19*

Talking about a picture

1 In the town or in the country?

A

B

a) Pick a picture (A or B) and describe it. Make notes. ▸ *Wordbank 2, p. 147*

1 Say where it is.	This is in a town / in the country.	
2 What can you see?	I can see a van There's a woman There are two horses	in the middle of the picture. on the left / on the right. in the foreground / background.
3 What are the people doing?	A woman is The men are	reading a … • chatting together. • waiting for … • crossing the … • going shopping. • talking to … • …

4 Make a general comment.

I like I don't like	life in town the country	because	there are lots of … / there aren't any … you can meet … / go … / see … it's (too) quiet / noisy / busy / boring / …

b) Use your notes and prepare a short talk about your picture. Then practise your talk.

c) Now tell a partner about your picture.

Partner A:
Give your talk.
Remember steps 1–4 in the tip.

Partner B:
Listen to your partner's talk.
Does he / she talk about points 1–4 in the tip?

Then swap roles.

Remember the steps in 1 a):
1 say **where** it is,
2 say **what** you can see,
3 say what the people are **doing**,
4 make a general **comment**.

▸ *Skills file 9, p. 135*

▸ *Workbook 9–10, pp. 20–21*

Linkers and time phrases

Linkers and time phrases make your writing more interesting. You'll practise using them on this page.

▸ *Skills file 8, p. 133*

1 Alfie's ideal place

a) Alfie wrote this comment on the internet forum *My ideal place*. Read his text. What does he think about London?

I came to London two years ago. At first I didn't really like it. But now I think it's a great place. I'll tell you why.

In London you can go everywhere on the Tube or by bus. That's cool because you don't need a car.

Also, I really like my neighbourhood. When I want to meet my friends, I can walk to their houses. So we usually meet every evening.

And London is an amazing city for sport. I always go to football games at the weekend.

So London is my ideal place to live.

b) Copy the table. Write the red words in Alfie's comment in the table.

TIME WORDS	LINKERS
two years ago	But
...	...

2 Rob's ideal place

a) Now read Rob's comment on the internet forum. It doesn't have linkers and time phrases. Write it again. Put the linkers and time phrases from the box into the text at numbers 1–8.

Also • because • But • For example • So • last August • every Saturday • At first

I moved to the Cotswolds (1). (2) I didn't like it here. (3) now I think it's cool. The people are friendly. (4) the neighbours help you if you have a problem. (5) the towns in the Cotswolds are nice. Stratford is a famous town. I go to Stratford with my friends (6) (7) there are great shops there. (8) the Cotswolds are my ideal place to live.

b) Is Rob happy in the Cotswolds now?

3 NOW YOU

More help p.101

Now write your comment for the internet forum *My ideal place*. Write as many sentences as you can. Put your text in your DOSSIER.
Ideas: Is it in a town or in the country? Why do you like it? What are the people like?

Düsseldorf is a big city in the west of Germany. My uncle and aunt live there, and I think it's a great place to live. I like the shops ...

▸ *Workbook 11, p. 22*

1 READING

Read sentences 1–5 and the notices A–F below. Then pick the best notice for each sentence. You won't need one notice.

1 You're a tourist in the Cotswolds and you want to listen to music.
2 You're in the country and you have a problem with your bike.
3 You're 17 and you love sport.
4 You're tired and hungry. So you want a place to stay and something to eat.
5 Your little brother or sister would like a new pet.

A

KITTENS – 9 WEEKS OLD
ALL BOYS
NEED LOVING HOMES
READY TO GO.
01386 [illegible]

B

The Bantam Tea Rooms

We offer home made cakes, biscuits, scones, tea cakes and toast all day (10 am – 5 pm).
At lunchtime we serve home made soup and sandwiches.

We also have a variety of teas, coffees and hot chocolate, and soft drinks, including local apple juice.
In summer months, sit in our garden and enjoy a slice of cake or a cream tea.

We also have rooms and can offer bed and breakfast accommodation. Please ask for details.

C

MOBILE BICYCLE service and repair

We come to you.
Most services carried out on site at home/work.
Prices from £15 per bike.
Collection and delivery services available.
Call David
07927 [illegible]

D

Listen to *North Cotswolds Community Radio* for up-to-the minute news, event information, lots of music and much more.

NCCR
Entertainment you'll love
Information you'll need

E

Mickleton Rangers FC

Training at 7 pm every Thursday at sports field Stratford Road.
If interested, phone Lewy: 841408
Players must be 16 or over.

F

Help! We need more actors for our Christmas pantomime, Dick Whittington.
Village Hall, Mondays 7.30 pm
The Mickleton Players

2 MEDIATION On holidays in the Cotswolds

a) You're on holidays in the Cotswolds with your friend Arif. But Arif doesn't understand a lot of English. Look at the *Bantam Tea Rooms* notice and answer his questions – in German.

1 Wann haben sie geöffnet?
2 Es heißt *Tea Rooms*. Gibt es nur Tee oder auch andere Getränke? Welche?
3 Es ist jetzt Mittagszeit. Ich habe Hunger, möchte aber keinen Kuchen essen. Was gibt es sonst?
4 Es ist warm heute. Können wir draußen sitzen?
5 Es ist schön hier. Kann man hier vielleicht übernachten?

b) Tell your friend the most important information about *Mobile Bicycle* – in German.

► *Skills file 11, p. 137*

► *Text file 2, pp. 118–120*

1 A visit to grandad's farm

In this film our four friends from Unit 1 visit a farm.

Before you watch: Look at the photos in exercise 2, then think about these three questions:

1 What are the names of the four friends?
2 Where do the friends live? What will be new for them on the farm? Collect ideas.
3 Do you think they will like life on the farm? Why (not)?

2 Chill in the country

a) Watch the film.

b) Now work with a partner. Copy and complete the captions. Write as much as you can.

Scene 1: The four friends plan a visit to …

Scene 2: The friends arrive at …

Scene 3: The kids have …

Scene 4: But first they have to …

Scene 5: In the evening they …

Scene 6: The next morning they …

3 NOW YOU What do *you* think?

a) Read the five sentences below.

1 The kids had a good time in the country.
2 They enjoyed the work on the farm.
3 Alfie's grandad wasn't very nice.
4 The kids had lots of fun in the evening.
5 They'll all come back again next weekend.

b) Now talk about the sentences with a partner. Do you agree?

Say why you agree or don't agree.

I agree because … *I don't agree because …*

Yes
I agree.
That's true.
You're right.

No
I don't agree.
That's rubbish.

1 Molly's questionnaire

Students in Molly's class are finding out about other students in their class.

a) Copy Molly's questionnaire.

		me	Partner 1: Hana	Partner 2: Ali	Partner 3: Noah
Have you ever	visited a farm?	lots of times!!			
	ridden a donkey?	once			
	been on a plane?	twice			
	moved house?	no			

b) Listen to Molly. Complete the answers for her three partners.

c) Now read her report. Find three mistakes in it.

Two students have visited a farm and I live on a farm. But Noah hasn't visited a farm.
Only one person has ridden a donkey – me! The others have never ridden a donkey.
We have all been on a plane. Hana has been on a plane five times.
Two students have moved house. I haven't moved house.

2 The present perfect

a) Complete the rule.

FOCUS

Das ***present perfect*** besteht aus zwei Teilen:

I You	have	+	visited a farm once. never mov... house.
He She It	has		been on a plane once. rid... a donkey twice.
We They	have		

Regelmäßige Verben erhalten die Endung ...

Einige Verben haben unregelmäßige Formen. Diese musst du lernen, z.B. ***be*** – ..., ***ride*** – ...

Mit dem ***present perfect*** sagst du, dass du etwas schon einmal, mehrmals oder noch nie gemacht hast.

Signalwörter sind:
ever, never, once, twice, lots of times.

Statt ... kann auch die Kurzform **'ve** stehen.

b) Copy and complete the table for regular verbs.

I work	I've worked
I start	I've ...
I finish	...
I text	...
I open	...
I cook	...

c) Look at the list of irregular verbs on page 200 and complete the table.

I buy	I've bought
I meet	I've ...
I speak	...
I have	I've had
I am	I've been
I ride	...
I see	...
I find	...

► *Language file 4, p. 141*

3 Molly and Rob

a) Read the sentences and pick the right form of the verb.

1 I know that Rob has / have seen a fox once.
2 And I know that Molly has / have saved sheep from a river.
3 Molly and Rob has / have been to Stratford lots of times.
4 Rob and his sister has / have lived in a block of flats.
5 And Molly? No, she hasn't / haven't lived in a block of flats.

b) O NOW YOU What about you? Write six sentences about yourself. // ● p.102

I've … once / a few times / lots of times. I've never …

ridden a horse

spoken to a star

been to a beach

had a disaster

found money in the street

worked on a farm

More practice 6 p.102

4 YOUR TASK Find out about students in your class

a) Make a questionnaire with four questions.
O Use the questions below. ● Make your own questions.
Put your own information under *me*. Leave space for three partners.

		me	Partner 1: …	Partner 2: …	Partner 3: …
Have you ever	lost money?	once			
	met a famous person?	no			
	been to the sea?	no			
	seen a game of rugby?	no			

b) Walk around: Ask the questions and make notes of your partners' answers.

c) Look at your notes and write what you have found out. Write sentences like this:

Only I Two / Three students	have	visited … ridden… met … been to … had … found … talked … played …
One student / Nobody	has	

STOP! CHECK! GO!

Ein Lösungsblatt für die Aufgaben 1–4 kannst du von deiner Lehrerin/deinem Lehrer erhalten. Den Hörtext (S. 45) findest du auch auf der Audio-CD im Workbook.

1 WORDS Town and country words

a) Copy the diagram. Then put the words from the green box into your diagram.

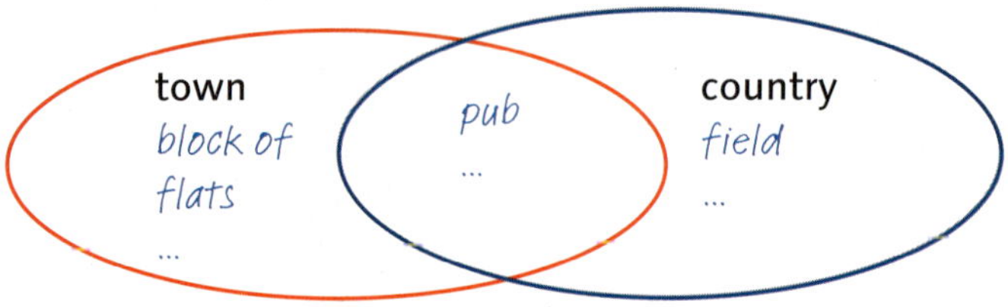

block of flats • bushes • church • crossroads • farm • farm gate • *field* • high street • park • *pub* • sheep • stadium • station • track • van • river • village • wood

b) Can you find more words for your diagram?

c) **Partner check:** Compare your diagram with other students.

Where is post office in your diagram?

In the middle. You can find post offices in the town and in the country.

Oh yes, that's right!

2 WORDS How many differences can you find?

Partner B: Go to page 90. **Partner A:** Look at this page.

a) Make a list of eight things in the picture and write where they are:
in the foreground / background, in the middle, on the left / right, behind, in front of, next to, near, ...

Things in the picture	Where in my picture?	In my partner's picture
a wood	*in the background, on the left*	
	...	

b) Now talk to your partner about your pictures.
Find at least five differences. Make notes in the third column of your table.

There's a ... in the background on the left.

In my picture it's on the right.

3 LANGUAGE A visit to *Cotswold Farm Park*

What's the missing word: *has* or *have*?

Rob's sisters Jodie and Evie are at *Cotswold Farm Park*. They ... (1) seen lots of things in the park. They're excited because Adam Henson ... (2) come into the farm park.

They know Adam, the owner of the park, from TV.

Jodie ______ Oh hello, Adam. We always watch you on TV!
Adam ______ Hi! ... (3) you had a nice day so far? What ... (4) you seen?
Evie ______ We ... (5) just been to see the rabbits. They're so cute.
Jodie ______ And the pigs! I ... (6) never been so near a pig before. They're cool.
Adam ______ Well, enjoy your visit. Nice to see you. Bye.
Jodie + Evie _ Bye, Adam.

Adam Henson

4 Telephone language

a) You're a tourist. You phone *Mobile Bicycle*.
What do you say? What does the other person say?
Write the dialogue.

MOBILE BICYCLE
service and repair
We come to you.
Call David 07927

Tourist:

Hello. Can / I / please / to / David / talk / ?
(Sage hallo und frage, ob du mit David sprechen kannst.)

Mobile bicycle:

to the phone / he / can't / I'm sorry / come / right now.
(Sage, dass David gerade nicht ans Telefon kommen kann.)
I / a message / take / Can / ?
(Frage, ob du etwas ausrichten kannst.)

Tourist:

a problem / I / my bike / have / with
(Du hast ein Problem mit deinem Rad.)
Can / David / me / help / ?
(Frage, ob David helfen kann.)

Mobile bicycle:

give / your message / him / I'll
(Sage, dass du es ausrichten wirst)
your name / What's / where / and / are you?
(Frage nach dem Namen des Anrufers und wo er oder sie gerade ist.)

Tourist:

(Sage deinen Namen und buchstabiere ihn.)
in Chipping Campden / outside / I'm / the church
(Sage, wo du bist.)

Mobile bicycle:

be / in an hour / David / will / there
(Sage, David wird in einer Stunde da sein.)

Tourist:

(Bedanke dich und verabschiede dich.)

Mobile bicycle:

(Sage: „Bitte, gern geschehen", und verabschiede dich.)

b) Practise the dialogue with a partner. Swap roles.

5 A picture story

a) Look at the pictures A–F and put them in the right order.

A

• Mr Jones' dog found rubbish in the field next to the sheep.

B

Mr Jones phoned Rob's dad. "I'm busy", said Rob's dad • "I can come on Saturday."

C

• Mr Jones, a farmer, found a sheep in his field. It couldn't stand. • Its leg was sore.

D

• Mr Jones and his family talked about the problem.

E

• Mr and Mrs Jones watched the monitors. • They saw two people and a car.

F

• Rob's dad came with his cameras. • Mr and Mrs Jones put CCTV cameras in the fields.

b) Partner check: Now compare your answers with a partner.

– I think picture B is number 1.

– I don't agree! I think picture ... is number 1.

c) WRITING Copy and complete the story in A–F.

• = Write a time phrase • = Write a linker (*and, because, so, but, when, ...*)

One day in September, Mr Jones, a farmer, found a sheep ...

d) ● WRITING Finish the story. For help, look at the story on pages 34–35.

Mrs Jones ...

Mr Jones drove his tractor ...

"OK. We'll take these men".

6 LISTENING Is it better to live in the country or in the city?

a) You're going to listen to a radio programme. Before you listen, copy these names in a list:

Anna:
Thomas:
Nina:
Karan:
Joe:

b) Now listen and find out:
Where do the callers live?
(Make notes: co = country, ci = city)
Do they like living there?
(likes it = ☺, doesn't like it = ☹)
Example: *Anna: co, ☹*

c) Listen again and write down why they like it or don't like where they live:
Anna: co, ☹, bus to school – an hour

7 APPOINTMENTS Have you ever met a famous footballer?

a) Copy the table. Think of three more questions and add them. (They can be funny!)

Have you ever ...	*me*	*1 o'clock partner*	*2 o'clock partner*	*3 o'clock partner*
played tennis?				
visited another country?				
been to hospital?				
seen a real elephant?				
spoken to a famous person?				
...				

b) Answer the questions for yourself. Then make an appointment with three partners and ask them your questions. Note their answers. Yes = ✓ or no = ✗.
Have you ever ... – Yes, I have. (✓) / No, I haven't. (✗)

c) Tell another partner / the class what you have found out:
Malte has (never) been to hospital. Svenja has ...

8 My learner log

Copy and complete your learner log. Then put it in your DOSSIER.

My learner log for Unit 2

Now I can ...
- talk about pictures: 😃 😐 ☹
- take or give a message on the phone: ...
- say where I have been: ...
- say what I have never done: ...
- use time phrases and linkers: 😃 😐 ☹

After Unit 2
- I know a bit about country life in the Cotswolds.
- I know some English teen language.
- These pages were easy: ...
- These pages were difficult: ...

After Unit 2 my English is: GREAT! 👍 / OK 👉 / NOT VERY GOOD 👎

► *Workbook (Portfolio), p. 25* ► *Workbook (Revision), p. 26* ► *Workbook (Test preparation), pp. 27–28*

Plans for next weekend – using the future tense

1 Plans

a) Read this email from your English friend Andy. What does he want to do in August?

b) The future

Die Zukunftsform bildest du mit *will* oder *'ll*.

1 Copy four examples from Andy's email.

Verneinungen verwenden das Wort *won't*.

2 Copy two examples from Andy's email.

Fragen beginnen mit *Will...?*

3 Copy one example from Andy's email.

▸ *Language file 5, p. 142*

Hi Burak!

Hooray! We have a week's holiday!
I think I'll stay at home today. Maybe I'll be good and tidy my room. But tomorrow I'll go into town with some friends, and in the evening we'll watch the new Sherlock Holmes film. I hope it won't be too American!

And next Friday I'll start my new job. I'll get up early and do my first paper round. I hope it won't rain!

I'd really like to come and see you in Germany this week, but I won't have the money. But I'm sure I'll have more money in summer, so maybe I could visit you in August.
When will your summer holidays begin?
Do you have plans for this weekend? Will you stay at home, or will you visit your grandma again?

Best wishes, Andy

2 100 weekend activities

a) What will you do next weekend?
Write ten sentences with the words from the table.

Hier sammelst du Ideen für Wortschatz, den du in ex. 4 benutzen kannst.

Maybe I'll	buy • do • go • make • meet • start • travel • tidy • visit • watch	to Berlin • my grandparents • some new clothes • into town • my new job • a special dinner • a film • my friends • my homework • my room

b) Think: Write sentences with the same verbs, but with different endings.
Write as many as you can.

1 Maybe I'll buy a new laptop / tickets for a concert / ...
2 I think I'll make a cake / a birthday card / ...
3 I'm sure we'll go to the water park.

c) Pair: Compare with a partner.

d) Share: Write your ideas on the board.

Do you have a 100 ideas for weekend activities?

3 The weather

Andy lives in Leeds, in the north of England.
On Monday you look on the internet and find the five day weather forecast for Leeds.

Today: Mon	Tues	Wed	Thurs	Fri
10° C	15° C	18° C	12° C	18° C
5	6	1	15	14

a) Look at the online information. What will the weather be like in Leeds this week?

1 It will be sunny / cloudy tomorrow in Leeds, but it will / won't rain.
2 Tomorrow will be warmer / colder than today.
3 On Wednesday it will be sunny / cloudy.
4 And it won't be windy / sunny on Wednesday.
5 On Thursday it will be rainy / foggy and it will / won't be very windy.
6 Thursday will be warmer / colder than Wednesday.

b) Andy will do his paper round on Friday.
What can you say about the weather on Friday?

Friday will …
It will …
It won't …
I think it will be a good / bad day for Andy's paper round because …

4 NOW YOU

a) Read Andy's email in exercise 1 again. What questions does he ask you?

b) Write to Andy and answer his questions. Write at least six sentences.

Hi Andy
Thanks … I hope we'll meet …
My holidays start …, so maybe you could come …
You ask for my plans …
On Saturday I'll…
On Sunday …
How is your new job?
I hope …
…

Say what you will do or what you won't do.
You can find ideas in Andy's letter and in exercise 2.

Maybe you can also write what you did yesterday (1–2 sentences). Then you'll need the *simple past*. Look at pages 26–27 for help.
Example:
I didn't read your email yesterday because I went to a party. It was good fun, but it was late when I got home.

c) **Partner check:** Show your email to a partner and check your partner's email. Check especially the verbs with *will* and *won't*.

Unit 3

Liverpool – the world ...

A

B

C

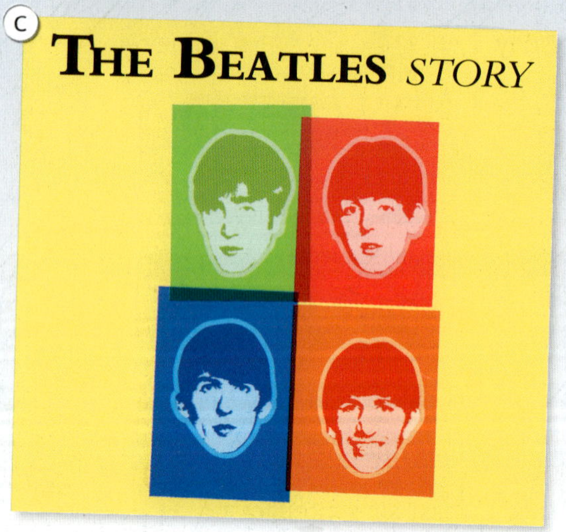

D

1 About Liverpool

a) Listen to six sound files. Match them with six of the pictures of Liverpool (A–H).

b) Listen again and pick the right answer.

1 When was the Titanic disaster? A 1900 B 1912 C 1932.
2 What's the colour of Liverpool FC? A white B blue C red.
3 When did people start to come from China to Liverpool? In the A 1850s B 1900s C 1950s.
4 Ships from Liverpool took slaves from Africa to A Europe B China C America.
5 What can you find in Liverpool ONE? A a harbour B a museum C shops and cafes.
6 Lots of people from Liverpool went to America and A Turkey B Australia C Germany.

▸ Text file 3, p. 121 ▸ Workbook 1, p. 29

E

F

H

G

The ferry across the river Mersey

2 PEOPLE AND PLACES The Beatles

Watch the film and find out:

a) What are the names of the four Beatles?

... Lennon ... Mc Cartney

... Harrison ... Starr

b) When did the Beatles sing together?

- In the 1960s.
- In the 1980s.
- In the 1990s.

c) What are the full song titles?

- She ... you, yeah, yeah, yeah!
- Eight days a ...
- Let it ...
- Baby, you can drive my ...

▸ *Workbook 2–3, p. 29*

Ben is in trouble

1 Trouble at school

a) Talk to a partner about the pictures. What's the right order of the pictures? More help p.103

I think picture ... is first.

Yes, and then it's picture ...

Really? I don't agree. I think picture ... comes before picture ...

A

B

C

D

b) Now listen to the story and check.

c) Read sentences 1–4. Match them with pictures A–D. You can listen again and check your answers.

1 "You aren't allowed to sell junk food."
2 "A packet of crisps, please."
3 "Hey, what are you kids doing?"
4 It was a very heavy school bag today.

d) Listen again and finish these sentences. //● p.104

1 Ben does not want to meet (A) his friends (B) the teachers (C) the principal.
2 He tries to sell (A) sausages (B) chicken (C) crisps.
3 **One** packet of crisps costs (A) 50p (B) 55p (C) £1.
4 When the teacher comes Ben puts his bag behind (A) his bicycle (B) his friend (C) his back.
5 Ms Hall takes Ben to (A) the classroom (A) the principal's office (C) his father.
6 At this school you aren't allowed to (A) sell (B) bring (C) buy crisps and chocolate bars.

2 A letter from school

a) The principal asks Ben's dad to do two things. What are they?

b) Find these words in the letter. Then pick the right meaning from the box.

1 sell	4 less
2 healthy food	5 school rules
3 junk food	6 yours sincerely

A best wishes
B opposite of *more*
C sweets, crisps, burgers, etc.
D what the school says you must do
E opposite of *buy*
F food that is good for you

South Liverpool High School

Monday, 10th January

Dear Mr Chung

We only sell healthy food here at school. This is very important because young people are eating more and more junk food. We want them to eat less junk food and as much healthy food as possible.

Today your son, Ben, brought junk food to school and sold it to other students. This is against our school rules. Please talk to Ben about this. If he sells junk food in school again, I will send him home for a week.

Please come to the school, and we will of course give you Ben's junk food.

Yours sincerely

Roger Bell

3 Trouble at home

Read what Ben's father said. Then put Ben's answers in the right order and act the dialogue.

Dad
Ben, what happened at school?
What sort of food?
Why did you sell junk food?
But it's against the school rules!
You must never do this again, Ben!

Ben
– Oh, Dad. It was nothing.
I sold some food at school.
– I know! I'm really sorry, Dad.
– Er ... crisps.
– OK, Dad.
– I wanted to make some money.

4 WORDS

a) Match the pictures with words in the box. Example: *A – cereal bars B – ...*

- biscuits
- cereal bars
- chocolate bars
- chips
- energy drinks
- fruit
- hot dogs
- sweets

More practice 1 p.104

b) Walk around: Talk to other students about food at your school. What do *you* think? And what do *they* think? ▸ Wordbank 3, p. 148

We can't buy ice cream at school. I think that's bad.

Really? I think ...

More practice 2 p.105

▸ Workbook 4–5, p. 30

Good at selling things

1 What's wrong?

a) How does Ben feel? And can Mrs Fox, his business studies teacher, help him? Read the dialogue and find out.

Mrs Fox Oh, Ben, I'd like to talk to you, please.
Ben Yes, Miss?
Mrs Fox You aren't as active in class as you were last term. What's wrong?
Ben Well, Miss, I'm not doing very well at school this term.
Mrs Fox But everybody is good at something. I hear that you're the best salesperson in the school!
Ben Ha, ha, ha, Miss. Very funny!
Mrs Fox Seriously, Ben. I think you could be good at business.
Ben If I sell things at school, I'll be in trouble again.
Mrs Fox You shouldn't sell junk food. Look ... I've heard of a competition. It's for people who are interested in business. Perfect for you!

Ben It sounds good, Miss. But I don't know what I can sell.
Mrs Fox If you take part in the competition, I'll help you as much as I can.
Ben I'll think about it, Miss.
Mrs Fox You'll find more information if you look in the school newsletter.

b) Which sentences of Mrs Fox tell you ...

1 that she wants to chat with Ben?
2 that Ben isn't taking part in her lessons very much this term?
3 that she knows Ben has tried to sell junk food?
4 that she wants to help Ben?
5 where he can read about the competition? More practice 3 p. 105

c) WORDS

Look again at the dialogue in 1a) and find the missing words. Each word has only **two** letters.

1 Ben, I'd like to talk ... you, please.
2 Ben isn't ... active in class ... he was last term.
3 Mrs Fox says that Ben could be good ... business.
4 ... Ben sells things at school, he'll be ... trouble.
5 But if Ben takes part in the competition, Mrs Fox will help him ... much ... she can.
6 Ben will find more information ... he looks ... the school newsletter.

▸ Workbook 6, p. 31

2 A competition

a) Read about the competition. What must students do?

SOUTH LIVERPOOL HIGH SCHOOL
NEWSLETTER

SL HS

BIZ 4 KIDZ – a school competition

The competition:
- Work in teams. Teams begin with £75.
- Try to make as much money as you can.
- Teams who make the most money win.

On TV: The TV programme BIZ 4 KIDZ will film you at school. So if you take part, you'll be on TV.

The prize: If you win the competition, your team will visit London for a weekend!

Talk to Mrs Fox today about your ideas for a business!

b) Sentences 1–6 are wrong. Read the newsletter again and correct the sentences.

1 You take part alone.
2 You try to make £75.
3 Teams who make £75 win the competition.
4 If you take part, you'll go to London.
5 If you win, your team will go to the USA.
6 Phone the TV people if you want to take part.

3 YOUR TASK Are you good at business?

Make teams of three or four. Each team has to think of a good business idea and present it on a poster.

Step 1 Ideas
Decide what you can make or sell.
Find a name for your business.
Decide where you can sell.

Step 2 Money
Decide these things in your team:

We need:	*Cost?*	*We can sell:*	*Price?*	*Profit:*
50 balloons	*4 €*	*50 balloons*	*1 € per balloon*	*50 €*
pens	*5 €*			*– 9 €*
	Total: 9 €			*Total: 41 €*

Step 3 Present your business plan More help p. 105

Make a poster with your business plan. Then present it to the class. Vote for the best idea.

BIZ 4 KIDZ
Our business plan:
Make and sell animal balloons
What do we need?
Balloons, pens
How much will they cost?
50 balloons cost 4 euros.

Here are some ideas for your presentation:

Here's our business plan. It's for animal balloons.

We think that we can sell ...

We must buy ...

▸ Workbook 7, p. 31

1 Before you read

Match the captions with pictures 1–5.

a) Not many people want to buy cakes. b) Show me the photo!
c) A good talk with dad d) A messy kitchen e) At the market

Something special

Ben looked around the kitchen. There was flour everywhere. And there was a broken egg on the table.
"If Dad comes home now, I'll be in trouble," Ben thought.
Then Ben's dad came home. He was earlier than usual.
"What has happened to this kitchen?" he asked. He looked angry.
"Take it easy, Dad," Ben said. "I made these cupcakes with my friends. It's for a business competition at school. If we win, ..."

But Ben's father wasn't impressed.
"Forget the competition," he said. "You have to work hard at school. If you work hard at school, you'll get a good job."
"But Dad, I want to leave school as soon as I can – at 16. I want to work in the shop with you," Ben answered.
Ben's father sat down. "Listen, Ben," he said. "Your grandfather left China when he was a boy. He came to Liverpool and worked hard. And I left school when I was 16. Now I have to work seven days a week in the shop!"
"Dad," Ben said. "I don't want to hear these boring old stories!"
"But you can learn from them!" his dad answered. He was angry now. "You aren't going to leave school at 16. You're going to work hard at school and get a better job!"
Ben and his dad didn't talk again that evening.

The next day Ben and his friends brought the cupcakes to school. But in an hour they only sold six cakes. What a disaster!
Ben was very fed up at home that evening. His dad felt it.
"I'm sorry that I was so negative last night," he said.
"Thanks, Dad," Ben said. Then he told his father about the disaster.

"Please try a cupcake, Dad," he said. "I have 44 cakes here!"
Ben's dad laughed. He took a cake and tried it.
"Hmmm, it's good," he said. "But it isn't good enough!"
"What do you mean, Dad?" he asked.
"Well, I mean it's as good as the cupcakes in my shop. But if you want to sell your cakes, they'll have to be something special!"
"You're right, Dad. I'll think about that," Ben said.

1

2

3

The next day Ben took the bus to school. He remembered his father's words. How could the cupcakes be 'something special'? Then the bus stopped outside a music club, and Ben saw a poster. "Maybe this is an idea for our business," he thought. He took a photo. When the other kids saw the photo, they were very excited. "We can do something with this," they all agreed.

4

On the day of the competition, lots of schools from Liverpool sent a team to a market in the city centre. They tried to sell as much as they could. The team with the biggest profit could stay in the competition and represent Liverpool. Ben was very excited about his team's new idea. What was their idea? And could they win the competition?

If you want to find out, listen to the radio programme in 3.

5

2 What's the right answer? p.106

Copy the sentences and complete them correctly – A, B, C or D.

1 Ben's dad was unhappy at first because A Ben ate the cakes. B Ben had no friends. C the kitchen was messy. D the cakes were bad.
2 Ben's dad thinks school is A important. B not important. C a waste of time. D easy.
3 Ben's dad thought the cakes were A fantastic. B better than the cakes in his shop. C terrible. D OK, but could be better.
4 Ben got his new idea from A his friends. B Mrs Fox. C a poster. D a text message.

More practice 4 p.106

3 The end of the story

a) Listen to the radio programme. Who won the Liverpool competition?
b) Listen to the programme again. Put pictures A–D in the right order.

A

B

C

c) Listen again. More help p.106
Note what the three teams sold and what profit they made.

More practice 5 p.106

D

▸ Workbook 8–9, p. 32

SKILLS TRAINING Note-taking

1 Natasha Jonas

a) First read the notes.

Natasha Jonas
Where she is from: ______________
Sports: __________ *and* __________
In 2012: ______________
Why she is special now: ______________
What's bad about boxing: ______________
What's good about boxing: ______________

When you read a text, it's useful to take notes. They help you to find out the most important information.

b) Now read the article about Natasha Jonas. Work with a partner and find out: Is the underlined information useful for the notes above or not? *1 not useful 2 ...*

Liverpool girls want to be like Tasha!

1 Natasha Jonas, who was born in 1984, is from
2 Toxteth in Liverpool and she's a top British
3 sportswoman. She started as a footballer, but
4 then she changed to boxing.

Female boxers weren't allowed to fight in the
5 Olympics before 2012. But at the London
6 Olympics in 2012, Tasha was one of three British
7 women boxers in the British Olympic team.

8 Natasha is a great role model for young people
in Liverpool. Her motto is: 'Respect your talent.'
In other words, find what you're good at and be
the best you can. For her it was boxing.

9 Of course, some people think people shouldn't box.
10 They say that boxers can get hurt. That's true, but
11 footballers and rugby players can get hurt too.

Lots of girls watched Natasha and the other female
boxers at the Olympics and they saw that boxing
12 makes you fit and strong. And now they want to
be like Tasha!

c) Copy and complete the notes about Natasha.

d) Use your notes and give a short talk about Natasha.

► *Skills file 10, p. 136*

To find out the most important information in a text:
- Read the text.
- Underline **important** facts for your task.
- Write **short** notes.

► *Skills file 4, p. 127*

► *Workbook 10, p. 33*

Giving opinions – for or against

1 Two comments about Natasha and boxing

a) Read the two comments about the article on page 56 and answer the questions:

1 Who doesn't like boxing?
2 Who thinks Natasha is a great person?

I think that the article about Natasha is very interesting for lots of reasons.

In my opinion Tasha is an amazing woman. She is a really good role model for young people. I also think that Natasha looks good.

In a word, I would like to be like Tasha!

Hannah, Liverpool

When you write a comment, follow these three steps:
- Give your opinion.
- Then give reasons.
- Think of a good ending.

I really don't like boxing. I don't think that it should be an Olympic sport.

The first thing is that boxing is dangerous. Even Natasha says that. And the second thing is that it's violent. In my opinion people shouldn't fight!

I really hope that young people will prefer different sports.

Sam, London

b) Read Hannah's and Sam's comments again. Find the English phrases for:

1 Ich denke, dass ...
2 Meiner Meinung nach ist Tasha ...
3 Ich denke auch, dass ...
4 Kurz gefasst möchte ich ...
5 Und zweitens ist es ...
6 Ich hoffe sehr, dass ...

2 NOW YOU

○ Write your own comment on Natasha and boxing.

● Choose your own sport and write a comment about it. More help p. 107

a) Write a first draft. Follow the three steps *(opinion – reasons – ending)*.

I think	*boxing is a great / stupid sport for women.*
In my opinion	*it's a violent sport and women shouldn't fight.*
	it makes you fit and strong.
	women can do the same sports as men.
I also think that	*other sports are more interesting.*
	other sports make you fit.
	boxing is very popular with men and women.
I really hope that	*more women will start boxing.*
	all boxing will stop.
	boxing for women will stop.

Remember:
- Use sentences from the comments in exercise 1, but change some words:
  She is a really good role model.
  => She is a terrible role model.
- Use linkers:
  I think boxing is a great sport. It's exciting.
  => I think boxing is a great sport because it's exciting.

b) Partner check: Read your partner's comment and check:

1 Did your partner follow the three steps *(opinion – reasons– ending)*?
2 Did he / she use phrases from exercise 1 *(In my opinion, I think, ...)*?
3 Did he / she use linkers *(because / and / so ...)*?

c) Now correct and rewrite your comment. Then put it in your DOSSIER.

▸ Skills file 8, pp. 132–134

▸ Workbook 11, pp. 34–35

1 At the tourist office

Two German tourists are at a tourist office in Liverpool. The boy doesn't speak English well.

a) Look at the poster and read the boy's questions in German.

b) Now read questions 1–4. There is often more than one way of asking the same question. With a partner, decide which **two** ways are correct.

1 Excuse me, please,
- A are there cheaper tickets for students?
- B we're students. Can we get less expensive tickets?
- C can students buy tickets?

2 And can you tell me:
- A how long is the tour, please?
- B how is the tour, please?
- C how long is the trip on the ferry?

3 And can you also tell me, please,
- A is there a cafe on the ferry?
- B do you sit inside or outside on the ferry?
- C can we sit inside on the boat?

4 And one more question, please.
- A We only have euros. Is that OK?
- B Where can we get euros?
- C Can we pay in euros?

c) Now listen to the dialogue. Which questions do you hear – A, B or C? More practice 6 p.108

> Es ist wichtig, höflich zu sein! Sage z.B.:
> *Excuse me, please, ...*
> *Can you tell me, please, ...*
> *And one more question, please, ...*
> Und sage immer *please* und *thank you*!

2 The man in the tourist office p.108

a) Listen to the dialogue again. This time, listen to the man in the tourist office. What are the right answers?

1 If you're under 15, a ticket is only A £2.50 B £4.50 C £4.75.
2 The next ferry leaves at A 10.00 B 11.00 C 11.30.
3 You can sit inside **or** outside. Outside you A pay more B pay less C see more.
4 There's a bank near here, in A Water Street B Walton Street C Warbury Street.

b) Now give your partner the information – in German. Then listen and check.

Der Mann sagt, dass die Karten nur ..., wenn wir ...
Die nächste Fähre ... Wir können ... Es gibt eine Bank ...

▸ Skills file 11, p. 137

▸ Workbook 12, p. 36

1 The 'SW6 Olympics'

a) Before you watch: Look at the photos of Sam, Tally, Ruby and Alfie. Who is in which photo? And what will you see in this film?

A A football match in the park. B A sports competition. C A sports lesson at school.

A

B

C
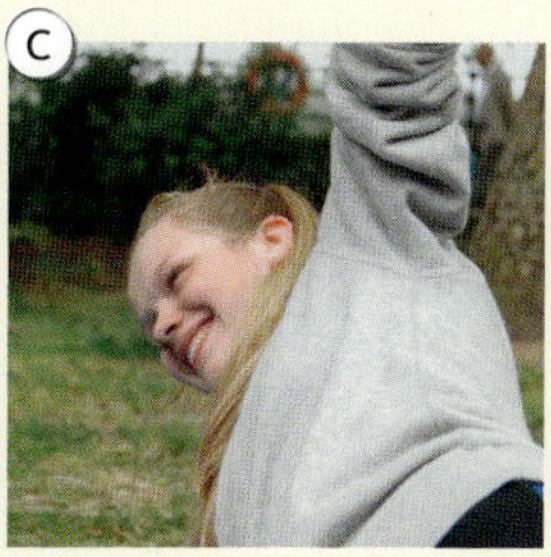

D

b) Now watch the film and check your answers in a).

2 Who said what?

a) Work with a partner. Who said sentences A–F? Write the names.

A

B

C

Scene 1
- A We want to go to town.
- B We all know that you're the football champion.

Scene 2
- C You can do it!
- D Get ready. Steady. Go!

Scene 3
- E That was fun today.
- F Yeah, I guess you're right.

b) Now watch the film again and check your answers. More practice 7 p.109

3 The message of the story

a) What do you think is the message in this story?

- Some sports are better than others.
- The most important thing is to have fun.
- Sport is a waste of time.
- It's most important to be good at sport.
- All sports are good.

b) Compare with two partners. Do they agree with you?

I think the message is ...

Really? I think ...

I agree. I think ...

1 Good business ideas!

Mrs Fox is talking to a different group of students about their ideas.

First look at the picture and make a list of the five business ideas.

2 If …

a) Read the FOCUS-box.

FOCUS

Mit *if*-Sätzen sagst du, was unter bestimmten Bedingungen passieren wird:
If it's cold, people will want hot soup.

Der Satz besteht aus zwei Teilen:
Einem Nebensatz mit *if* im *simple present* + einem Hauptsatz mit *will (Kurzform 'll)* oder *won't*.

If it's cold, *people will want hot soup.*

Der Nebensatz mit *if* kann vorne oder hinten stehen:
People won't buy it if it's cold.

b) Now look again at the sentences in exercise 1. Write the six sentences with *if*.

1 *If it's sunny, …*
2 *But people won't …*
3 … 4 … 5 …

► Language file 11, p. 145

3 Ben's plans for Saturday

Put the sentence parts together.

1 If the weather is nice, I'll ...
2 But if the weather is bad, I'll ...
3 If I have enough money, I'll ...
4 If my friends are free, I'll ...
5 But if I have lots of homework, I won't ...

... meet them in town.
... ride my bike in the park.
... go out. I'll stay at home and work.
... stay at home and watch a DVD.
... go bowling. Bowling isn't cheap!

4 What are Ben's ideas for Sunday?

p. 109

Finish the sentences.

1 If it ... (rain) on Sunday, Ben will stay at home. *If it rains, ...*
2 But if Ben ... (stay) at home, he'll be bored.
3 If Ben's friends ... (come) to his house, they'll have fun.
4 If Ben ... (have) some milk, eggs and flour, they'll make more cupcakes.
5 And if the cupcakes ... (look) nice, Ben's friends will eat them. They don't need any cakes for the competition now!

More practice 8 p. 109

5 What will happen if ...?

a) Think: Write as many sentences about the picture as you can.

If the cat jumps, the baby will be surprised.
If the baby is surprised, the ice cream will fall.
If the ice cream ..., the dog will jump.
If the dog ..., ...

b) Pair: Compare your sentences with a partner.

c) Share: Read your sentences to the class. Who has the best sentences?

STOP! CHECK! GO!

Ein Lösungsblatt für die Aufgaben 1–4 kannst du von deiner Lehrerin/deinem Lehrer erhalten. Den Hörtext (S. 64) findest du auch auf der Audio-CD im Workbook.

1 WORDS A quiz about countries

a) Look at the flags. Write the country for each flag.

Australia • China • Britain • Denmark • France • Spain • Turkey • the USA

b) Now compare with a partner.

I think number 1 is France.

Really? I think you're wrong. I think it's ...

Yes, I think you're right!

c) Which two countries do you want to visit? Why? Write two sentences.

I'd like to visit ... because there are good beaches / they have great food / it's always sunny / ...

2 WORDS Business words

a) Match the words on the left with the phrases on the right: *take part in a competition*

take part in	+	as much money as you can
be good		your bike to a friend
advertise		your business online
make		a good idea
have		*a competition*
sell		at business

b) Choose verbs from a) and make your own sentences – as many as you can.

1 I make money with my Saturday job. I work in a garden center and I ...

2 I took part in a competition last summer. I went to ...

3 REVISION An interview with a footballer

Blue verbs are regular (+ *-ed*). Red verbs have a special form. You can check them on page 200.

Ben writes for a football magazine. He interviewed footballer Tarik in Liverpool. Complete the interview. Use the *simple past*.

Reporter — Hi Tarik. Great to meet you! You ... (come) to Liverpool last year from Germany. Are you German?

Tarik — Yes, I am. I was born in Germany and I ... (start) to play football in Germany. But later I ... (play) for a Turkish club.

Reporter — When ... you ... (leave) your Turkish club? And why?

Tarik — I ... (leave) them in September 2012 because I ... (want) to go back to Germany. First I ... (miss) my old club, but soon I ... (find) new friends and ... (feel) at home in my new club.

Reporter — And when ... you ... (start) in Liverpool?

Tarik — I ... (arrive) in the last week of August 2013. My first match ... (be) in September.

Reporter — You ... (make) people happy with your two goals last Saturday.

Tarik — Yes, lots of Liverpool fans ... (write) to me after that. I'm glad they're happy because I like Liverpool a lot!

▸ Language file 3, p. 140

4 LANGUAGE Comparing

a) Compare these things.
Write like this:
Ferry A is bigger than ferry B.
Ferry C is the biggest.

1 Plymouth (258.700 people) – Liverpool (445.200 people) – Manchester (503.100 people) *big*
2 Beatles Museum (£15.95) – River trip (£4.70) – Liverpool bus tour (£10) *cheap*
3 the River Mersey (112 km) – the River Weser (452 km) – the River Thames (246 km) *short*
4 skiing – swimming – football *easy*

b) Expressions with *as … as …* can make texts more interesting. Match some of the expressions in the box with the pictures (1–7).

as big as a house
as green as grass
as strong as a lion
as hungry as a bear
as cold as ice
as quiet as a mouse

▸ *Language file 10, p. 144*

c) Make up your own comparisons.

1 Our cat is as black as …
2 He ran as fast as …
3 I was as tired as …
4 The film was as boring as …
5 The river was as deep as …
6 The house was as big as …

5 LANGUAGE Your plans for next weekend

a) Use the ideas below and make a questionnaire. Choose at least four questions.

What will you do if …
… friends suddenly arrive at your house?
… it rains all weekend?
… you get lots of homework on Friday?
… you're not well and have to stay in bed?
… you're not allowed to watch TV?
… you're alone at home on Saturday evening?

What will you do if …	*me*	*Partner 1: …*	*Partner 2: …*	*Partner 3: …*
… you get lots of homework on Friday?	*I'll be very angry*			
…	…			

b) Answer the questions for yourself. Then talk to three partners. Ask them your questions and answer their questions.

c) Write about your partners. Write as many sentences as you can.
If we get lots of homework on Friday, three of us will … and one will …

6 SPEAKING Making plans in Liverpool

Partner B: Look at page 91.

Partner A: You want to spend the day with a friend in Liverpool. You want to go to the places below. Your friend has different ideas.

a) Tell your partner
- where you want to go,
- what you want to do there,
- what it costs.

Partner A _ I'd like to ...
Partner B _ Oh? Why?
Partner A _ Because I like ... / it's ...

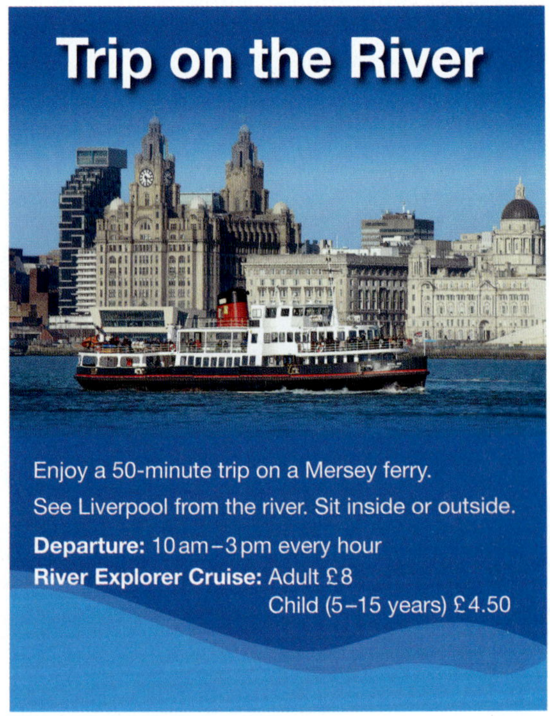

b) Listen to your partner's ideas and take notes.

c) Talk to your partner and choose two things that you want to visit together.

Partner A _ In my opinion we should ...
Partner B _ Really? I disagree. I think ...
Partner A _ Oh, ..., OK. I agree. Let's go to ...

7 LISTENING and MEDIATION *City Explorer Bus Tour*

a) Du bist mit deiner Familie in Liverpool. Ihr plant eine Bustour. Höre dir die Ansage an und mache Notizen. Deine Familie möchte wissen:
- wie lange die Tour dauert,
- wann die erste Tour am Morgen startet,
- wie viel die Karten für Erwachsene und Kinder kosten,
- ob es auch ein Familienticket gibt und wie viel das kostet.

b) Überprüfe deine Notizen beim zweiten Hören.

8 READING and WRITING More sport at school?

a) Read these online comments. Who likes more sport at school and who doesn't?

In my opinion everybody should have two sport lessons a day. Sport makes you active and strong.
And at school you can try different sorts of sport like rugby, basketball, or hockey.
Students like sport because it makes them feel great!
I really hope all the students will have as much sport as possible. **(Kelly, 14)**

I believe sport lessons are as important as maths and English. We need sport to stay healthy. Most of our sports are team sports. You don't have to be good at the sports, you do your best for your team. So I say: more sport, please! **(Jordan, 13)**

You can do sport outside school if you want to be fit. I like ice skating and canoeing – so I don't need sport at school. Sport lessons are boring because there aren't enough really good sports like zumba or yoga.
I really think we should have less school sport. **(Evie, 14)**

b) Copy the table. Then read the comments in a) again and complete it. Make your notes as short as possible!

More help p. 110

reasons for more sport	*reasons against more sport*	*linkers*
makes you active and …	*boring*	*In my opinion …*

c) Write your own comment about more school sport. Remember the three steps: Give your opinion – give reasons – find a good ending.

d) Put all the comments up on the wall. Who has the best arguments?

9 My learner log

Copy and complete your learner log. Then put it in your DOSSIER.

My learner log for Unit 3

Now I can …
- present a business idea:
- find important facts from a text and take notes:
- give my opinion when I agree or disagree: …
- talk about things if something happens: …

After Unit 3
- I know some facts about Liverpool.
- I know more food words.
- These pages were interesting: …
- These pages were difficult: …

After Unit 3 my English is: GREAT! / OK / NOT VERY GOOD

▸ Workbook (Portfolio), p. 39 ▸ Workbook (Revision), p. 40

Writing about you or your family – using the simple present

You met a nice boy last week. His name is Angelo and he's Italian.
Angelo doesn't speak German and you don't speak Italian – so you write in English.

1 Angelo's first email

a) Read the email. What does Angelo write about?

1 his family 2 his parents 3 his sister 4 his brother 5 his pet 6 his school 7 his hobbies

Hi,

Thanks for your email and your photos. I like the photo of your funny hamster!
I don't live in a house – we live in a flat. My parents work in the city of Bologna. My dad helps in a home for old people and my mum works in the big post office in the centre of town. I have an older brother, Luigi. He doesn't have a job, but he sometimes helps in a garden centre.
My school isn't too far from our flat. School is OK, but we get homework every day. Does your school give you lots of homework too?
After school I chat with my friends and we sometimes go bowling or swimming together. When I'm at home, I listen to music. I really like music. Do you have a favourite singer?
That's all for now. Please write soon!
Angelo

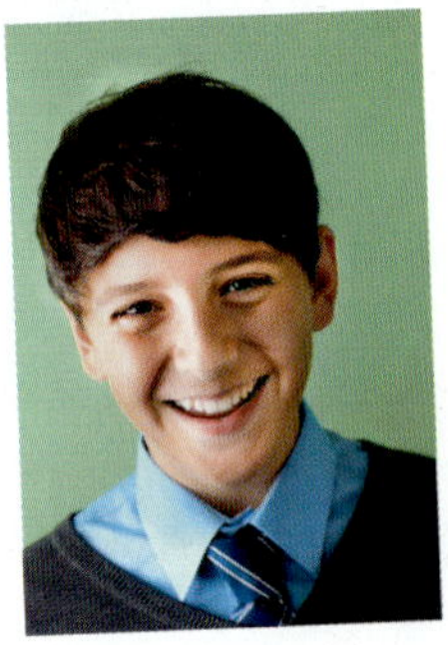

b) The simple present

Verben nach *I, you, we, they*

1 Copy eight verbs in the simple present from the email: *I ... we ... my parents ...*

Verben nach *he, she, it* enden auf *-s*.

2 Copy three examples from the email:
my dad ... my mum ... he ...

Verneinungen bildest du mit *don't* oder *doesn't*.

3 Copy two examples from the email:
I ... he ...

Fragen beginnen mit *Do ...?* oder *Does ...?*

4 Copy two examples from the email.
Does ...? Do ...?

► *Language file 1, p. 138*

2 O Angelo's second email

Read the email and pick the right form of the verb.

Hi,
I want/wants (1) to send you a photo of our dog, Mona. She's so cute! Mona like/likes (2) running in our park. Luigi take/takes (3) her there every morning and I go/goes (4) with her in the evening. Mona often dive/dives (5) into the water there because she love/loves (6) swimming.
We all love/loves (7) Mona!
Angelo

Mona sleeps in the kitchen.

3 Angelo and his family

Your brother tries to tell your parents about Angelo. But he gets everything wrong! Look at the correct information in exercises 1 and 2 and write correct sentences with *doesn't* or *don't*.

Remember:
I / you / we / they + don't
he / she / it + doesn't

Angelo and his parents live in a house.

1 No, they don't live in a house! They live in a flat.

Angelo's parents work in a village.

2 No, they ... in a village! They work ...

Angelo's brother Luigi has a job.

3 No, he ... a job! He helps ...

Angelo gets home-work once a week.

4 No, he ...! He ...

Angelo and his friends always go home after school.

5 No, they ...! They ...

Mona, Angelo's dog, sleeps in his room.

6 No, she ...! She ...

4 A video chat with Angelo

You have some questions for Angelo.
What are the missing words?

How • What • When • Where • Who • Why

Bei Interviews brauchst du meist Fragewörter und das *simple present*. Achtung:
Where? = Wo?
Who? = Wer?

You:	Angelo:
1 ... does your school begin?	– At 8.30 am.
2 ... do you go to school?	– I walk.
3 ... is your favourite lesson?	– Art.
4 ... do you like this lesson?	– Because the teacher is nice.
5 ... do you have lunch?	– I have lunch at school.
6 ... are your best friends at school?	– Luciano and Carlo. They're fun!

5 NOW YOU

a) Look again at Angelo's email in exercise 1. Then write an email to Angelo. Answer his questions and write about your family, your school and your hobbies. Write as many sentences as you can.
Ask a question. Look at exercise 4 for ideas.

Hi Angelo!
Thanks for your two emails and for the photo of Mona. She's cute!
I have ... brothers and sisters. My dad works in ... and my mum ...
I go to school ... After school I ... and I sometimes ...

Use some sentences in ex. 1, 2 or 3 and change them for your text. Example:
My mum works in the big post office.
=> My dad works in a hospital.
We live in a flat.
=> We live in a flat too.

b) **Partner check:** Show your email to a partner and check your partner's email:
Is there information about family, school and hobbies?
Should there be more information? If so, what sort of information: about brother / sister, ...?

Unit 4 Scotland is different

A

Scotland is famous for its castles.

B

Glasgow

BEWARE OF THE MONSTER

C

The Scottish word for *lake* is *loch*. Here is Loch Ness.

D

E

F

Shinty is a Scottish game, a bit like hockey.

G

How far can he throw it?

H

1 Talk about the photos

What can you see in photo A? — I can see ...

a bridge • a castle • a lake • people • a grey sky • flags • modern buildings • hills • woods • ...

What are the people doing? — I think they're ...

dancing • playing a game • jumping • taking part in ... • throwing ... • ...

2 YOUR TASK Find out about Scotland

a) Work in groups of three. Read all the question cards together. Write down any answers that you know.

A Scottish geography
1 What's the capital of Scotland?
2 What's the biggest city in Scotland?
3 Which Scottish lake has a monster?

B Scottish history
1 Does Scotland have its own a) football team b) parliament c) money?
2 What are the colours of the Scottish flag?

C Scottish life
Give Scottish examples: a) clothes b) sport c) a language d) a musical instrument

b) Each student in the group takes one question card (A–C). Go to pages 122–123. Find the answers to your questions and write them down.

c) Sit in a new group with three students who worked on the same questions (all three A, all three B, etc). Compare your answers.

d) Go back to your first group. Tell your group the answers to your questions.

► *Text file 4, pp. 122–123*

► *Workbook 1–2, p. 41*

Time for a change

1 News for the MacDonalds

The MacDonald family lives in Scotland.

a) Listen and pick two answers:

Do the parents and children sound (A) happy? (B) sad? (C) surprised?

b) Listen again and find out:

1 What are the names of the family (A–D?) Match the names from the box with the photos.

(A)

(B)

Kate
Jamie
Alec
Kara

(C)

(D)

2 Where do they live?
3 Does the dad have a job?
4 Does the mum have a job?

2 Bad news for Inverness

a) Read the article. Find out: Is it good or bad news for the MacDonalds?

INVERNESS NEWS

Another Inverness shop closes

Today the doors of MacBean's in Church Street in Inverness closed for the last time. MacBean's was the number one shop in Inverness for sports clothes and equipment.

"Now most of our customers like to go to big shopping centres or shop online," Alec MacDonald, the manager of MacBean's, said to *Inverness News*.

"Eight people including me are unemployed now and there are no jobs here."

Two other shops closed in Inverness centre last month – a hairdresser's and a toy shop. This is bad news for the town centre and bad news for Inverness.

b) Read the article again and take notes:

1 Name of shop: ...
2 Address: ...
3 What you can buy there: ...
4 Why it is closing: ...
5 How many people worked there: ...

c) WORDS

Find these words in the article:

1 you open them when you go into shops
2 things that you wear
3 people who buy things in a shop
4 the person who is the boss in a shop
5 when somebody has no work
6 a person who cuts your hair

More practice 1 p. 110

► Workbook 3, p. 42

3 Hard times

a) Talk to a partner. What do you think the MacDonalds should do?

A Mr MacDonald should take a job in Glasgow. B The family should go to Glasgow.

C Mr and Mrs MacDonald should look for work nearer home.

b) Now read and find out what their ideas are.

The next evening, the MacDonalds had dinner in the kitchen. But it wasn't a very happy meal!

Kara — Dad, we know you're fed up about your job. But don't blame yourself.

Dad — Maybe I'll have to go to Glasgow. I can be a manager in MacBean's Glasgow shop.

Jamie — No, Dad. It's too far away.

Kara — Yeah, we should stay together in hard times. We're the MacDonalds. And the MacDonalds always look after themselves!

Dad — Your mum and I talked about things and we asked ourselves – how can we all stay here in our home? And mum had an idea ...

Mum — Well, first I told myself – we live in a beautiful place. And lots of tourists come here to visit Loch Ness and the Highlands. And they need places to stay where they can enjoy themselves ...

Jamie — Like hotels ...

Mum — And bed and breakfast places.

Kara — Yes ... and ...?

Mum — That's my answer! We have a big old house with lots of rooms. We can start a B&B!

Jamie — But we don't know anything about B&Bs!

Kara — We can learn. We can teach ourselves!

Dad — Let's think about it. Now the soup is getting cold, so help yourselves!

c) True, false or not in the text?

1 The kids think their dad should go to Glasgow.
2 Mum and dad had a new idea.
3 Tourists think Loch Ness is more beautiful than Glasgow.
4 Tourists only stay in hotels.
5 The MacDonalds are thinking about starting a B&B.
6 Jamie loves the new idea.

d) Find all the words with *-self* and *-selves* in the text. Example: *yourself, ...*

e) Copy and complete this table.

I tell	...
you blame	...
he helps	himself
she enjoys	herself
we ask	...
you help	...
they look after	...

► *Language file 8, p. 143* More practice 2 p. 111

► *Workbook 4–5, pp. 42–43*

The MacDonalds are open for business

1 The new website

a) Look at the website for the new B&B.

1 Does it give (A) the phone number? (B) prices? (C) the number of rooms?

2 Does it tell you about (A) the family? (B) activities for tourists? (C) equipment in the rooms?

Bed and breakfast next to Loch Ness

Welcome to our family-friendly bed and breakfast near Dores, next to Loch Ness!

Urquhart Castle and Loch Ness

It's a great place for water sports and there are lots of places to visit: the Loch Ness monster exhibition, beautiful Urquhart Castle, the RockNess music festival, etc.

We have a family room (for four guests), a twin room and a single room. The rooms have TV, DVD player, hairdryer, kettle to make tea or coffee and Wi-fi. There's also a room where you can dry your coats and boots.

£25 per person per night. (Children: under 10 free, 10–16 years old £10, 16–18 £20.)

Email: macdonaldfamily@lochside.com Telephone: 01463

RockNess

Lochside B&B

The twin room

b) Details about the B&B.

1 How many guests can stay in the B&B?

2 What equipment is there in the rooms?

3 How do you know that families are welcome?

4 What activities are there for tourists near the B&B?

5 What does one night cost for two parents and a child under 10?

6 How do you know that the weather can often be wet?

2 Canadian guests

a) Listen to this Canadian family.

1 Who finds the MacDonalds' website?

2 Is there a room free for the Grants?

b) Listen again and note the missing information A–G.

c) Now write the full email.

From: Abigail Grant To: Lochside B&B

Hi!
We're a family of ... (A) people – two adults and ... (B) teenage kids (... (C) and ... (D) years old). We'd like to book your ... (E) room for ... (F) nights from ... (G)
Will the room be free? Thanks a lot.
The Grant family

► Workbook 6, p. 43

3 Our first guests!

a) Read the dialogue. How will the Grants find their B&B?

Mrs Grant – Hello, is that *Lochside B&B?*
Jamie – Yes, that's right. This is Jamie MacDonald.
Mrs Grant – Hi, Jamie. This is Michelle Grant. I'm phoning to confirm our reservation for 22nd July.
Jamie – Oh right, great. That was the family room for two nights, right?
Mrs Grant – Yes, that's right. Two nights from tomorrow.
Jamie – OK. What time will you arrive?
Mrs Grant – I'm not sure. Maybe about 7 pm tomorrow.
Jamie – Do you need directions?
Mrs Grant – I think we'll be OK. We have a GPS.
Jamie – OK, well just take the road to Loch Ness and Dores. Phone us if you have a problem.
Mrs Grant – Great. See you tomorrow evening then.
Jamie – OK, bye!

Telephone messages

Who rang? ____________
How many nights? ________
Will arrive on: ______ at: ______
Room: single ☐ twin ☐ family ☐

b) Copy and complete the telephone message. More practice 3 p. 111

4 ROLE-PLAY Phoning *Lochside B&B*

a) Partner B: Go to page 92.
Partner A: You phone *Lochside B&B* to confirm your reservation:
– a single room for 2 nights
– you'll arrive 2nd August between 6 and 7 pm

– Hi. This is ... I'm phoning to confirm my ... for ....
– That's right, a ... room.
– I'd like to stay ...
– I'll arrive between ...

If you don't understand, say: *Sorry, can you say that again, please?*

b) Now you're Jamie. Copy the telephone message above. Then answer the phone and write the message.

– Let me see. That was the twin room, right?
– How many nights?
– Yes, that's fine. What time will ...?
– No problem. Thank you.

5 PEOPLE AND PLACES Welcome to Scotland

a) Before you watch: What things could you see in a film about Scotland? Look again at pages 68 and 69 and make a list. Then compare with a partner.

b) Now watch the film. How many of the things on your list were in the film?

c) Read these questions, then watch the film again and try to answer them.

1 Where does Mehdy start his trip? A In Glasgow B In Edinburgh C In Inverness.
2 You can wear a knife with a kilt. You put it in A your sock B your shoe C your hat.
3 How much do Mehdy's Scottish clothes cost? A Less than £500 B £500 C More than £500.
4 What didn't you see in the DVD? A Food B Cycling C Dancing D Shinty E Bagpipes.

▸ Workbook 7–10, pp. 44–45

1 JIGSAW A story in four parts

Your teacher will put you in groups of four. Each student in your group reads a **different** part of the story (A, B, C, D). Try to answer these questions and take notes.

1 *Who was in the text?*	2 *When did it happen?*	3 *Where did it happen?*	4 *What happened?*
…	…	…	…

Ghosts don't exist

(Careful! Parts A, B, C and D are not in the right order!)

A

The Grant family came into the big old house. The old man took them upstairs to a room with four beds. "Make yourselves comfortable," he said.
Duncan and Abi were very excited. "This is a real Scottish castle," Duncan said.
"Maybe there are ghosts!" Abi said and laughed.
"Ghosts don't exist," her mum answered.

Later in the evening the family went down to a kitchen with a warm fire and big table that had lots of food on it. Some people played music and some people danced. The Grants chatted, enjoyed the food and danced too.
"Our family left Scotland more than 200 years ago," Mr Grant said.
"Then you're welcome home," the old man said.

But the next morning, the Grants found the place empty and the castle looked lonely. When the Grants went outside to their car they heard the lonely music of the bagpipes. And they saw the old man on the walls of the castle. He was alone.
The Grants waved and shouted "Thanks!" But the old man just played his bagpipes.

B

It was the Grant family's first night in Scotland. But their plane was late and the sky was dark grey when they landed at Inverness. Then one of their bags was missing. And when they wanted to hire a car, Mrs Grant couldn't find her driving licence.
"It's OK," Mr Grant said. "I have mine."
But, when he began to drive, the other cars all hooted.
"Dad, you have to drive on the left!" the kids shouted.
Mr Grant stopped quickly and luckily nothing happened.

The Grants drove to Inverness and looked for the road to Dores, the village where their B&B was. But it wasn't so easy because it was dark. Mrs Grant looked for the map of Scotland – but it was in the missing bag, with the GPS!
"Dores is near Loch Ness, so let's find the road that goes to the lake," Duncan said. And that's what they did.
They soon saw a sign to Loch Ness. "Ah! Things are looking better," Mr Grant thought to himself.

C

The Grants found the right road to Dores and arrived at *Lochside Bed and Breakfast* at about 11 am. They told the MacDonalds about the old man and the castle. Then they looked at a map and Mrs Grant put her finger on Urquhart Castle.
"I think that's the place that we visited last night," she said.
"It can't be – it's a ruin!" Kate MacDonald said. "But ... the last family who lived at Urquhart Castle was the Grant family!"
The Grants from Canada were very excited. "Let's go there!" Abi said.

So in the afternoon the Grants parked at Urquhart Castle. Was it the car park from the night before? They weren't sure. Then they walked around the ruins. It really was a beautiful old castle – about 1500 years old.
"So maybe our family came from here a long time ago," Mr Grant said.
"Yes, I can feel the ghosts of the Grants here," Duncan smiled.
"But ghosts don't exist," the others answered and laughed.

D

The rain started at about 10 pm. The sky was black now and the road was narrow. So it was very difficult for Mr Grant to drive. After 20 minutes the Grants began to worry. Dores is only about 10 miles from Inverness. But they didn't find a village – only woods and fields.
"I'll stop at this car park," Mr Grant said. "We have to find someone who can help us."
"Let's phone the MacDonalds," Mrs Grant said. "But my mobile doesn't work. Can we try yours, Abi?" "Sorry, mine doesn't work either", Abi said.
"It must be the mountains," Mrs Grant thought to herself.
It was after 11 o'clock and everybody was tired.

Then Mrs Grant said, "Look! There's a light over there!"
She and Mr Grant ran in the rain to the end of the car park and came to a building. An old man was at the door. The Grants told him about their problems.
"Och, come in. You can stay here for the night," he said in a Scottish accent.

2 What's the story?

a) Find three other students who read the same text as you. Talk about the questions in exercise 1.

1 The people in the story were ...
2 It was in the morning at ...
3 They were in a castle / in ...
4 They went / met / drove / saw / thought / couldn't find ...

b) Go back to your first group. Tell your group about your text. Listen to the others. What's the right order of the texts A, B, C, D?

I think that text C is first because ...

I don't agree. I think that text B is first because ...

c) Now close your books and listen to the whole story. Enjoy it!

More practice 4+5 p. 112

► Workbook 11, p. 46

Writing a story

1 An amazing day

Back in Canada, Duncan writes about his holiday for *Hi guys* magazine which has prizes for short stories.

a) Read the first part of his story.

An amazing day

Last July I flew to Scotland with my parents and my sister. We landed at Inverness late in the evening, so it was dark on the roads. Then we couldn't find our B&B because we had no map. We felt tired and scared.

Suddenly there was a light. And then we saw a man. Mum and dad talked with him and he said we could stay in his house. We felt so happy!

b) What's good in Duncan's text? Work with a partner and find the answers for 1, 2 and 3 in Duncan's text.

First part of story

1 **WH-questions**
Make notes:
– Who was in the story?
– When did it happen?
– Where did it happen?
– What happenend?

2 **Time phrases and linkers**
Copy and complete the table.

time phrases	*linkers*
last July	*so*
...	...

For examples of time phrases and linkers see Unit 2, p. 37.

3 **How people felt**
Which two sentences tell you how Duncan and his family felt?

2 NOW YOU

Finish Duncan's story. More help p.113

a) Look again at the story on pages 74–75. Write notes for the next parts of the story. Example:

At the castle → *Who? When? Where? What?*

b) Use your notes and write your story.

c) **Partner check:** Swap your story with a partner. Check your partner's story. Then write a good version of your story and put it in your DOSSIER.

OR

Write your own story for *Hi guys*.

1 Think of an amazing day in your life
2 What are the parts of your story?
3 Write ideas for each part.

Example:

A great birthday → *Who? When? Where? What?*

Check:
1 Are there answers to the *wh*-questions?
2 Are there time phrases and linkers?
3 Does the text say how people felt?

▸ *Skills file 8, pp. 132–134*

▸ *Workbook 12–13, p. 47*

1 Who is Amy Macdonald?

a) Listen to the radio programme about Amy Macdonald. Choose the best answers.

1 Amy Macdonald (A) plays football for Scotland (B) is in the British Olympic team (C) is a Scottish singer.
2 Amy's biggest hobby is (A) music (B) football (C) cars.
3 Amy is very proud when (A) she sings at football matches (B) she meets famous bands (C) she sings in big cities.
4 Amy's song *Pride* is about (A) Glasgow (B) her first teachers (C) singing for Scotland's football team.

b) Listen again. Make notes about Amy Macdonald: More help p.113
her work? born in …? big hits? instrument? hobbies?

2 Pride

a) Listen to the song and look at the text.

1 Is it a happy or a sad song?
2 What instruments do you hear?

the drums

the guitar

the bass guitar

the piano

b) Listen again and look at the text.
What words or phrases tell you that …

1 this song is about a football game?
2 the singer is nervous at first?
3 she then feels proud?
4 this song is about Scotland?

More practice 6 p.113

Verse 1
I never felt like this before
Try to hold it back and I feel it even more
Sweat drips down my spine
And my knees are weak
I cannot move, I cannot speak.

Verse 2
But then you came
And I held it together again
I managed to stumble through
Fifty thousand voices singing in the rain
There's nothing that I wouldn't do.

Chorus
'Cause I'd move mountains
If you asked me to
I'd swim the seven seas
I'll be the one to hold your torch again
I'll do anything you ask of me.

Verse 3
I never knew how proud I would feel
Just standing in the rain
These three words mean everything to me
And I'll sing them again and again.

Verse 4
Well the blue and the white
Of the flag shines bright
And it's blowing there for me
With my hand on my heart,
The honest truth
There's nowhere I'd rather be.

(Text by Amy Elizabeth Macdonald)

1 Loch Ness brochures

a) First read these three tourist profiles.

b) Then skim the two brochures and find out:
- Which brochure is useful for which tourist (A, B, C)?
- Which tourist has no brochure?

When you **skim** a text:
- Look at headings, pictures and captions.
- Don't read every word – you don't need to understand everything.

Tourist A
You're on holiday and want to spend two or three days near Loch Ness with a friend. You don't have a lot of money, you need a cheap place.

Tourist B
You're staying in Inverness with your family. You love Nessie stories, so you would like to visit a good Nessie museum.

Tourist C
You've just arrived in Scotland with some friends. You'd like to visit the Loch Ness region – quickly. You only have one day!

1

Sightseeing tours through the Highlands

Around Loch Ness

Your complete Loch Ness experience

Tour around Loch Ness
We offer a fully guided day tour around Loch Ness with castle visit and a boat trip on Loch Ness.

Highland Highlights
This is a fully guided day tour of the Highlands including Clava Cairns, Culloden, Inverness, Loch Ness with options for a castle visit and a boat trip on Loch Ness.

2

Comfortable rooms

Outdoor sports

The perfect place to stay in the Highlands.

Rooms
Double rooms, twin rooms or less expensive beds in four- and six-bed dormitories.

Food
Self-catering kitchen, or we can provide breakfast, packed lunches and evening meals.

We have bikes for hire.

c) Talk to a partner. What helped you to pick the right brochures?
Headings? Examples: … Pictures? Examples: … More practice 7 p. 114 ▸ *Skills file 6, p. 130*

2 WORDS

Now look for details. What words in the *Maggie's Lodge* brochure tell you that …

1 you can cook your own food.
2 you can buy picnic food.
3 you can have dinner.
4 you can borrow bikes.
5 they have some cheaper rooms.
6 they have rooms with one bed for two people.

 ▸ *Workbook 14, p. 48*

1 Tally's video diary

a) Before you watch:
Which of these things do you think are different between Scotland and England?

accents • dancing • food • houses • shopping • money • music • sport

b) Watch the film. Which of these things do we learn about?

2 Four scenes

a) Think: Look at the four pictures and read the questions. Can you answer some questions?

A

1 What meal is Tally making?
2 Will Hamish like it?
3 Does Tally use salt or sugar?

B

4 What's Ruby's problem?
5 What does the Scottish word *wee* mean?
6 Who helps Ruby to understand Hamish?

C

7 Why does Alfie need money?
8 Why is Alfie surprised?
9 Can you use Scottish money in England?

D

10 Does Hamish play the bagpipes?
11 What are the kids doing in this picture?
12 Who do you think will fall?

b) Pair: Watch the film again. When you see the four scenes above, stop the film and answer all the questions with a partner.

c) Share: Compare your answers with another pair. Then compare your answers in class.

1 Tourist questions

Read the tourist questions. What words do they need?
Look at the pictures and write the words. *1–kettle, 2 …*

1 What's the thing that we use to make hot water for tea?

2 Do you have the thing that you use to dry yourself after a shower?

3 What's the thing that you use to look at yourself in the bathroom?

4 What do you call the person who is the boss in a hotel?

5 I need somebody who can help me with my car.

6 What do you call the man or woman who brings the food in a restaurant?

A 
a waiter/waitress

B 
a manager

C 
a mechanic

D 
a mirror

E 
a towel

F 
a kettle

2 Who / That

a) Work with a partner. Look at the speech bubbles above. What's the difference between the sentences on the left (1–3) and on the right (4–6)?

b) Now copy and complete these rules.
You'll find example sentences in exercise 1.

FOCUS

Mit Relativsätzen beschreibst du eine Sache oder eine Person noch genauer,
z. B.: *Wie nennt man das Ding, das …?* *Wie heißt der Mann, der …?*
Auf Englisch benutzt du *that* oder *who*.
Wenn du über **Dinge** redest, benutzt du …
Beispielsatz: …
Wenn du über **Menschen** redest, benutzt du meistens …
Beispielsatz: …

► *Language file 12, p. 145*

3 More questions

p.114

Pick the answers to these questions.

1 What do you call visitors who spend the night in your house?
2 What's the white stuff that you use to make bread or cake?
3 What do you call the thing that you use to cut food?
4 What do you call a person who wins a sports competition?
5 What do you call a person who sells things like cars?
6 What's the thing that you wear when you go outside and it's cold?

A 
a coat

B 
guests

C 
a champion

D 
a knife

E 
flour

F 
a salesperson

4 ROLE-PLAY What is it?

a) **Partner B:** Go to page 92.
Partner A: Listen to your partner.
What words does he/she mean?

> Oh, you mean a waiter/the sky/ a bus driver/a diswasher/a B&B.

b) Now ask your partner the words for these people and things.

1 

2 

3 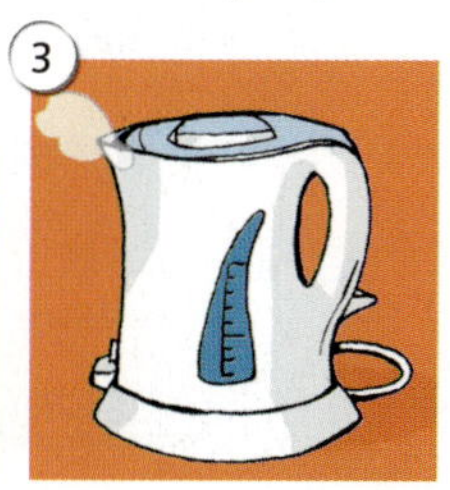

4 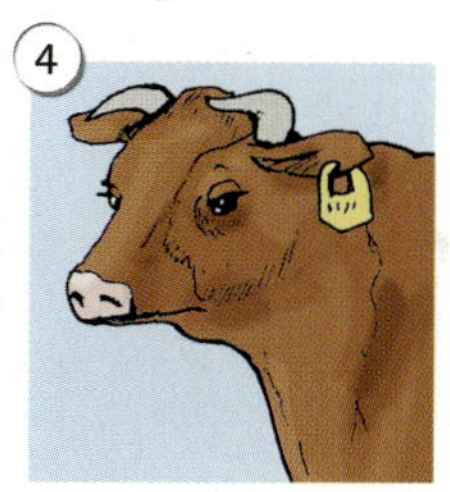

5 

What do you call	the small animal	who / that	eats cheese?
	somebody		works on a farm?
	the machine		makes hot water in the kitchen?
	the big animal		gives milk?
	somebody		buys things in a shop?

5 WORDS

a) Copy and complete the network with words from these two pages.

b) Work with a partner. Can you add more words to the network? ▸ *Wordbank 4, p. 149*

Useful words for tourists
- in a hotel
  - bathroom
  - room
- people who work for tourists
- at a restaurant

▸ *Workbook 15–16, pp. 49–51*

STOP! CHECK! GO!

Ein Lösungsblatt für die Aufgaben 1–5 kannst du von deiner Lehrerin / deinem Lehrer erhalten.

1 REVISION If the weather is good, …

The Grant family are telling Kara MacDonald about their plans for tomorrow. Copy and complete the sentences.

Mrs Grant — If the weather … (be) good, we … (stay) here two more days. *If the weather is good, …*

Kara — That's great! If you stay here longer, what … (you, do)?

Duncan — If it isn't too expensive, we … (hire) a canoe for a tour of Loch Ness.

Abi — Perhaps we … (see) Nessie if we go out early enough!

Mr Grant — But if the weather isn't good, we … (not stay).

Duncan — Yes, if the weather is bad, we … (go) to Edinburgh.

Mrs Grant — And if we visit Edinburgh, we … (go) to the castle.

Abi — If we find a nice kilt shop, we … (look for) a kilt for dad's birthday.

Kara — Are you sure he … (wear) a kilt if you find one for him?

Duncan — You're right. If we buy a kilt, he … (not wear) it!

2 ○ LANGUAGE What do you call …? //● p.115

Eight tourists can't think of the word in English. Copy and complete what they say or ask.

1 "I need a paper *that shows where places are.*"

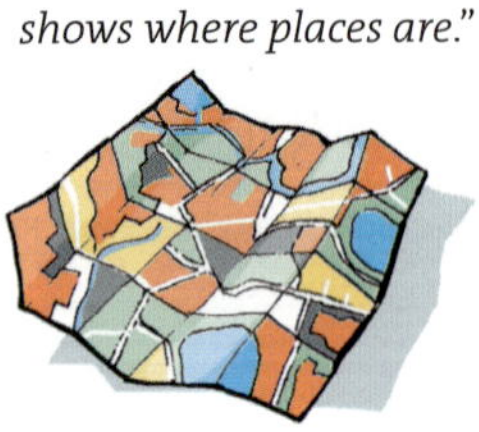

"It's a map."

2 "What do you call a person …"

"You mean an adult."

3 "What's the boat …"

"It's a ferry."

4 "What do you call the people …"

"Firefighters."

5 "What's the name of the person …

"A hairdresser."

6 "What's the white stuff …"

"Oh, you mean salt."

7 "What do you call the things …"

"You mean socks."

8 "Can you tell me the word for the person …"

"It's a mechanic."

… who fight against fire?
… who helps when your car is broken?
… who is not a child?
… who cuts or styles your hair?
… that you wear on your feet under your shoes?
… that you put on rice or potatoes or eggs?
… *that shows where places are.*
… that takes people across a river?

3 LANGUAGE Enjoy yourselves! p.115

Jamie and Kara want to go camping. They are talking to their parents.
Pick the right word: *myself, yourself, herself, …*

> If you need help, look at
> ▸ *Language file 8, p. 143*.

Jamie — Mum, Kara and I want to go camping.
Mum — Camping? Is that a good idea? That's what I ask myself / herself.
Dad — Oh, I'm sure the kids can look after himself / themselves, Kate.
Jamie — Of course we can look after ourselves / yourselves!
Kara — Don't forget Jamie has taught myself / himself to cook!
Dad — Ah yes, I hear you're good at cooking soup for myself / yourself, Jamie!
Mum — Well, OK then. You two go camping and enjoy themselves / yourselves.
But I won't blame myself / herself if you come back hungry!

4 WRITING and SPEAKING Booking a B&B

Dolby B&B

Our beautiful B&B is located in beautiful country near Aberdeen. We have single rooms, double rooms and a family room with four beds. >>> More details

To book online click here

From £35 price per room per night

a) You want to stay eight nights in this B&B from 14th July to 22nd July. There are four of you in your family. You'd like the family room. Write the email to the B&B.

> Hi!
> We are a … of four: two … and two …
> We'd like to book …
> Will the room be …? Many thanks.
> Simon Koch

b) You phone the B&B to confirm the reservation. Write your sentences.

You — Hi. is / Simon Koch / This
phoning / our reservation / I'm / to confirm
B&B — Thanks for phoning. I'm sorry, but our family room isn't free. But we can give you two double rooms for the same price.
You — OK / double / Two / rooms / are
B&B — Great. Two double rooms from 14th to 22nd July.
You — pay / we / euros / Can / in / ?
B&B — Yes, no problem. It's a total price of 610 euros.
You — with / breakfast / Is / that / ?
B&B — Yes, including breakfast. What time will you arrive?
You — arrive / evening / We'll / the / in
B&B — In the evening is fine.
You — very / you / Thank / much
B&B — No problem. Bye.

5 READING Brochures

Read statements 1–7. Then skim the brochures A–E and choose the best brochure for each statement. Be careful: There are more statements than brochures – so you can use some brochures more than once.

1 You are a big Harry Potter fan and you want to see places that you know from the films.
2 You like going on organised group bike tours.
3 You are a good mountain biker and you want to try riding in more difficult country.
4 You like trips in old trains.
5 You are interested in Scottish history.
6 You like all kinds of water sports, but you have never tried rafting.
7 You want to buy presents for your friends and family.

A

Fancy a ride?

Bike hire … and so much more

Discover one of the most spectacular parts of the Scottish Highlands by bike – with one of our expert guides.

B

Experience the fun

Outdoor activities in Scotland

Quad biking
Experience riding a quad bike in some of the most beautiful settings in Scotland.

Canyoning
Canyoning is an adrenaline-filled adventure – jump from cliffs and abseil from waterfalls.

White-water rafting
Experience the best white-water rafting trip in Scotland.

C

Edinburgh – explore the jewel of Scottish cities

Edinburgh has something for everybody!

Discover Scotland's past
Visit Edinburgh Castle, The Royal Scottish Museum or Old Town with its narrow streets and learn something about Scotland's history.

A dream for shoppers
Shopping in Edinburgh is a fantastic experience as you can browse the shops of several great spots including Princes Street, George Street and the St James Centre.

D

Jacobite Steam Train

Follow in the footsteps of Harry Potter along the route used by the Hogwarts Express.

- See the carriages that were used in the Harry Potter films.
- Travel to Mallaig along the line used in the films.
- Cross the famous Glenfinnan Viaduct, a unique landmark for all Harry Potter fans.

It's a great day out for all the family.

E

Wolftrax Trails and Activities

Located in one of the most beautiful parts of Cairngorms National Park, Laggan:

- Our exciting, off-road mountain bike park. There are trails for all abilities.

- The Haflinger Pony-Trekking Centre with various lovely trekking trails.

Booking:
Mountain Bikes: 01528
Pony-Trekking: 07926

6 WRITING A story about Slains Castle

a) Look at the pictures of Slains Castle. Imagine you and your family went there for a trip. Write your story:

Last August I travelled to ... with ...
We stayed in a hotel / ... near ...
One day we visited ...
It was a sunny / foggy / ... day. The sky was ...
Suddenly I saw something white / ...
I heard a noise / something / ...
I felt nervous / excited / scared / ...
Was it a ghost? No, of course not! It was only ...
Silly me! We all laughed when I told my family about it!

– Answer the questions *Who? When? Where? What?*
– Use time phrases and linkers *(so, but, because, ...)*
– Write how you felt. If you need help, see page 76.

b) Work with one or two partners. Compare your ideas. Maybe a partner has a good idea for you?

c) Put the new ideas in your story. Then put your story in your DOSSIER.

7 My learner log

Copy and complete your learner log. Then put it in your DOSSIER.

My learner log for Unit 4

Now I can ...
- understand words in a B&B advert: 😃 😐 😟
- write an email to book a room: 😃 😐 😟
- phone a B&B to confirm a reservation: 😃 😐 😟
- use some tips to write a good story: 😃 😐 😟
- ask for things even if I don't know the word: ...

After Unit 4
- I know some things about Scotland.
- I understand a Scottish accent.
- I have listened to a Scottish song.
- My favourite part of this unit was ...

After Unit 4 my English is: GREAT! 👍 / OK 👉 / NOT VERY GOOD 👎

A German student in Dublin

In May, Maike Hoffmann travelled from Berlin to Dublin to spend one week with the O'Briens. She wanted to practise her English – but she also learned lots of things about living in another country.

Part 1 Maike arrives at the O'Briens

Mrs O'Brien, her son Dara and her daughter Ciara met Maike at the airport. They then drove her to their house – a small, cute house, in a line of other houses. Inside, Maike met two younger boys. They looked shy[1].

"I'm Maike," the visitor said and she put out her hand. But the boys didn't take her hand. They only looked at her and smiled shyly.
"That's Liam and Sammy," Mrs O'Brien said. "Say hello to Maike, boys."
The boys said hello, then a small girl and a dog came out of a room.
"And that's Tess – with Milo the dog," Mrs O'Brien said.
Maike smiled at Tess but she didn't put out her hand this time.

"I'll make some tea," said Dara. "Milk and sugar, Maike?"
"No, thanks – just black, please," Maike answered.
Dara was surprised. And Maike was surprised when she tried the tea. It was very, very strong.
"Oh, I will some sugar, please," she said.
"You mean I'd like some sugar, please," Mrs O'Brien said. "Is it OK if I correct your English?"
"Yes, please, Mrs O'Brien," Maike said. "That's good for me."
"OK, Maike. But don't call me 'Mrs O'Brien'. My name is Nora, so please call me Nora."
"OK, Mrs O'Brien ... erm, I mean Nora."
Maike was surprised. She liked Nora O'Brien already.

Maike had some presents – marzipan sweets for the kids and a *Black Forest* ham[2] for Mrs O'Brien.
"Oh, thanks very much," Mrs O'Brien said and put the ham in the fridge[3].

Maike's Blog (1)

Endlich in Irland angekommen ... es ist schon irgendwie alles anders und neu hier! Aber die Familie ist echt nett, besonders Nora, die Mutter.
Morgen gehe ich mit Dara in die Schule und bin schon sehr gespannt!
Einiges habe ich hier schon gelernt, z.B. ...

Part 2 Maike's first day at school

Peep – peep – peep ... Ciara woke up[4] with a shock. "What's that?" she thought. "It's only 7 o'clock." It was Maike's alarm clock on her mobile.
"Oh, Maike, it's too early! School starts at 9 o'clock," Ciara said and went back to sleep.

But Maike got up. She was excited because this was her first day at school in Dublin. She was in Dara's class, because Maike and Dara were both 16.

[1] shy *schüchtern* [2] Black Forest ham *Schwarzwälder Schinken* [3] fridge *Kühlschrank* [4] she woke up *sie wachte auf*

At 8 o'clock Maike was in the bathroom. Three O'Brien kids were outside the bathroom. They wanted to go to the toilet – it wasn't funny! When Maike came out at last, she understood the problem. "Oh I'm sorry," she said. "I forgot that there was only one toilet in the house."

Nora had a school uniform for Maike. Maike looked great in it. It was a new experience[5] for her and Dara had to help her with the school tie.

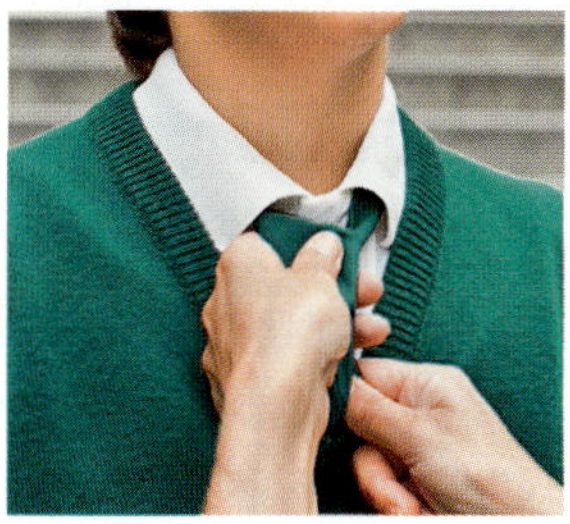

Maike was really excited and a bit nervous.

When they got to school, some of Dara's friends looked at Maike and smiled. "Is this your new girlfriend, Dara?" they asked. "I'm not his girlfriend!" Maike said. Dara went a bit red[6]. After that, the day at school was OK. Lots of kids asked Maike about Germany, her school, her family. She didn't understand everything, but it was fun.

> ***Maike's Blog (2)***
>
> Heute war ich in der Schule. Alle haben gedacht, dass ich Daras Freundin bin ☺. Auch heute habe ich ein paar Sachen gelernt, z. B. dass man in der Schule …

Part 3 **After school**

It was a long day at school. Lessons finished at 4 pm, and they got home at 5 pm. "Hi, Maike," called Nora. "It's tea time." "Tea time?" Maike asked Ciara. "I'm tired – but I'm very hungry!" Ciara smiled. "Don't worry. We say 'tea', but we mean dinner."

Maike found Dara in the kitchen. "Guess what's for tea," he said to Maike with a smile. "It's your *Black Forest* ham." He showed Maike a big pot on the cooker. The ham was in hot water. "Oh no!" Maike said. "You don't cook this ham. You eat it cold!"

Ciara looked at Dara. Dara looked at his mum. And Nora looked at Maike. Then they all laughed. So they didn't have *Black Forest* ham that evening. (Milo, the dog, had a very nice surprise for his dinner!) Dara cooked sausages, eggs, tomatoes, beans and potatoes. "Good appetite,"

Maike said – and Dara's brother Liam laughed. "Did I say something wrong?" Maike asked. "No," Nora answered. "We understood you, but we don't say 'Good appetite'. We say 'Enjoy your meal'." "Oh, OK. Enjoy your meal," Maike said.

After tea, Dara had a question for Maike. He was a bit shy, but in the end he asked her. "Hey Maike, there's a disco on Friday. My friends want to go. It's for kids under 18. There's no alcohol and it's over[7] before 12 pm. Would you like to come?" Dara asked. "Yes, OK," Maike said. "But I don't have the right clothes." "That's no problem," said Ciara. "I'll phone some friends."

---

[5] experience *Erfahrung* [6] go red *rot werden* [7] it's over *es ist vorbei*

On Friday after school three girls brought some disco clothes and other things to the house. Maike had lots of fun with the girls. She tried different clothes and shoes. They did her hair too. She soon looked very different.
At the disco Maike met more of Dara's friends. They were very nice and they all had lots of fun that evening.

> ***Maike's Blog (3)***
>
> Mittwoch abend hat Nora den Schwarzwälder Schinken gekocht ... das war lustig. Wenigstens hat sich Milo darüber gefreut ☺. Heute war ich mit Dara in der Disco, das war voll genial. Ein paar Mädels haben mir Anziehsachen geliehen und Schminke – das war richtig cool! Ich habe wieder was dazu gelernt, z.B. ...

Part 4 The last day

The day before Maike left, she and Dara went into Dublin centre on the bus. They walked along the busy Dublin streets and went into some shops. Maike bought presents for her family and friends at home. She bought a silly hat for her sister.
Then they saw some street musicians and they listened to some good Irish music.

At lunchtime Maike said she was hungry.
"Can we eat something Irish?" Maike asked.
"OK," Dara said. "I have an idea!"
So Dara took Maike to the old part of Dublin, with narrow streets and old buildings.

There they found a place called Leo Burdock.
"It's the best fish and chip shop in Dublin!" Dara said.
They waited, and then Dara asked for two fish and chips.
"Do you want salt and vinegar[8] on the chips, love[9]?" the friendly woman asked them.
"Vinegar on my chips?" Maike said, shocked. "No thanks!"

They took their food to St Patrick's Park. It was nice there. The fish and chips were fresh, hot and very good.
"Try my chips with vinegar," Dara said to Maike. She tried one ... and she liked it!
"What do you put on chips in Germany?" Dara asked.
"Tomato ketchup or mayonnaise," Maike answered.
"Mayonnaise on chips? Yuck![10]" Dara said, shocked.
"When you come to Germany you can try it. It's great!" Maike answered and smiled.
"You learn a lot when you travel," she thought, "things that you can't learn at school."

1 Maike's blogs

a) Pick one of Maike's blogs (1–3). Find examples of things that she learned.

b) You're Maike. Write a blog for Part 4 of the story – in English or in German.

[8] vinegar *Essig* [9] love *hier: meine Liebe (freundliche Anrede)* [10] Yuck! *Igitt!*

1 People and places **Welcome to Dublin, the capital of Ireland**

a) Before you watch, look at these places in Dublin.

1 Where can you – buy fruit? – take a bus? – listen to street musicians?
– go shopping? – relax? – see the river? – look at the sea?

2 What's the name of a famous old ship?

b) Then watch the film. Make a list of the places in the brochure in the right order.

A TOUR OF DUBLIN – in three hours

Grafton Street

O'Connell Street

The Jeanie Johnston

Moore Street

Temple Bar

Molly Malone

Stephen's Green

The Ha'penny Bridge

Dublin Bay

c) Match these sentences with your list of places from b). Watch the film again and check.

A This is a quiet place in the city centre.
B It's very important in Dublin's history.
C It goes across the River Liffey.
D It's the oldest part of Dublin.
E Poor people travelled on it to the USA.
F It's Dublin's most popular shopping street.

d) Imagine you're in Dublin with a partner. Agree on three places to visit. Say why.

I'd like to visit ... because I like ...

I don't really want to go to ...

So we want to visit ...

... looks fun / quiet / exciting / nice / ...

I think you can go shopping in ...

Unit 2

3 ROLE-PLAY Talking on the phone ▸ *Unit 2, p.33*

b) Partner B: You are the babysitter for the Smiths, a family in England. First copy the notepad. Then answer the phone and listen to your partner.

- Say Mrs Smith can't answer the phone right now.
- Ask if you can take a message.
- Make notes on your notepad.

Messages

Who phoned? ________

Wanted to speak to: ________

Message: ________

____

____

c) Swap roles. You are staying in England with your host family, the Smiths. Now you want to phone and tell Mr Smith that you'll be outside school at 6 o'clock. Ask if Mr Smith can meet you there, at the big gate.

- First practise what you want to say.
- Then make the phone call.

Hello. This is ... Can I ... Mr Smith, please?

I'll be ... at 6 o'clock.

Can Mr Smith ... me there?

2 WORDS How many differences can you find? ▸ *Unit 2, p.42*

Partner B

a) Make a list of eight things in the picture and write where they are: *in the foreground / background, in the middle, on the left / right, behind, in front of, next to, near, ...*

Things in the picture	Where in my picture?	In my partner's picture
a wood	*in the background, on the right*	
	...	

b) Now talk to your partner about your pictures.
Find at least five differences. Make notes in the third column of your table.

There's a ... in the background on the left.

In my picture it's on the right.

6 SPEAKING Making plans in Liverpool ▸ Unit 3, p. 64

Partner B: You want to spend the day with a friend in Liverpool.

a) Find out
- what your partner wants to do,
- why,
- what it costs.

Listen to the answers and take notes.

Partner B — What would you like to do?
Partner A — I'd like ...
Partner B — Oh? Why?
Partner A — Because I like ... / it's ...
Partner B — What does it cost?
Partner A — ...

b) But you have different ideas. You want to go to the places below. Tell your partner where you want to go, why and what it costs.

What about 170 shops, cafes and restaurants?

1 LIVERPOOL ONE

Liverpool ONE is the biggest shopping centre in the city. Here you'll find the ODEON cinema and two hotels. The ODEON cinema is open until late.

Entry to the shopping centre is free.

Merseyside Maritime Museum

Everything about Liverpool's seafaring history. Real boats, ship models, pictures and films bring Liverpool's shipping stories to life. And of yourse you can learn everything about the story of the Titanic.

Free entry!

c) Talk to your partner and choose two things that you want to visit together.

Partner A — In my opinion we should ...
Partner B — Really? I disagree. I think ...
Partner A — Oh, ..., OK. I agree. Let's go to ...

Unit 4

4 ROLE-PLAY Phoning *Lochside B&B* ▸ Unit 4, p. 73

a) Partner B: You work in the B&B. Your partner is a tourist. Copy the telephone message. When your partner phones, talk to him or her and note the information.

Partner A — Hi. This is ... I'm phoning to confirm my reservation for ...
You — Let me see. That was the single room, right?
Partner A — ...
You — How many nights?
Partner A — ...
You — Yes, that's fine. What time will you arrive?
Partner A — ...
You — No problem. Thank you.

Telephone messages

Who rang? ______________
How many nights? ______________
Will arrive on: ______ at: ______
Room: single ☐ twin ☐ family ☐

b) Now you ring Lochside B&B to confirm your reservation:
- a twin room for one night
- you'll arrive 1st September late in the evening (about 9 pm)

You — Hi. This is ... I'm phoning to confirm our ... for ...
Partner A — Let me see. That was the twin room, right?
You — ...
Partner A — How many nights?
You — We'd like to stay for ... night.
Partner A — Yes, that's fine. What time will you arrive?
You — We'll arrive ...
You — No problem. Thank you.

If you don't understand, say: *Sorry, can you say that again, please?*

4 ROLE-PLAY What is it? ▸ Unit 4, p. 81

a) Partner B: Ask your partner the words for these people and things.

1 
2 
3 
4 
5 

What do you call	the blue	who / that	is over us?
	the machine		washes cups and glasses?
	somebody		brings food to people in a restaurant?
	a small house		has rooms for guests?
	somebody		drives a bus?

b) Now listen to your partner. What words does he/she mean?

Oh, do you mean a cow / customer / farmer / mouse / kettle?

Unit 1

More practice 1 Which advert is best? ▸ Unit 1, p. 12

Read the sentences below. Then pick the best advert (A–G) on page 12 for each sentence.

1 You love music, especially pop music. And you're free this evening!
2 You watched the 2012 Olympic Games on TV. Now you want to see where they happened.
3 You like clothes and you love interesting food. But you don't want to spend lots of money.
4 You want to travel around London for a day and you want the cheapest ticket.
5 You love the theatre and music. But you don't really like pop music.
6 Your hobby is shopping and you love English shops.
7 You're a football fan and you'd like to visit a famous English stadium.

More help 2 ACTIVITY London plans ▸ Unit 1, p. 13

Step 2: Agree with partners in a group.

Work in a group. Talk to your partners and agree on three (or more) ideas. Write them down. Write why you want to go there. You can use some of these ideas:

You should	visit go to see	…	because	it's	cheap • free • interesting good • fun • very popular amazing • famous great for football / sport fans
				you can	buy presents / do some shopping there. see a great show there. see the hottest fashion there. listen to cool music.

More practice 2 About the story ▸ Unit 1, p. 15

a) Which sentences give the main points of the story?

About me	A Sherlock is different from his friends.	B Sherlock likes books.
Disaster on the Tube	A The friends ran to the train.	B Alfie didn't get on the train.
Shopping disaster	A The kids had to leave Harrods.	B Things are expensive in Harrods.
Disaster in Hyde Park	A Alfie kicked a ball.	B The friends had trouble with some teenagers.
In the museum, at last	A Everybody liked the museum.	B The museum has dinosaurs.

b) What do you think was Sherlock's best idea? Talk to other students – do they agree?

I think Sherlock's best idea was … on the Tube / in Harrods / in Hyde Park / the Natural History Museum.

Yes, I agree.

I don't agree. I think his best idea was …

Unit 1

More help 4 Why and what?

▸ Unit 1, p. 15

Complete the sentences with the right endings A–F.

1 Sam's friends call him *geek* because ...
2 His friends said BORING! when ...
3 Alfie missed the Tube train because ...
4 They had a problem at Harrods because ...
5 The teens in the park ran away when ...
6 They went to the museum because ...

A they heard a noise like a police car.
B they had no money and the museum was free.
C Alfie had a rucksack and they weren't with an adult.
D he likes things like books, history and museums.
E he was too slow.
F Sherlock wanted to go to the Natural History Museum.

More practice 3 Alfie's story

▸ Unit 1, p. 15

You're Alfie. Read the paragraph *Disaster on the Tube* again.
Then write about your experience in about six sentences. The sentences below will help you.

Denk daran: Du bist Alfie und erzählst die Geschichte aus Alfies Sicht:
Wo warst du?
Was hast du gemacht?
Wie hast du dich gefühlt?
Was kannst du nicht wissen?

Sherlock's story	Alfie's story
We went to the Tube station in Fulham.	Hier bleibt alles gleich.
We ran to our train but ~~Alfie~~ was too slow.	Hier musst du die Person ändern: → ... *I was too slow.*
The train left and ~~poor Alfie~~ was still on the platform.	Hier musst du wieder die Person ändern: → ... *I was still on the platform.*
~~We tried to phone, but our mobiles didn't work on the Tube. Then I had an idea.~~	Du kannst das alles nicht wissen, also weglassen!
~~We'll~~ get out ~~at the next station~~ and wait for the next train.	Hier musst du Person und Zeit ändern: → *My friends got out ... and waited ...*
~~And that's what we did.~~	Das gehört nicht zu deiner Geschichte, also weglassen.
Ten minutes later the next train came and ~~Alfie was~~ on it.	→ *I got on.*
~~He~~ was happy to see ~~us~~.	→ *I was happy to see my friends.*
~~"Very clever, Sherlock," Tally said. So I was happy too.~~	Auch das gehört nicht zu deiner Geschichte, also weglassen.

More practice 4 Find the right order ▸ Unit 1, p. 15

Here's a short version of the story. What's the right order of the sentences?

A After Harrods they went to Hyde Park.
B Sam, Tally and Ruby got the Tube train, but Alfie was too slow.
C On Saturday Sam met his friends Ruby, Alfie and Tally.
D Then they went to the Natural History Museum.
E They went to Fulham Tube station.
F They all really liked the museum, especially the earthquake room.
G When they got out of the Tube they went to Harrods.
H They had trouble with some teenagers because Alfie kicked a ball into their picnic.
I They had trouble with a security man because Alfie had a rucksack.

More help 1b Ideas for a text about your neighbourhood ▸ Unit 1, p. 16

Add 20 of these words to your list or network about your neighbourhood.

bank • bike shop • bus station • bus stop • cake shop • cinema • farm • fields • flats • gardens • hairdresser's • harbour • houses • museum • park • post office • restaurant • school • second-hand shop • sports centre • stadium • supermarket • swimming pool • taxis • theatre • traffic lights • train station • video shop

More help 2 NOW YOU ▸ Unit 1, p. 16

a) First read this example text.

*I live in Wimbledon. It's not far from London.
The best thing about Wimbledon is the tennis.
There are lots of great shops here.
And there's a train station near our house.
But there aren't any swimming pools near us.
I think Wimbledon is great.*

b) Now tell Ruby or Darren about your neighbourhood. Change the words in orange.
Write about 40 words.

*I live in Lüneburg. It's not far from Hamburg.
The best thing about Lüneburg is ...*

Unit 1

More practice 5 Two articles ▸ Unit 1, p. 17

There are some new words in these articles. Can you guess what the red words mean in German? Think of English words that you already know or German words. Pick a) or b).

a) ○

Everybody was very muddy after the five kilometre fun run in the park this weekend. The winner was May Keating. She is a bus driver in Wimbledon.

There were no losers in this fun run, but there was a bag of prizes at the finish for everybody.

b) ●

German footballers surprised

The well-known German team Borussia Dortmund got a surprise last night when they played against a little-known team from Dublin – Shamrock Rovers. More than one hundred Irish fans travelled to Dortmund and sang noisily in the half-full German stadium. It was a rainy day and the field was very muddy.

The Dortmund players didn't start well. They all looked sleepy and played like sleepwalkers. Shamrock Rovers looked dangerous, and after 11 minutes one of the Shannon Rovers players put the ball in the back of the Borussia net. 1-0 to Shamrock Rovers! That was a wake-up call for Dortmund.

After that they played much better and they won 2-1. So it was a good win for the German team, but the Irish fans were good losers – they sang all through the match!

More help 1a Is fashion important? ▸ Unit 1, p. 18

Serena and Andy are talking about shopping and fashion. Listen to them and read the dialogue. Do you agree with Andy or Serena?

Andy — Hey, Serena. I'm going shopping. Do you want to come?
Serena — No thanks, Andy. I'm not interested in fashion.
Andy — Why not?
Serena — Because fashion is a waste of money.
Andy — That's rubbish! Fashion is so important!
Serena — Why is fashion so important for you, Andy?
Andy — If you look good, you feel good!
Serena — I don't agree. You don't need expensive clothes to feel good!
Andy — OK, Serena, but you don't have to spend a lot of money on fashion.
Serena — You're right. But **you** spend all your pocket money on clothes!
Andy — You're wrong! I always buy cheap clothes. Erm, ... Serena, can I borrow some money?
Serena — Oh!!! Not again!

More practice 6 Emma and Habib are good friends ▸ Unit 1, p. 18

Copy and complete the dialogue with words from the box.

have • if • expensive • interested • rubbish • waste • wrong

Emma — Oh, Habib! I'm going to the new shopping centre in town. Do you want to come too?
Habib — No thanks. I'm not ... (1) in fashion.
Emma — Why not?
Habib — Because it's a ... (2) of money.
Emma — You're ... (3)! Fashion is really important! ... (4) you look good, you feel good!
Habib — That's rubbish! You don't need ... (5) clothes to feel good!
Emma — But you don't ... (6) to spend a lot of money on fashion.
Habib — That's true. But you always spend a lot of money, Emma!
Emma — That's ... (7)! I always buy cheap clothes. But, Habib, can I borrow some money?
Habib — Oh, Emma!!! Not again!

//● 4a A letter to buzz ▸ Unit 1, p. 21

Complete the letter with *has to / have to / don't have to.*

Dear buzz
My friend often visits me in the evening, but then she ... (1) walk home alone. Her mum and dad can't pick her up because they ... (2) work in the evenings. The problem is that she ... (3) walk along dark streets. She says that I ... (4) worry about her, but I worry a lot. I ... (5) be sure that she's OK, so I phone her on her mobile.
A nervous friend

More practice 7 Tips for visitors in your town ▸ Unit 1, p. 21

Write tips for British visitors in your town. Use the ideas from exercises 1 and 5 and your own ideas. Put the text in your DOSSIER. Think about these questions:

- What's famous / interesting / fun / popular in your town?
- Do you have to travel by car?
- Where can you watch or do sports / go shopping?
- What do you have to wear in winter?
- What parts of the town aren't interesting for tourists?
- What food or drink should tourists try?

Unit 2

More practice 1 **WORDS** **Teen talk** ▸ Unit 2, p. 30

When teenagers talk together, they often use special phrases.

a) Copy each phrase onto a piece of card.

All's good. | Cool! | That's good. | It sucks!

Oh, come on! | You're joking! | Sounds good. | What a pain!

Pick the correct German phrase from the box and write it on the back of the card.

Spitzenwitz! • Na, komm schon! • Das ist gut. • Voll blöd! • Klingt gut. • Das nervt! • Alles ist gut. • Cool!

b) Pick good answers from your cards for these sentences:

1 I met a really nice boy at the youth club yesterday. – ?

2 How's life? – ?

3 You have to help your dad in the kitchen. – ?

4 What's your new school like? – ?

5 Do you have 50 euros for me? – ?

c) Walk around:

Half the class (partners A):
- Walk around with your English book.
- Say one of the sentences in b).
- Then go on to another partner.

The other half of the class (partners B):
- Walk around with your *Teen Talk*-cards.
- Listen and answer with a phrase on one of your cards. Show the card too.
- Then go on to another partner.

After a few minutes, partners A and B swap roles.

More help 2d This isn't a park!

► Unit 2, p. 31

Find the right answers for the five questions.
Be careful! You won't need two answers.

1 Is that your car?
2 How old are you?
3 Can you drive?
4 Where are you from?
5 Do you like it here in Mickleton?

Because I like sheep. | With my dog. | Yes, it is. | No, not really. | Yes, I can. | I'm from London. | I'm 14.

More practice 2 The story

► Unit 2, p. 32

a) What are the missing words in sentences 1–9?

The story

father • Police officer Butler • daughter

Who did what?
1 Molly, the ... of farmer John Taylor, saved three sheep.
2 John Taylor, Molly's ... was proud of her.
3 ... spoke to the newspaper.

proudly • hard • well • calmly

How Molly did it
4 She walked ... into the water.
5 She worked ...
6 Her father spoke ... and said Molly did ...

deep • dangerous • heavy • wet • brave

How things were
7 Molly was ... when she walked into the water.
8 The water wasn't too ... or ... for Molly.
9 The sheep were ... because they were ...

b) Now look back at page 32 and check your answers.

c) Look again at your sentences and tell a partner the story of Molly and the sheep:
Molly, the daughter of farmer John Taylor, saved three sheep.
She walked ...
...

Unit 2

More practice 3 NOW YOU ▸ Unit 2, p. 32

What can *you* do well? Write as many sentences as you can.

I can cook well.
I can play the guitar well.
I can ...

//● 2 You're a reporter ▸ Unit 2, p. 35

a) Finish the sentences with the right words.

car • dog • farm • home • idea • night • Rob • rubbish

A Rob ran to Molly's field with his ...
B Molly phoned ...
C The two police officers couldn't drive ...
D The police said the CCTV was a good ...
E Rob wrote the number of the ...
F Rob and Molly saw lights of a car at ...
G Rob's dad put CCTV cameras on the ...
H Rob's dog, Wally, found some ...

b) Now put sentences A–H in the right order and tell the story for a newspaper.

More practice 4 Who was it? ▸ Unit 2, p. 35

a) Copy the sentences and write the missing name(s).

The fox • Missy • Molly (3x) • Molly's dad • Molly's mum • police officers (2x) • Rob (3x) • Robs's father • Wally

1 ... wasn't well and had to stay in bed.
2 ... and ... ran along the track to Molly's farm.
3 The sheep ran into the next field and ... and ... came behind them.
4 ... and ... put up CCTV cameras on the Taylors' farm.
5 ... and ... saw the fox.
6 ... had a chicken in its mouth.
7 Much later ... went to the door.
8 Two ... spoke with her.
9 The ... couldn't go home because ...'s car was at the end of the track.

b) Look back at the story and check your answers.

More practice 5 An exciting night! ▸ Unit 2, p. 35

Imagine that you're Rob or Molly. Write your diary about the night at the Taylors' farm.
- Before you write, first decide if you're Rob or Molly.
- Then write like this:

Rob's story
Saturday night was very exciting!
I watched a DVD with Molly and then
we checked the CCTV monitor.
Suddenly we saw ...
We ran to the chickens and suddenly
we saw ...
Molly parked the car at the end of ...,
so the big black car couldn't ...
I wrote down ...
Then I went back to ... and waited
for Molly.
Later two ... came to the door.
They spoke with ...
They couldn't go home because ...

Molly's story
Saturday night was very exciting!
I watched a DVD with Rob and then
we checked the CCTV monitor.
Suddenly we saw ...
We ran to the chickens and suddenly
we saw ...
I parked the car at the end of ...,
so the big black car couldn't ...
Rob wrote down ...
Then Rob went back to ... and waited
for me.
Later two ... came to the door.
They spoke with ...
They couldn't go home because ...

More help 3 NOW YOU ▸ Unit 2, p. 37

Now write your comment (40–60 words) for the internet forum *My ideal place*.
Put your text in your DOSSIER.
Copy the sentences from the Düsseldorf text, but change the words in red and write about *your* ideal town.

Düsseldorf is a big city in the west of Germany. My uncle and aunt live there, and I think it's a great place to live.
I like the shops.
Also, you can go everywhere by bus.
That's great when I want to visit my friends.
So Düsseldorf is my ideal place to live.

Do you remember the *Writing Course* from Unit 1?
You can use sentences from your English book and change them.
For example from Alfies's text on page 37:
You can go everywhere by bus.
=> You can go to town / to the beach / to the park / to the shops ... by bus.

Unit 2

//● 3b Molly and Rob ▸ Unit 2, p. 41

NOW YOU What about you? Write six sentences about yourself.

I've ... once / a few times / lots of times. I've never ...

(ride) a horse

(speak) to a star

(be) to a beach

(have) a disaster

(find) money in the street

(work) on a farm

More practice 6 Chores ▸ Unit 2, p. 41

The table shows you how often Molly, Rob and his sister Jodie have helped at home over the last few days.

a) Look at the table. Then copy and complete the sentences.

1 ... has helped a lot.
2 ... and ... haven't helped a lot.

	Molly	Rob	Jodie
hoover house	I	never	never
fill dishwasher	IIII	never	never
wash car	I	never	never
clean kitchen	II	I	never
cook lunch	II	I	never

b) Now copy and complete the sentences.

1 Molly has ... (hoover) the house.
2 And she has ... (fill) the dishwasher.
3 She has ... (wash) the car too.
4 Molly and Rob have ... (clean) the kitchen.
5 And they've ... (cook) lunch.
6 And what about Jodie – has she ... (help) at home? – No, she hasn't. Not once!

Diese Verbens sind alle regelmäßig. Endung also: *-ed*.

Unit 3

More help 1a Trouble at school

► Unit 3, p. 50

Talk to a partner about the pictures. What's the right order of the pictures?

1 First talk about these questions:

Who is in each photo? Where are they? What is happening?

A

B

C

D

In picture A there are some kids. They're at school. One boy has money. Maybe he's buying something?

In picture B there are two teachers. One teacher is talking to the boy from picture A. Maybe he is the principal and the boy is in trouble.

In picture C a ... is coming to school. He has a big .... His bag is ... than the other students' bags. What's ... his bag?

In picture D there are some ... and a .... She's talking to the students. Maybe they have done something wrong?

2 Then talk about the order of the pictures.

I think picture ... is first.

Yes, and then it's picture ...

Really? I don't agree. I think picture ... comes before picture ...

Unit 3

1d Trouble at school ▸ Unit 3, p. 50

Listen again and finish these sentences.

1 Ben does not want to meet the ...
2 He tries to sell ...
3 **One** packet of crisps costs ...p.
4 When the teacher comes Ben puts his bag behind his ...
5 Ms Hall takes Ben to the ... office.
6 At this school you aren't allowed to ... crisps and chocolate bars.

More practice 1 WORDS ▸ Unit 3, p. 51

a) Copy the network. Then write food and drink words for the five blue boxes. Write as many words as you can.

Use the words in the green box and use your own ideas too.

biscuits • bread • cake • cereal bars • cheese • chicken • chips • chocolate bars • crisps • fruit • hot dogs • ice cream • jam • juice • lasagne • milk • potatoes • salad • sausages • energy drinks • soup • tea • toast • vegetables • water

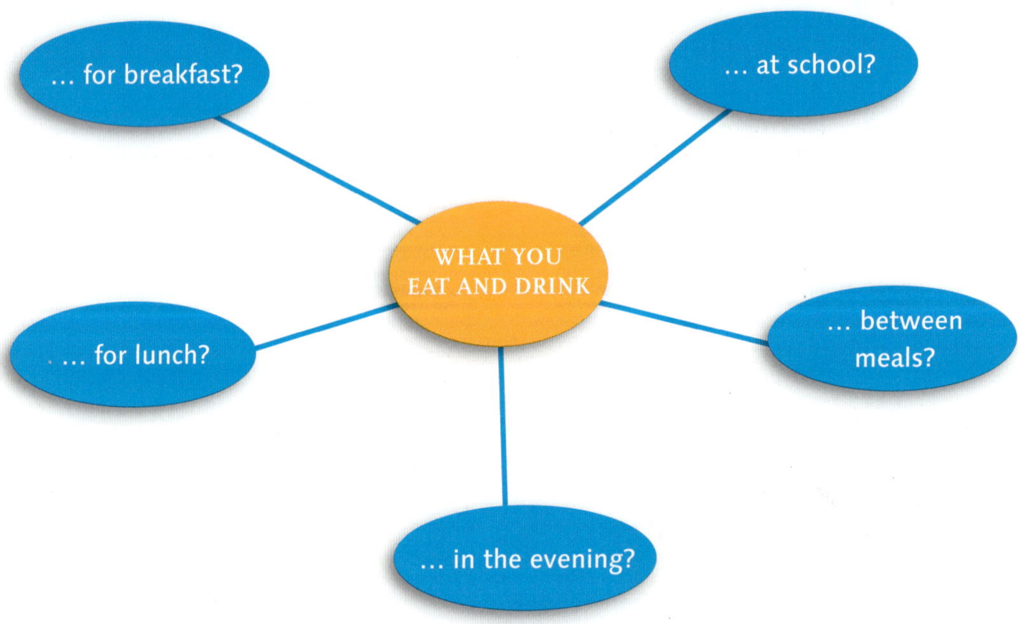

b) Now complete these sentences. Give as many examples as you can in each sentence.

1 I should eat less ...
2 I should drink less ...
3 I should eat more ...
4 I should drink more ...

More practice 2 Food at your school ▸ Unit 3, p. 51

What did you learn in your walk around? Report to the class:

I talked to four / six / ... people.
Two people said we can / can't buy ...
Two people think this is good / bad.
Three others think ...

More practice 3 Ben and Mrs Fox ▸ Unit 3, p. 52

Read these sentences. Are they true, false or not in the dialogue?

1 Ben was better at school last term.
2 Mrs Fox says Ben isn't a good salesperson.
3 Ben is the best at maths.
4 Ben wants to sell things at school again.
5 Mrs Fox heard about the new competition on the internet.
6 There's information about the competition in the school newsletter.

More help 3 YOUR TASK Are you good at business? ▸ Unit 3, p. 53

Here are some ideas for your poster:

BIZ 4 KIDZ

Our business plan:
make and sell animal balloons

What do we need?
balloons, pens

How much will they cost?
50 balloons cost 4 euros.
4 pens cost 5 euros.

How much money do we need?
only 9 euros

How many balloons can we sell?
maybe 50

How much can we get for the balloons?
1 euro

How much profit can we make?
41 euros

And here are some ideas for your presentation:

Here's our business plan. It's for animal balloons.

We must buy the balloons and some pens – about 9 euros.

We think that we can sell about 50 balloons. People have to pay 1 euro for each balloon.

If we sell 50 balloons, we'll make 50 euros. That's a profit of 41 euros.

That's our business plan. Thank you for listening.

Unit 3

//● 2 What's the right answer? ▸ Unit 3, p. 55

Copy and complete the sentences about the story.

1 Ben's dad was unhappy at first because the kitchen ....
2 Ben's dad thinks school is ...
3 Ben's dad thought the cakes were OK, but ...
4 Ben got his new idea from a ...

More practice 4 Tell the story ▸ Unit 3, p. 55

Put the sentences in the right order and tell the story.

A Ben's dad tried a cupcake and said it was OK – but it had to be something special.
B Ben and his friends made cupcakes in Ben's kitchen.
C Ben got an idea for his business on the way to school – from a Beatles poster.
D Ben and his friends didn't sell many cupcakes at school, so Ben was fed up.
E Ben told his dad about the competition, but his dad wasn't impressed.
F The kitchen was messy and Ben's dad was angry.

More help 3c The end of the story ▸ Unit 3, p. 55

Copy the table into your exercise book. Then listen again to the radio programme and complete your table.

	King Richard	Woodlands	South Liverpool
What are they selling?	...	...	cupcakes
What's their profit?	£...	£153	£...

More practice 5 Tell the end of the story ▸ Unit 3, p. 55

● Finish the sentences to tell the end of the story.

First Kiera Patel, the TV reporter, talked to the kids from ...
They had different sorts of milkshakes, for example ...
Kiera tried a milkshake and it was ...

Next Kiera talked to the team from ...
They had lots of ...
The books weren't expensive because ...

Then Kiera talked to the kids from South Liverpool High School. They looked like ...
Their cupcakes were ...
And they looked good too because ...

In the end, Ben and his friends didn't win the competition. They got ...

More help 2 NOW YOU

▸ Unit 3, p. 57

I think	diving dancing football gymnastics hang gliding hiking ice hockey judo skateboarding skiing swimming street surfing tae kwon do table tennis	is	a an	amazing great terrible boring exciting dangerous stupid	sport	for everybody. for women. for men. for young people.

In my opinion	its too dangerous. it's too violent. it's expensive. it's a waste of time. it makes you fit and strong. it's a great team sport.

I think	women men young people	can do the same sport as	men. women. older people.

I also think that	it's a very popular sport. other sports are more popular. …

I really hope that	(more) women (more) young people everybody	will	do this sport. stop doing this sport.

Unit 3

More practice 6 Mediation ▸ Unit 3, p. 58

Du sollst dolmetschen, aber weißt das Wort nicht?

a) Versuche es mit dem Gegenteil. Beispiel:

Mein Haus ist klein. => *My house isn't big.*

1 Das Wasser ist heiß. (Du weißt *hot* nicht.)
=> *The water isn't c...*

2 Mein Freund ist traurig. (Du weißt *sad* nicht.)
=> *My friend isn't h...*

3 Deine Tasse ist leer. (Du weißt *empty* nicht.)
=> *Your cup isn't f...*

4 Ich glaube, Arsenal wird verlieren.
(Du weißt *lose* nicht.)
=> *I think Arsenal won't w...*

5 Das war ein spannender Film!
(Du weißt *exciting* nicht.)
=> *The film was not b...*

6 Ich bin anderer Meinung.
(Du weißt *disagree* nicht.)
=> *I don't a...*

Wenn du für jemanden dolmetschen sollst, brauchst du nicht jedes Wort zu übersetzen. Es reicht, wenn du den Sinn wieder gibst.

b) Versuche, dich anders auszudrücken. Verwende Wörter aus dem grünen Kasten, die dasselbe bedeuten.

an apple, banana or orange • hard • mother's sister • quickly • sells things • who aren't children

1 Meine Hausaufgaben sind schwierig.
(Du weißt *difficult* nicht.) => *My homework is ...*

2 Meine Tante hat angerufen.
(Du weißt *aunt* nicht.) => *My ... phoned.*

3 Du schreibst schnell.
(Du weißt *fast* nicht.) => *You write ...*

4 Möchtest du etwas Obst?
(Du weißt *fruit* nicht.) => *Would you like ...?*

5 Was zahlen Erwachsene?
(Du weißt *adults* nicht.) => *How much is it for people ...*

6 Meine Schwester ist Verkäuferin.
(Du weißt *salesperson* nicht.) => *My sister ...*

Vielleicht kennst du ein Wort mit ähnlicher Bedeutung? Beispiel:
on the ferry => on the boat
Oder du kannst dasselbe mit anderen Worten sagen? Beispiel:
Can we pay with euros? => We only have euros. Is that OK?

//● 2 The man in the tourist office ▸ Unit 3, p. 58

a) Listen to the dialogue again.
This time, listen to the man in the tourist office. What are the right answers?

1 If you're under 15, a ticket is only ...
2 The next ferry leaves at ...
3 You can sit inside or outside. Outside you ... more.
4 There's a bank near here, in ... Street.

b) Now give your partner the information – in German. Then listen and check.

Der Mann sagt, dass ...

More practice 7 A summary – with mistakes!

▸ Unit 3, p. 59

a) Read the summary. Then correct the mistakes in red.

The three friends meet in North Park. Alfie plays basketball there.
Then they have a competition, and Sam wins.
The next week they meet again in the street.
They play three games – skipping, pilates and jogging.
Tally is very good at jogging. Sam is very good at pilates. And Ruby is good at skipping. Alfie is good at all three sports.
In the end they all play tennis together.

b) Now watch the film again and check your answers.

//● 4 What are Ben's ideas for Sunday?

▸ Unit 3, p. 61

Im *if*-Satz: *simple present*
Im Hauptsatz: *will-future*

Finish the sentences.

1 If it ... (rain) on Sunday, Ben ... (stay) at home.
2 But if Ben ... (stay) at home, he ... (be) bored.
3 If Ben's friends ... (come) to his house, they ... (have fun).
4 If Ben ... (have) some milk, eggs and flour, they ... (make) more cupcakes.
5 And if the cupcakes ... (look) nice, Ben's friends ... (eat) them. They don't need any cakes for the competition now!

More practice 8 NOW YOU

▸ Unit 3, p. 61

What can you say about next weekend? Complete the sentences.
Use your own ideas if you can.

1 I'll be very happy if ... I have no homework / there's a good show on TV / ...
2 But mum and dad won't be very happy if ... my music is too loud / dad can't find work / ...
3 I'll stay in bed late if ... we don't go on a trip / I'm tired / ...
4 But I'll get up early if ... we visit my uncle and aunt / I go swimming with my sister / ...
5 I'll go to town if ...
6 I'll be a bit sad if ...

Unit 3 Stop! Check! Go!

More help 8b READING and WRITING More sport at school? ▸ Unit 3, p. 65

Copy the table.

reasons for more sport	*reasons against more sport*

Now put the phrases from the green box in the correct column.

> makes you active and strong • need sport to stay healthy • lots of sports are boring • do your best for your team • not enough really good sports • as important as maths • can try different sorts of sport • don't need sport at school • feel great • can do sport outside school

reasons for more sport	*reasons against more sport*
makes you active and ...	*boring*

Unit 4

More practice 1 Sports clothes and equipment ▸ Unit 4, p. 70

What things did MacBean's sell?

a) Match the photos (A–H) with the right words. Example: *A: first aid kits*

Rain jackets from £12.99

Trainers only £9.99

Walking boots from £39.99

Sunglasses from £4.99

First aid kits £4.99

Sleeping bags from £8.99

Tents from £29.99

Rain trousers from £8.99

b) Work with a partner. Pick **A** or **B**.

A

Cover the words in the yellow bubbles.
Partner A draws one of the things A–H on paper.

Partner B writes the word for each thing next to the picture.

B

Cover the words in the yellow bubbles.
Partner A spells one of the things A–H.

T–E–N–T

Partner B writes the word(s) on paper.

Now look at the words and check that Partner B has written them correctly.
Then change roles.

More practice 2 How to run a B&B

▸ *Unit 4, p. 71*

Read Kara's comments about their new *bed and breakfast*. Write the correct sentences.

1. "We must teach ourselves / themselves business," said mum.
2. And mum bought herself / himself a book – *How to run a B&B.*
3. "You'll have to look after themselves / yourselves in the morning," mum said to Jamie and me, "because we'll be busy."
4. Jamie said, "I want to help, so I'll teach myself / yourself how to cook nice meals."
5. Jamie put tea and coffee in the visitors' rooms, so they can help themselves / ourselves .
6. And dad has stopped blaming herself / himself for what happened at MacBean's!

More practice 3 More visitors for *Lochside B&B*

▸ *Unit 4, p. 73*

Write the names of the visitors. Then listen and write the correct date next to each name.
● Write the times too.

1 Perry
2 Brown
3 Johnson
4 Taylor
5 Jones
6 Schmidt

27th July | 31st July | 1st August
15th August | 16th August | 27th August

Unit 4

More practice 4 Tell the story

▸ Unit 4, p. 75

Copy and complete the network with the right adjectives.

1

When the Grants landed
- The plane was …
- The sky was …
- One bag was …

dark grey • late • missing

2

On their way to Dores
- The sky was …
- The road was …
- The Grants were …

narrow • black • tired

3

At the castle
- The rooms were …
- The kids were …
- The food was …

comfortable • good • excited

4

The next morning
- The place was …
- The music sounded …
- The Grants were …

lonely • empty • surprised

More practice 5 WORDS

▸ Unit 4, p. 75

Be careful: The verbs are in the wrong sentences!
Write the sentences with the six verbs in the right sentences.

1

The plane ~~laughed~~.

2

She ~~waved~~ a warning.

3

They all ~~hired~~ happily.

4

The old man ~~hooted~~.

5

The car isn't mine. I ~~landed~~ it.

6

The young man ~~chatted~~ goodbye.

More help 2 NOW YOU
▸ Unit 4, p. 76

You're Duncan.

a) Read the story *Ghosts don't exist!* again (pages 74/75).

b) Then write your story. The sentences below will help you.

We came into a big old ...
My sister and I were very excited because ...
First we went upstairs to our room. Then we went ...
Some people played music and some people danced.
We ... too.

But the next morning, the castle was ...
When we went outside, we heard ...
We saw ... But he was alone.

At about 11 am we arrived at our ...
Then we found the castle on a ....
It was ... castle.

In the afternoon we visited ...
It was a ruin. But the last family who lived at Urquhart Castle was ... !
So maybe we saw the ghosts of the Grants?

More help 1b Who is Amy Macdonald?
▸ Unit 4, p. 77

Listen again. Make notes about Amy MacDonald.

– First copy the headings on the right in your exercise book.
– Then listen and make short notes (1–4 words per answer).

Amy Macdonald
Her work: She's a ...
Born: (year) ...
Country: ...
First hit: ...
Instrument: ...
Hobbies: ...
Favourite groups:

More practice 6 A famous Scottish person
▸ Unit 4, p. 77

a) Find information about a famous Scottish person: age, hobbies, where he/she lives, why he/she is famous, what he/she does or did, etc. Here are some ideas:

Alexander Bell – scientist
Sean Connery – actor
Arthur Conan Doyle – writer
Robert Burns – poet
Kenny Dalglish – footballer
Amy Macdonald – singer

b) Now write a text about him or her for an online magazine. Write as many sentences as you can.

My famous Scottish person is ...
He/She was born on [date] in ...
He/She is/was a famous singer/actor/football player/film star/writer/...
He/She is famous because he/she ...
He/She also likes/liked ...
He/She is/was good at ...

Alexander Bell

Robert Burns

Unit 4

More practice 7 Holidays in Scotland

▸ Unit 4, p. 78

a) Read these statements. Then pick the best brochure from page 78 (*Around Loch Ness* or *Maggie's Lodge*) for each statement.

1 You'd love to visit a Scottish castle.
2 You're a big mountain biking fan.
3 You want to go for a walk in the Highlands, but you don't have any food.
4 You want to see as much of Loch Ness and the Highlands as possible.
5 You enjoy trips on lakes.
6 You need accommodation, but you don't have enough money for your own room.

b) ● Read the three tourist profiles below again and complete these sentences.

1 Tourist A will choose Maggie's Lodge because ...
2 Tourist B won't be very happy because ...
3 I think that tourist C will take the ... tour because ...

Tourist A
You're on holiday and want to spend two or three days near Loch Ness with a friend. You don't have a lot of money, you need a cheap place.

Tourist B
You're staying in Inverness with your family. You love Nessie stories, so you would like to visit a good Nessie museum.

Tourist C
You've just arrived in Scotland with some friends. You'd like to visit the Loch Ness region – quickly. You only have one day!

//● 3 More questions

▸ Unit 4, p. 81

Pick the answers to these questions. You won't need two words.

1 What do you call visitors who spend the night in your house?
2 What's the white stuff that you use to make bread or cake?
3 What do you call the thing that you use to cut food?
4 What do you call a person who wins a sports competition?
5 What do you call a person who sells things like cars?
6 What's the thing that you wear when you go outside and it's cold?

champion • coat • cook • guests • flour • knife • mirror • salesperson

//● 2 LANGUAGE What do you call ...? ▸ *Unit 4, p. 82*

a) Eight tourists can't think of the word in English. What do they say or ask? Write the correct sentences.

1 I need a paper that / who shows where places are.
2 What do you call a person that / who is not a child?
3 What's the boat that / who takes people across a river?
4 What do you call the people that / who fight against fire?
5 What's the name of the person that / who cuts or styles your hair?
6 What's the white stuff that / who you put on rice or potatoes or eggs?
7 What do you call the things that / who you wear on your feet under your shoes?
8 Can you tell me the word for the person that / who helps when your car is broken?

b) Now look at the pictures below. Write the right word after each sentence in a).

salt

mechanic

hairdresser

firefighters

socks

map

ferry

adult

//● 3 LANGUAGE Enjoy yourselves! ▸ *Unit 4, p. 83*

Jamie and Kara want to go camping. They are talking to their parents. Pick the right words from the box and complete the dialogue.
– You won't need all the words.
– You'll need one word twice.

myself • yourself • herself • himself
ourselves • yourselves • themselves

Jamie — Mum, Kara and I want to go camping.
Mum — Camping? Is that a good idea? That's what I ask ... (1).
Dad — Oh, I'm sure the kids can look after ... (2), Kate.
Jamie — Of course we can look after ... (3)!
Kara — Don't forget Jamie has taught ... (4) to cook!
Dad — Ah yes, I hear you're good at cooking soup for ... (5), Jamie!
Mum — Well, OK then. You go camping and enjoy ... (6).
But I won't blame ... (7) if you come back hungry!

TF 1 London facts

Travel …

… by Tube

The Tube is the popular name for London Underground trains. It's the oldest underground train system in the world – it opened in 1863! Today there are 270 stations and 11 lines. Over 3 million people go on the Tube every day.

… by a London bus

London's red double-decker buses are famous. The city has more than 700 bus routes and most Londoners live only 400 metres away from one of the 19,500 bus stops. Teens from 11–15 travel free – but they need a special photo card.

… or by taxi

Taxi drivers must take a very difficult test. To pass the test[1] they must know 25,000 streets in London. Drivers learn for the test for two to four years.

Buckingham Palace

The king or queen lives and works here. When the Queen is at home, you see her flag on top of[2] the palace.

You can see the guards change in front of the palace at 11.30 am every day in summer, or every second day for the rest of the year. It's free to watch the guard ceremony.

The palace has 240 bedrooms, 78 bathrooms and 775 rooms in all. About 800 people work in or for the palace: cooks, cleaners[3], gardeners, drivers, etc.

Guards[4] (soldiers[5]) with black and red uniforms and big, black hats stand outside the palace.

Buckingham Palace is **open** from July to the end of September. **Travel** by bus, or take the tube to St James' Park, or walk! It's only 15 minutes on foot from Big Ben.

[1] pass a test *eine Prüfung bestehen* [2] on top of *oben* [3] cleaner *Reinigungskraft* [4] guard *Wache* [5] soldier *Soldat/in*

Wembley Stadium

Wembley Stadium, the home of the England national football team, opened in 2007. With space for 90 000 fans and 310 fans in wheelchairs, it's the second largest stadium in Europe. It has 688 places where fans can buy food and drink, and 2,618 toilets.

Wembley is a stadium for lots of different sports, especially American football, rugby and athletics. It's also a famous place for music concerts.
It's open every day, but not over Christmas and on 1st January, or when there is a game or concert. **Travel** by tube or bus. It's 12 kilometres from the centre of London to Wembley!

London Eye

About 3.5 million people ride the London Eye every year. It's 135 metres tall and a tour takes 30 minutes. The Eye moves[6] so slowly that it doesn't stop when people get on. **It's open** every day (but not on Christmas Day). **Travel** by tube to Waterloo. Or walk over the river from the Houses of Parliament.

Harry Potter

There are lots of Harry Potter film places in London. The way into the Leaky Cauldron is at Leadenhall Market, Harry speaks to a snake in London Zoo, and the train to Hogwarts goes from platform 9¾ at Kings Cross Station.

Big Ben

Dong, dong, dong, dong! For many people Big Ben is the most famous sound of London. When Londoners say "Big Ben" they

usually mean the clock tower – but Big Ben is really the name of the very large bell. You can hear Big Ben very well if you stand next to the Houses of Parliament.

Sherlock Holmes

Sherlock Holmes lived at 221B Baker Street ... No! That's not true! Sherlock Holmes wasn't a real person. He was a famous detective in books by Arthur Conan Doyle. The first Sherlock Holmes story came out in 1887.

But today, 221B Baker Street is a great museum about Sherlock Holmes.
It's open from 9.30 am to 5.30 pm. **Travel** by tube to Baker Street, and see the statue of Sherlock Holmes outside the station!

[6] move *sich bewegen*

TF 2 Dick Whittington – a Christmas pantomime

What is a pantomime?

In Britain a pantomime (or 'panto') is a funny show. The characters[1] in a panto talk, shout and sing. Pantos are in every theatre at Christmas time and also in small villages, schools and clubs. And they are very, very popular.

The stories are traditional children's stories, but pantos aren't just for kids – everybody loves them!

Pantomimes have some very special rules:

- A big man in colourful clothes plays a woman. This character is always very funny. He (or she?!) makes lots of silly jokes and sings a silly song.
- The audience[2] laughs and shouts a lot! For example, the people shout "Boo!" when they see the bad guy.
- There's always a bad guy who tries to make trouble. But everything is always OK in the end.

The audience at a pantomime

Everything is OK in the end.

1 It's all wrong!

Correct these sentences.

1 In pantomimes the characters don't talk.
2 They're only for children.
3 The people who watch a panto have to be quiet.
4 The ending is sad.

[1] character *Figur* [2] audience *Zuschauer, Publikum*

Scene 1 **Welcome!**

Narrator[3] – *(to audience)* Hello everybody!

Audience — Hello!

Narrator — Welcome to our pantomime! It's the story of Dick Whittington. Look! Here he is. Hi Dick! But you look sad ... What's wrong?

Dick — I'm sad and tired. You see, I tried to find work in London, but I couldn't find a job. So I'm going home to the Cotswolds!

Cat — *(comes in)* No work in London? You're wrong!

Dick — What? You're a cat, ... but you can talk?

Cat — Yes, I'm Tommy the cat. And I know there's work for you in London. Listen to the church bells.

Dick — The bells?

Tommy — Yes! Listen!

Dick — *(to audience)* Hm. Are the bells right? Well, I'll go back to London and I'll look for a job again.

Tommy — And I'll come with you.

Scene 2 **A London market**

(Characters: Dick, Tommy the cat, Alice)

Dick — *(to his cat)* Oh Tommy! I need a job! But nobody at this market can help me.

Tommy — Oh, I'm sure you'll find work soon. Remember the bells. They're never wrong.

Dick — Oh, I don't know ...

Alice — Hello. You're beautiful[4], aren't you!

Dick — *(surprised)* Oh, hello. Thank you!

Alice — No, not you. I'm talking to your cat! What's his name?

Dick — Ah, the cat. This is Tommy. He's a very intelligent cat. He can talk.

Alice — *(laughs)* Oh no, he can't.

(Narrator holds a sign for the audience: Oh yes, he can!)

Audience and Tommy — Oh yes he can!

Alice — *(surprised)* Oh, you're right! He can talk! That's very clever. My name is Alice Fitzwarren. What's your name?

Dick — Dick Whittington. I'm looking for a job.

Alice — Really? My dad needs somebody to help him in his shop. Come on. It's this way. *(They leave.)*

Scene 3 **Mr Fitzwarren's shop**

(Mr Fitzwarren has a problem with rats in his shop. Sarah, the cook, is running after the rats – but they're not scared of her!)

Sarah — *(sings)* I don't like you rats!
You eat my cheese!
So run away please!

Sarah — *(to audience)* Can you help me? Maybe if you sing my song, all the rats will run away!

Audience — *(sings)* I don't like you rats!
You eat my cheese!
So run away please!

Sarah — Yes, go away! We don't want you here!

---

[3] narrator *Erzähler/in* [4] beautiful *schön*

(Dick, Alice and Tommy arrive.)

Dick — Oh. That's not very nice!

Sarah — No, not you. The rats.

Dick — Oh, I see. My cat can help you.

Alice — Oh yes. Tommy can help you.

Sarah — Oh no, he can't.

(Narrator holds a sign for the audience: Oh yes, he can!)

Audience — Oh yes, he can!

Sarah — Oh no, he can't.

Audience — Oh yes he can!

Dick — Go on, Tommy!

(Tommy runs after the rats and they run away. Mr Fitzwarren arrives and sees this.)

Mr Fitzw. — That's a good cat. *(to Dick)* Would you like a job? You and your cat can live here if you like.

Dick — Oh, yes please!

Scene 4 King Rat

(Characters: Narrator, King Rat, Rat 2)

Narrator — Good! Now Dick has a job and lives in a nice house. But ... there's a problem. You see, this is a pantomime, and so there's a bad guy. And the bad guy is King Rat. He's very bad. Here he is.

(King Rat and Rat 2 arrive. The narrator holds a sign for the audience: Boo!)

Audience — Boo!

Narrator — Louder!

Audience — Booooo!!!

King Rat — *(to Rat 2)* I don't like cats! And I really don't like Tommy the cat!

Rat 2 — Yes, but what can we do?

King Rat — Listen to me! I have a plan.

Rat 2 — A plan?

King Rat — Yes. Tonight[5] we go to Alice's room. We take her diamond necklace ...

... and we put the necklace in Dick's room. OK?

Rat 2 — *(He's not sure)* OK. But ... why?

King Rat — You stupid rat! Because Mr Fitzwarren will find the necklace in Dick's room. Then he'll be angry. *(laughs)* Muw-ha-ha-ha-ha-ha-ha! And then Dick and his cat will have to leave the house!

(Narrator holds a sign for the audience: Boo!)

Audience — Boo!

What happens next in the story?

Well, bad King Rat takes Alice's necklace and puts it in Dick's room. When Mr Fitzwarren finds it, he calls the police.

Poor Dick! He and Tommy run away. They go to a country where there are lots of rats and mice[6] – but no cats. But when Tommy arrives, all the rats and mice run away! The people are very happy, and they give Dick lots of money.

When Dick comes back to London with his cat, he is very rich[7]. He marries[8] Alice and he is Lord Mayor[9] of London.

So everything is OK in the end. Hurray!

2 THEATRE TIME

In a group, act out one of the scenes of the pantomime for your class.

[5] tonight *heute Abend/Nacht* [6] mice *Mäuse* [7] rich *reich* [8] marry *heiraten* [9] Lord Mayor *etwa: Oberbürgermeister*

TF 3 Liverpool and the Titanic

The Titanic was a Liverpool ship. Liverpool's *White Star Line* owned[1] the Titanic and the Captain, Edward Smith, was a Liverpool man. Some of the 885 people who worked on the Titanic were from Liverpool too.
White Star Line made plans for the Titanic in 1908. They wanted a ship that was bigger and better than all other ships in the world.

People said that the new ship was the strongest and safest ship in history. They thought it couldn't sink.
The Titanic left England for New York on 10th April 1912, but this was its first and last journey[2].
On 14th April the ship hit an iceberg. Two hours later, the Titanic sank and more than 1500 people died.

There were three groups of passengers[3] on the Titanic: first-class (325 passengers), second-class (285 passengers) and third-class (706 passengers). The most expensive tickets cost £512 (about €60,000 today) and third-class tickets cost £3 to £8 (about €350 to €950 today). Third-class passengers were not allowed to visit the parts of the ship that were for first-class passengers.

There were not enough lifeboats[4] for everybody. You can see in the plan that third-class passengers were a long way from the lifeboats. When the Titanic sank, 38% of the first-class passengers died, but 75% of the third-class passengers lost their lives. In all, only about 700 people survived[5] and arrived in New York.

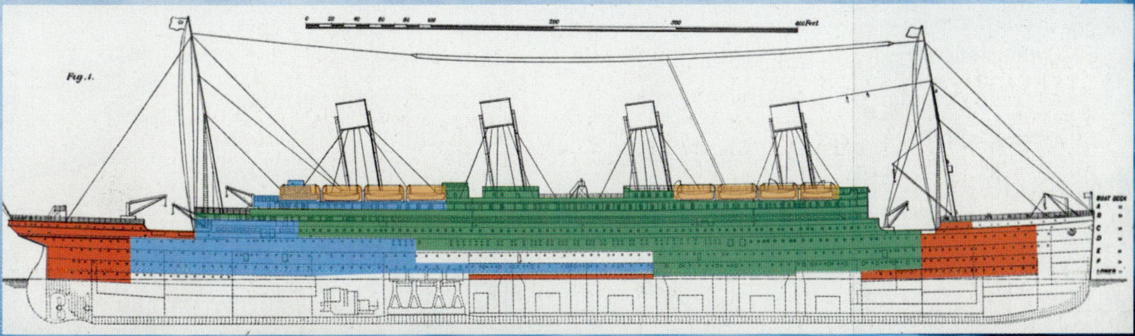

green: first class part of the ship, **blue:** second class part of the ship, **red:** third class part of the ship, **orange:** lifeboats

Erkläre diese Zahlen auf Deutsch: 885 – 1908 – 1912 – 1500 – 706 – 60 000 – 75% – 700
Beispiel: *885 Menschen arbeiteten auf ...*

[1] own *besitzen* [2] journey *Reise* [3] passenger *Passagier* [4] lifeboat *Rettungsboot* [5] survive *überleben*

TF 4 Scotland facts

A Geography

Scotland is the country north of England. It's about half as big as England.

Most people live in the south, in or near the big cities of Edinburgh (the capital) and Glasgow.
Aberdeen is the only big city in the north.

England + Wales + Scotland
=
Great Britain
+
Northern Ireland
=
United Kingdom (UK)

Number of people in Scotland's biggest cities:

Glasgow	**598,830**
Edinburgh	**486,120**
Aberdeen	**220,420**

Not many people live in the *Highlands* in the north and west. This is a region of hills and mountains: the highest mountain is Ben Nevis (1344 m).

Oil[1] and gas from the North Sea bring a lot of money and jobs to Aberdeen.

The longest river is the River Tay. There are 790 islands[2] (99 with people) and more than 30,000 freshwater lakes *(lochs)*. The biggest lake in cubic metres is Loch Ness (7,452 million m^3). Loch Ness is the most famous lake because some people think it has a monster.

B History

Scotland is part of the UK. But people from Scotland are proud to be Scottish, so don't call them English!

Older history

For hundreds of years, Scotland and England were two different countries. They often fought each other[3]. Sometimes England won, sometimes Scotland won.

In **1707** Scotland and England joined[4] and became[5] Great Britain. They had one Parliament – in London.

Modern history

Scotland has its own flag and national football team. The Scots have pounds like the English, but Scottish money looks a bit different.

1997: Scotland gets its own parliament again.

2014: The Scottish people vote about independence[6]. They decide to stay in the UK.

[1] oil *Öl* [2] island *Insel* [3] they fought each other *sie bekämpften sich* [4] join *sich vereinigen* [5] they became *sie wurden*
[6] vote about independence *über die Unabhängigkeit abstimmen*

C Life

Languages: Everybody in Scotland speaks English. But in the Highlands some people also speak Gaelic[7]. You'll see road signs in English and Gaelic.

Sport: Football is the most popular sport in Scotland. Golf is popular too – it started 600 years ago in St Andrews, near Edinburgh. Golf isn't an expensive sport in Scotland so everybody can play. In the Highlands you can see shinty and other traditional sports like tossing the caber[8].

tossing the caber

Festivals:
In Scotland there is a long tradition of singing and dancing, and Scottish music is very popular.

You'll also see these things at festivals in Scotland:

haggis

bagpipes

a kilt

The Loch Ness Monster

Loch Ness is a big long lake in the north of Scotland.

Is there a monster in Loch Ness? Most people say "no", but every year people take photos of something that looks like a monster.

This photo from 1934 is perhaps the most famous photo. For 60 years, people weren't sure if the photo was real or not. But in 1993 the true story came out.
It was a trick! It was really a toy submarine[9] with a model of a monster.

In 2012, Marcus Atkinson, a tourist boat captain, was on Loch Ness near Urquhart Castle. Something big followed his boat for more than two minutes. Marcus saw it on his sonar equipment, so he took a photo of the sonar picture. It looks like a big snake.

Marcus said: "I was shocked. I showed it to other boat captains and nobody knew what it was."

Experts said it was a photo of plankton (very, very small animals) in the water, but fans of the Loch Ness monster were very excited.

Stories like this explain why thousands of tourists come to Loch Ness every year to look for Nessie. Perhaps you could find Nessie too?

[7] Gaelic *Gälisch* [8] tossing the caber *Baumstammwerfen* [9] toy submarine *Spielzeug U-Boot*

SF 1 Vokabeln lernen

- Führe dein Vokabelheft oder deine Vokabelkartei aus Klasse 6 weiter.
- Lerne nur 5 bis 10 neue Vokabeln auf einmal.
- Versuche, jeden Tag 10 Minuten zu lernen.
- Lerne mit jemandem zusammen. Es macht mehr Spaß, und ihr könnt euch gegenseitig abfragen.
- Finde heraus, wie du am besten lernst: durch Hören oder Nachsprechen, mit Bildern, am Computer oder Handy?
- Schreibe die neuen Wörter auch immer auf.

Weitere Tipps zum besseren Merken:

1 Mache Wortfelder

Ordne die Wörter unter einem Oberbegriff. Du kannst eine Liste machen, ein *network* oder mit Karteikarten arbeiten.

2 Finde Gegensatzpaare

Sammle Gegensatzpaare und schreibe sie z.B. auf die letzte Seite deines Vokabelhefts.

3 Lerne *phrases* oder Beispielsätze statt Einzelwörter

Vor allem schwierige Wörter kannst du dir besser merken, wenn du sie als *phrases* lernst. *Phrases* sind Ausdrücke von zwei Wörtern oder mehr. Lerne z.B. nicht *cup*, sondern *a cup of tea*.

travel	→	*travel by bus*
spend	→	*spend money on clothes*
ago	→	*two years ago*

Oder merke dir kurze Beispielsätze:

especially	→	*I love sports, especially football.*
have to	→	*It's late. We have to go now.*

SF 2 Unbekannte Wörter verstehen

▸ Unit 1, p. 17

Du kannst englische Texte verstehen – auch wenn du nicht alle Wörter kennst.

1 Schau auf die Bilder

Bilder zeigen dir oft Dinge aus dem Text. Was bedeuten z.B. *screws, nails* und *screwdriver* im Text rechts?

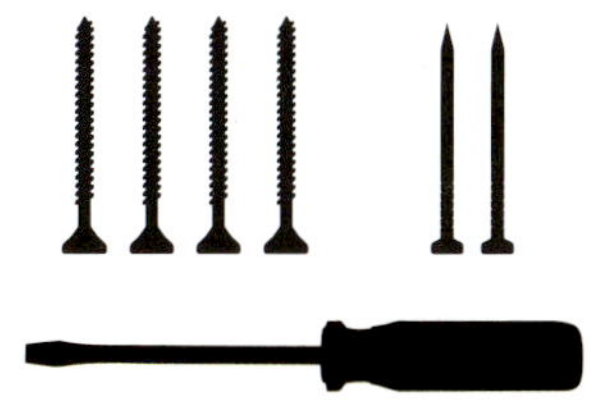

First check if you have all things:
4 screws, **2** long nails and a **screwdriver**.
You also need a **hammer** and some **sandpaper**.

2 Denke an ähnliche Wörter im Deutschen

Viele englische Wörter werden ähnlich wie im Deutschen geschrieben oder klingen ähnlich wie deutsche Wörter:

- *hammer* heißt auf Deutsch „Hammer"
- *sandpaper* bedeutet „Sand- oder Schmirgelpapier"

Was bedeuten die folgenden Wörter auf Deutsch?

balcony • cable • element • flexible • material • optimistic • quality • situation • typical

3 Schau auf den ganzen Satz

Du kannst ein unbekanntes Wort auch erschließen. Lies den ganzen Satz und überlege, welches Wort Sinn macht. Was könnten z.B. *share* und *population* bedeuten?

1 *In our hotel my parents had a room and I had to share a room with my little brother.*
2 *Berlin has a population of about 3 million people.*

4 Suche Bekanntes in unbekannten Wörtern

Manchmal steckt in einem neuen Wort ein anderes Wort, das du schon kennst. Wie heißen die folgenden Wörter auf Deutsch?

biker • buyer • dreamer • learner • loser • fruity • icy • smelly • watery • sunlight • haircut • high jumper

1: screws *Schrauben* nails *Nägel* screwdriver *Schraubendreher*
2: balcony *Balkon* cable *Kabel* element *Element* flexible *flexibel* material *Material* optimistic *optimistisch* quality *Qualität* situation *Situation* typical *typisch* 3: share *teilen* population *Bevölkerung*
4: biker *Fahrradfahrer/in* buyer *Käufer/in* dreamer *Träumer/in* learner *Lerner* loser *Verlierer/in* fruity *fruchtig* icy *eisig* smelly *übelriechend* watery *wässrig* sunlight *Sonnenlicht* haircut *Haarschnitt* high jumper *Hochspringer/in*

SF 3 Im Wörterbuch nachschlagen

1 Wörter alphabetisch ordnen

Alles im Wörterbuch ist alphabetisch aufgelistet:
- *U* kommt vor *V*
- *van* kommt vor *vegetables*
- *vegetables* kommt vor *verse*

usually ['juːʒʊəli] meistens, normalerweise III 2 (37)

V

van [væn] Transporter, Lieferwagen III 2 (30)
°**variety (of)** [və'raɪəti] Auswahl (an)
°**various** ['veəriəs] (mehrere) verschiedene
vegetables, *infml auch* **veg** ['vedʒtəblz], [vedʒ] Gemüse I
°**verse** [vɜːs] Vers, Strophe *(Lied)*

2 Zusammengesetzte Ausdrücke finden

Der Haupteintrag (z.B. *easy)* steht farbig oder fett am Anfang. Daneben oder darunter findest du oft zusammengesetzte Wörter oder Redewendungen (z.B. *take it easy*).

easy ▶ **take it easy** *(umgs)* sich nicht aufregen
▶ **easy-going** ungezwungen, gelassen

3 Unterschiedliche Wortbedeutungen beachten

Die Ziffern 1, 2 usw. bei einem Eintrag zeigen, dass ein Wort mehrere Bedeutungen hat.

Egal ob du ein englisches oder deutsches Wort suchst: Lies immer **alle** Einträge und entscheide dann, welches die richtige Bedeutung ist.

a) Englisch-Deutsch
Das Wort *enter* heißt am Computer *eingeben*. Was aber heißt *enter* in diesen Sätzen?

1 *When did you enter the USA? – Two weeks ago.*
2 *Please use the door on the right to enter the building.*
3 *Please enter your name here at the top of the list.*
4 *Lots of people were seasick, so they were happy when the ferry entered the harbour.*

enter *Verb*
1 (*Zimmer*) eintreten
2 (*Gebäude*) betreten, hineinkommen
3 (*Land*) einreisen
4 (*Hafen*) einlaufen
5 (*in Liste*) eintragen
6 (*Computer*) eingeben

b) Deutsch-Englisch
Welches sind die richtigen englischen Wörter für *anmachen* in diesen Sätzen?

1 *Kannst du den Salat anmachen?*
2 *Wieso machst du mich an? Ich habe nichts getan.*
3 *Bitte mach das Licht an.*
4 *Er machte einen Spiegel im Bad an.*

anmachen *Verb (umgs)*
1 (*anbringen*) put up
2 (*einschalten*) put on
3 (*anzünden*) light
4 (*Salat*) dress
5 (*kritisieren*) have a go at someone *(infml)*

3a): 1 einreisen; 2 hineinkommen; 3 eintragen; 4 einlaufen;
3b): 1 dress; 2 have a go at someone; 3 put on; 4 put up

SF 4 Texte markieren

▸ Unit 3, p. 56

1 Wie kannst du markieren?

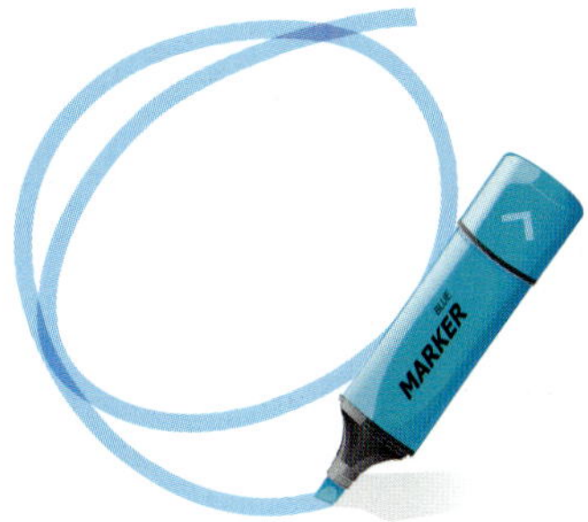

Wenn du Aufgaben zu einem Text bearbeiten sollst, solltest du wichtige Textstellen im Text markieren. Du kannst die Stellen

- umkreisen,
- unterstreichen,
- oder mit Textmarker hervorheben.

Aber das geht nur auf Fotokopien, nicht im geliehenen Schülerbuch.

2 Wie gehst du vor?

a) Lies zuerst die Aufgabe. Rechts ist ein Beispiel.

Read the text. Then tick the correct answers (a, b or c).

1 *In the 1980s Liverpool FC*
- *a) won two League Championships.* ☐
- *b) won three FA Cups.* ☐
- *c) won the "Double" in 1986.* ☐

2 *The Hillsborough disaster happened*
- *a) in 1991.* ☐
- *b) in the FA Cup final.* ☐
- *c) because too many people were in the stadium.* ☐

b) Dann lies den Text.
- Markiere nur die Informationen, die du brauchst.
- Die Textstellen für Frage 1 sind schon markiert. Welche Stellen würdest du für Frage 2 unterstreichen?

c) Jetzt ist die Lösung leicht: Welche Kästchen musst du bei Aufgabe 1 und 2 oben rechts ankreuzen?

The Hillsborough Disaster

In the 1980s Liverpool FC had a great time. The club won another three League Championships and two FA Cups. In 1986 they won the "Double", which is FA Cup and League Championship in the same year. But the club's great time ended with the Hillsborough disaster. It was a very sad day for Liverpool. In the FA Cup semi-final against Nottingham Forest on 15 April 1989 there was a panic in the stadium and hundreds of Liverpool fans were thrown against the fences. Ninety-four fans died that day; two people died some time later. A report later said that too many people were in the stadium.

2b: FA Cup semi-final; 1989; too many people were in the stadium.
2c: 1c; 2c.

SF 5 Prüfungen und Klassenarbeiten

1 Was musst du immer beachten?

Do – Lies alle Arbeitsanweisungen.

better – Unterstreiche wichtige Punkte.

in tests – Überprüfe am Ende, ob du alle Punkte abhaken kannst.

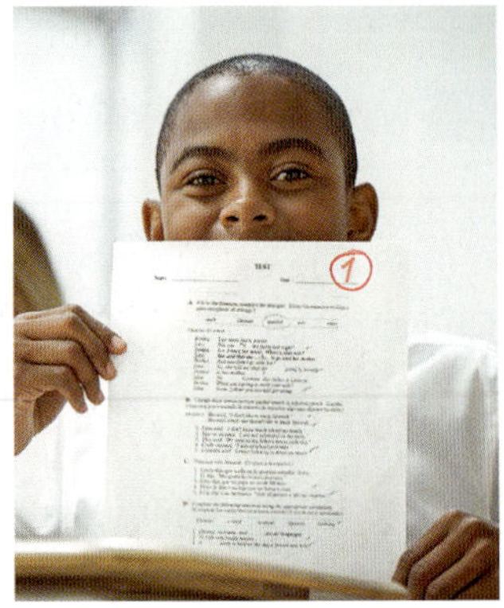

2 READING

First read the text.
Then do tasks 1-9.
Decide if the statements are true or false and tick the correct box.
Then finish the sentences. You can quote from the text.

I've lived in London since January. At first I didn't like the city, because it is very loud and noisy. After some time I really enjoyed it here and I think it's an amazing place for lots of reasons.
Firstly, you can go to many interesting places like the National History Museum where you can see dinosaurs. The best thing is: You don't have to pay to get in.
Secondly, you have nice parks, where you can have a break …

1. *He came to London at the beginning of the year. This statement is*
   a) ☐ *true*
   b) ☐ *false*
   because the text says
   ____
2. *Now he likes life in the city. This statement is*
   a) ☐ *true*
   b) ☐ *false*
   because the text says
   ____
3. …

Hier ist ein Beispiel für eine Leseaufgabe.

a) Lies zuerst die Arbeitsanweisung. Unterstreiche, was du tun oder beachten sollst. Hier ein Beispiel:

First read the text.
Then do tasks 1-9.
Decide if the statements are true or false and tick the correct box.
Then finish the sentences. You can quote from the text.

b) Was musst du bei dieser Aufgabe tun?
- eine Tabelle vervollständigen?
- Kästchen ankreuzen?
- Textstellen suchen?
- aus dem Text zitieren?
- falsche Aussagen korrigieren?

Du musst Kästchen ankreuzen, Textstellen suchen und aus dem Text zitieren.

3 LISTENING

Lies auch bei Höraufgaben die Arbeitsanweisung genau und unterstreiche das Wichtigste.

First read the tasks 1–6.	Was sollst du zuallererst tun?
Then listen to the discussion.	Was wirst du hören?
Tick the correct box or complete the sentences while you are listening.	Musst du bei jeder Aufgabe Kästchen ankreuzen?
Tick only one box.	Kannst du mehrere Kästchen ankreuzen?
At the end you will hear the discussion again.	Wie oft wirst du den Text hören?
Now read the tasks 1–6. You have 1 minute.	Wie viel Zeit hast du, um die Augaben zu lesen?

4 WRITING

Hier ist ein Beispiel für eine Schreibaufgabe.

Write an email to your English penfriend Steve. Tell him about your last class trip (two things or more).
Ask him two questions about his class trip.
Write 60 words or more.

1 Lies zuerst die Arbeitsanweisungen. Welche würdest du unterstreichen?

Dear Steve
How are you?
I feel great. We came back from a class trip last Friday.
It was fantastic. We spent a week in Norderney. It's an island in the North Sea.
We went simming and played beach volleyball.
One night we walked. It was dark and our teacher scared us. It was great fun because all the girls cried.
Where did you go on your last class trip? Tell me about it.

2 Lies Yasins email.
Hat er die Aufgabe richtig gelöst?
- Sind Anfang und Ende wie bei einer Email?
- Hat er mindestens zwei Dinge über seine Klassenfahrt geschrieben?
- Hat er zwei Fragen gestellt?
- Hat er mindestens 60 Wörter geschrieben?

1 Write an email to your English penfriend Steve. Tell him about your last class trip (two things or more). Ask him two questions about his class trip. Write at least 60 words.
2 Yasin hat zwei Dinge nicht befolgt: Er hat die Schlussformel der Email vergessen (Best wishes, Yasin) und er hat nur eine Frage zu Steves Klassenfahrt gestellt.

SF 6 Texte besser verstehen ▸ Unit 4, p. 78

1 Skimming

Mit dieser Technik kannst du dir schnell einen Überblick über einen Text verschaffen. Dabei liest du nur ganz kurz und schnell und achtest besonders auf **Überschriften, Bilder, Bildunterschriften** und **fett gedruckte Wörter**. Du brauchst nicht jedes Detail zu verstehen. Du bereitest z.B. einen Vortrag zum Thema *Shinty* vor und suchst allgemeine Informationen zu diesem schottischen Ballspiel. Welcher der beiden Texte eignet sich besser für dein Thema?

Strathglass Shinty Club

Where
The club is based in the village of Cannich near Loch Ness in the Scottish Highlands.

History and teams
The Shinty club has an amazing history. It started over 125 years ago and today has junior teams, a senior team, a reserve team and a women's team.

Success
The senior team presently plays in North Division 1. The village is very proud of its sports heroes.

Shinty

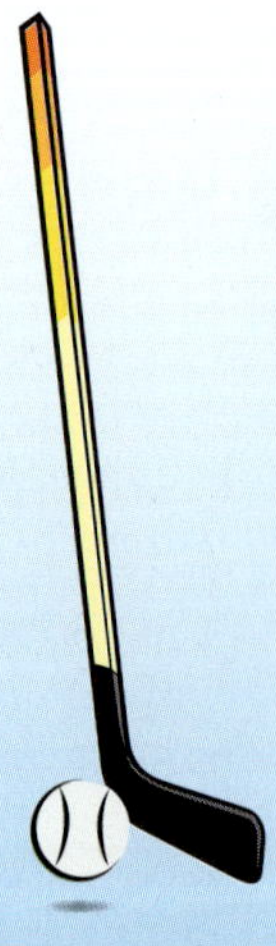

Game
Shinty is a team game played with sticks and a ball. It's a bit like hockey.

Rules
There are 12 players on each side.
Players can play the ball in the air and are allowed to use both sides of the stick.
They mustn't use their hands – only the goalkeeper can do that. The winner is the team that scores the most goals.

League system
At present there are these divisions:

2 Scanning

Mit dieser Technik kannst du einen Text nach ganz bestimmten Informationen durchsuchen.
- Du suchst dabei nur nach wichtigen Wörtern (Schlüsselwörtern) und lässt alles andere beiseite.
- Geh dabei mit den Augen und dem Finger schnell über den Text. Das gesuchte Wort wird dir „ins Auge springen". Lies nur dort weiter, um Näheres zu erfahren. Du möchtest z.B. wissen, wie viele Spieler es bei Shinty gibt. Suche also nach dem Wort *player*.
- Wenn du das Wort nicht findest, suche nach ähnlichen Begriffen.

SF 7 Hören und Notizen machen

1 Vor dem Hören

Lies immer <u>zuerst</u> die Aufgabe. Lies sorgfältig. Hier ein Beispiel:

- *Listen to a phone call. Sarah is phoning a B&B in Glasgow and wants to book a room.* → Überlege vor dem Hören: Was könnte Sarah sagen? (Tag der Ankunft, wie viele Nächte, wie viele Personen etc.)
- *Write down the information that she gives man at the B&B.* → Merke dir genau, was du tun sollst.
- *There is an example at the beginning.* → Schau dir das Beispiel an. Es hilft dir.
- *You will hear the recording twice.* → Es macht nichts, wenn du zuerst nicht alles hast – du hörst den Text zweimal.

Typische Aufgaben sind:
- *multiple choice*-Aufgaben
- *true/false*-Aufgaben
- Bilder nach einer Reihenfolge ordnen
- eine Tabelle oder Lücken in einem Text vervollständigen wie im Beispiel rechts

Example: *Name* The Hansen family
Number of nights: ______
Date of arrival: ______
rooms: ______
number of guests: ______
pets: ______
mobile phone: ______

2 Beim Hören

- Achte beim Hören auf die Wörter, die in der Aufgabe stehen. Achtung! Die Informationen könnten in einer anderen Reihenfolge auftauchen.
- Mache dir Notizen. Verwende Symbole oder Abkürzungen, z.B. *fam r* für *family room*.
- Gib nicht auf, wenn du etwas nicht verstanden hast. Bleib ruhig und höre weiter zu. Vielleicht verstehst du beim zweiten Hören mehr. Oder vielleicht brauchst du diese Information gar nicht.

3 Nach dem Hören

- Vervollständige deine Notizen sofort.
- Konzentriere dich beim zweiten Hören auf das, was du zuerst nicht gut verstanden hast.

SF 8 Eigene Texte schreiben

A Beachte: Welche Art von Text wirst du schreiben?

1 Persönlicher Brief oder Email

- Beginne mit einer persönlichen Anrede, z.B. *Dear Lily* oder *Hi Alex!*
- Frage, wie es deinem Freund oder deiner Freundin geht: *How are you?*
- Erzähle, wie es dir geht, und was bei dir Interessantes geschehen ist: *I'm tired because ... Yesterday we went ... Then we had ...*
- Frage, was bei deinem Freund oder deiner Freundin so passiert ist: *What did you do last week / in the holidays / ...?*
- Schreibe am Ende immer einen freundlichen Gruß, z.B. *Best wishes* oder *Lots of love* und deinen Namen.

Hi Alex!

How are you? I'm tired because I was very busy yesterday. I went shopping with my dad. Then I went to the cinema with my friend Charlotte. We saw a funny film and ate lots of crisps. It was great.
What did you do yesterday?
Were you busy too?

Lots of love
Anne

2 Persönliche Stellungnahme ▸ Unit 3, p. 57

Befolge diese drei Schritte:

1 Sage zuerst, was deine Meinung ist *(opinion):*
I think ... In my opinion...

2 Begründe deine Meinung *(reason):*
The first thing is that ... And the second thing is ...

3 Finde einen guten Schluss *(ending):*
In a word ... I really hope that ...

*I think that skiing is the best hobby.
The first thing is that you can go really quickly. A bike is too slow for me!
The second thing is that mountains are really cool. They are better than streets!
I really hope that I can go skiing in the winter.*

3 Story ▸ Unit 4, p. 76

Wenn du eine Geschichte schreiben sollst, denke an diese drei Punkte:

1 Mache dir Notizen zu den *wh-questions:*
Who was in the story?
When did it happen?
Where did it happen?
What happened?

2 Verwende *time phrases* und *linkers.*

3 Sage, wie sich die Personen gefühlt haben.

A great day
Last week I went to the theme park near our town with my friends. The roller coaster was too expensive so we went on the ghost train. First we felt scared, but then there was ...

B Folge diesen vier Schritten beim Schreiben:

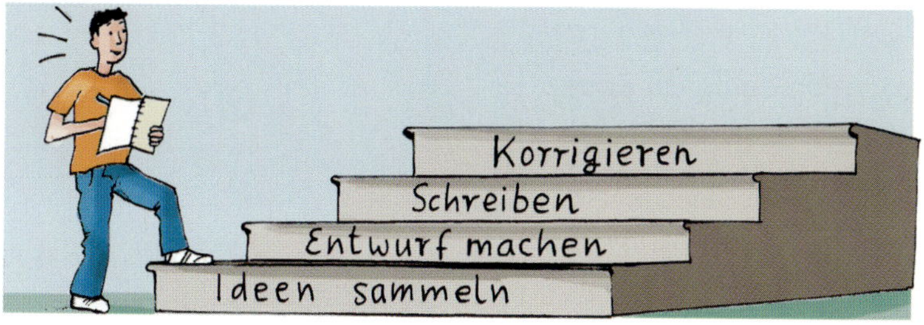

1 Ideen sammeln ▸ *Unit 1, p. 16*

Sammle zuerst wichtige Ideen und Wörter, z.B. in einem Gedankennetz oder einer Liste.

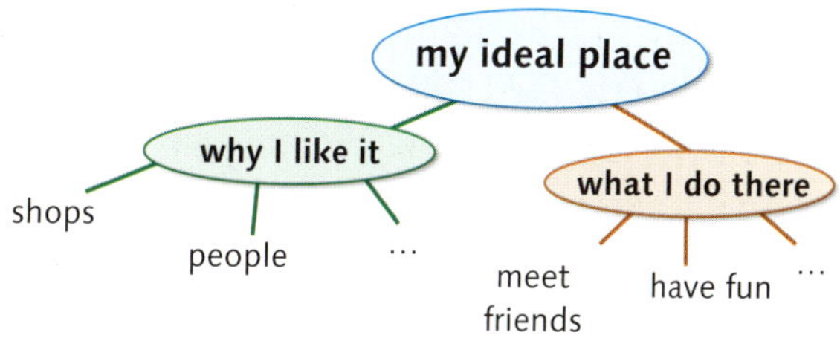

2 Textentwurf machen ▸ *Unit 4, p. 76*

Mache einen Textentwurf auf einem Zettel oder am Computer.

- Schreibst du einen Brief, eine persönliche Stellungnahme oder eine Geschichte? Beachte die Hinweise auf S. 132.
- Überlege dir eine sinnvolle Reihenfolge und mache Absätze bei neuen Punkten.
- Texte aus dem Buch sind oft ein gutes Muster. Schreibe sie aber nicht ab. Ändere sie und ergänze eigene Ideen.

3 Text schreiben ▸ *Unit 2, p. 37; Unit 4, p. 76*

Nun schreibe deinen Text. So wird dein Text besser:

- Verbinde deine Sätze mit *linking words (and, but, so* oder *because)* und *time phrases (yesterday, at first, then, …)*
- Wenn du eine Geschichte schreibst, sage, wie sich die Menschen fühlten *(happy, disappointed, scared, tired, …)*.

Vergleiche z.B. diese beiden Texte. Welcher klingt besser?

Holidays in Scotland
We flew to Scotland. We went to Loch Ness. We didn't see the monster. We spent a day in Inverness. Dad bought a kilt. We all watched a game of shinty.

Holidays in Scotland
Last July I flew to Scotland with my parents. We were very excited. On the first day we went to Loch Ness – but we didn't see the monster so I was disappointed. Then we spent a day in Inverness and dad bought a kilt. He felt so happy with his new kilt! The next day we all watched a game of shinty. That was fun!

4 Überprüfen und korrigieren

Ein Text ist noch nicht fertig, wenn du ihn zu Ende geschrieben hast! Lies ihn danach noch zweimal durch.

1 Groß- und Kleinschreibung

Im Englischen schreibt man fast alles klein. Prüfe also:

- Hast du Wörter wie *football*, *cinema*, *train*, … kleingeschrieben?

In diesen Fällen schreibt man aber groß – prüfe also:

- Hast du alle Satzanfänge großgeschrieben?
  Our school starts at 8 o'clock.
- Hast du das Wort *I* (= ich) immer großgeschrieben?
  I live in Germany.

2 Die richtige Zeitform

- Schreibst du über die Gegenwart? Oder über Dinge, die du regelmäßig machst? (Signalwörter: *today, often, always)* Dann brauchst du das *simple present:*
  I often meet my friends in the park.
- Oder schreibst du über Sachen, die schon passiert sind? (Signalwörter: *yesterday, last Friday)* Dann verwende das *simple past:*
  Last Sunday I went on a bike tour with my family.
- Schreibst du über Dinge, die du vorhast oder für die Zukunft plantst? (Signalwörter *tomorrow, next Monday)* Dann brauchst du das *going-to future:*
  Tomorrow I'm going to visit my grandma.

Partner check:
Falls dies möglich ist, suche dir einen Partner oder eine Partnerin und tauscht eure Texte aus.
Versteht ihr die Texte des anderen? Findet ihr noch Fehler?

SF 9 Bilder beschreiben ▸ *Unit 2, p. 36*

Wenn du ein Bild oder ein Foto beschreiben sollst, merke dir folgende Schritte:

1 Beginne allgemein

Sage zunächst in ein oder zwei Sätzen, was du allgemein auf dem Bild siehst:
Welcher Ort ist zu sehen?
Welche Menschen und wie viele?
In the picture I can see a beach with lots of people.

2 Sage, wo sich was befindet

Sage, was du im Vordergrund und im Hintergrund siehst und was links, in der Mitte und rechts auf dem Bild zu sehen ist.

In the foreground I can see a woman with a hat. She's on the left.

In the middle I can see two birds.

In the background there are some people in the water.

On the right there's a man with two ice creams.

3 Ordne die Personen und Dinge einander zu

Verwende Präpositionen:
There's a book in front of the woman with the hat. The three children are behind the woman.
There's a ball under the old man's chair. The man with the two ice creams is next to the old woman.
The two birds are between the woman with the hat and the old man and woman.

4 Beschreibe, was die Personen gerade tun

Verwende das *present progressive:*
The woman with the hat is sleeping. The three children behind her are playing in the sand.
The old woman is eating a sandwich.
The man in the water is taking a photo of his family. The woman next to him is surfing.
A boy and a girl are swimming in the sea.
The two birds are looking at the old woman with the sandwich.

SF 10 Einen Kurzvortrag halten

▸ Unit 3, p. 56

1 Erarbeitung

- Entscheide dich für ein Thema.
- Sammle Ideen zu deinem Thema und ordne sie:
  Was passt zum Thema und was nicht?
  Womit fängst du an?
  Welche Reihenfolge ist am besten?
  Womit hörst du auf?
  Schreibe das Wichtigste auf Karteikarten.

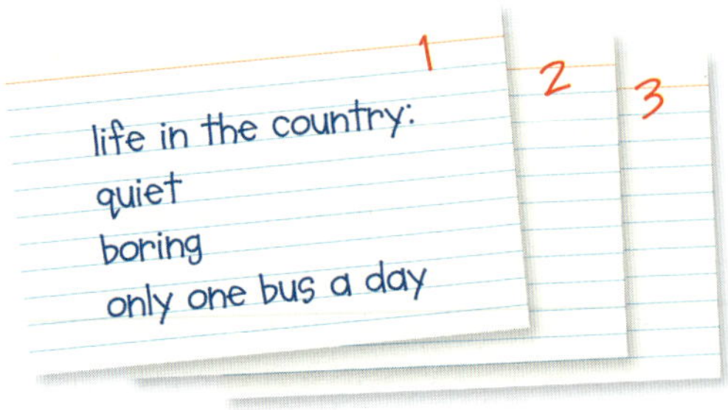

- Überlege dir, welche Bilder du zeigen kannst und wie du sie präsentieren möchtest – z.B. als Poster oder am Computer?
  Verwende dabei wenig Text.
  Schreibe groß und lesbar.
- Übe die Präsentation allein vor einem Spiegel oder mit einem Partner/einer Partnerin.
  Das gibt dir Sicherheit.

2 Durchführung

a) Am Anfang des Vortrags

- Überprüfe, ob alles vorbereitet ist:
  Ist das Poster aufgehängt? Ist der Computer bereit? Sind die Vortragskarten sortiert?
- Sage, worüber du sprechen möchtest.

b) Während des Vortrags

- Verwende typische Redewendungen und sprich langsam und deutlich.
- Schaue deine Zuhörer/innen an.
- Wenn du ein Poster oder Bilder benutzt, zeige während des Vortrags darauf.

c) Am Ende des Vortrags

- Sage, wann dein Vortrag zu Ende ist.
- Bedanke dich fürs Zuhören und frage deine Mitschüler/innen, ob sie noch Fragen haben.

SF 11 Mediation

▸ Unit 2, p. 38; Unit 3, p. 58

1 Worum geht es?

Mediation bedeutet, zwischen zwei Sprachen zu vermitteln, z.B.

- englische Informationen auf Deutsch weitergeben: Du bist z.B. mit deiner Familie in England. Dein Vater kann nur wenig Englisch und will wissen, was jemand gesagt hat oder was auf einer Broschüre steht.
- deutsche Informationen auf Englisch wiedergeben: Vielleicht ist bei dir zu Hause ein Austauschschüler zu Gast, der kein Deutsch spricht.

2 Worauf musst du achten?

- *Mediation* ist keine wörtliche Übersetzung. Deshalb gib nur das Wesentliche wieder und lasse unwichtige Informationen weg.
- Verwende kurze und einfache Sätze.

- Beachte die Wortstellung – sie ist im Englischen oft anders als im Deutschen.
- Wenn du ein Wort nicht kennst, sage es anders. Beispiele:
  außer Dienstags → *but not on Tuesdays*
  ermäßigte Eintrittskarten → *cheaper tickets*
  der Zug hat 10 Minuten Verspätung → *the train is 10 minutes late*
  Wie könntest du folgende Ausdrücke umschreiben?
  - *Gibt es hier Übernachtungsmöglichkeiten?*
  - *Fußballspielen verboten*
  - *Mindestalter 14 Jahre*

LF 1 REVISION Simple present

▸ p. 66/67

bejahte Sätze Yes

I You We They	start early.

Mit dem *simple present* (einfache Gegenwart) sagst du, was oft oder jeden Tag passiert und auch was selten oder nie geschieht:
I often go to the sports club.
We never have lunch at school.

He She It	starts early.

Mit ***he/she/it*** musst du immer ein *-s* ans Verb anhängen.
Achtung: bei einigen Verben wird *-es* angehängt:
do – does
wash – washes
watch – watches

verneinte Sätze No

I You We They	don't start early.

Wenn du sagen willst, dass etwas nicht passiert oder der Fall ist, setzt du ***don't*** vor das Verb.

He She It	doesn't start early.

Mit ***he/she/it*** verwendest du ***doesn't***.

He doesn't like dogs.

Fragen mit do/does ?

Do I Do you Does he/she/it Do we Do they	like crabs?

Fragen, auf die man mit *ja* oder *nein* antworten kann, beginnen mit ***Do*** oder ***Does***.
Mit ***I, you, we*** oder ***they*** verwendest du ***Do***.
Mit ***he/she/it*** verwendest du ***Does***.

Fragen mit Fragewörtern ?

Where do I go now?
Why do you do this?
What does he/she/it do?
When do we arrive?
How do they run?

Manche Fragen beginnen mit Fragewörtern. Nach dem Fragewort verwendest du:
do (bei ***I/you/we/they***)
oder
does (bei ***he/she/it***).

LF 2 REVISION Present progressive

I'm reading a comic.
Ich lese gerade einen Comic.

Dad is cooking dinner.
Papa macht gerade das Abendessen.

What are you doing at the moment?
Was machst du jetzt gerade?

Mit dem *present progressive* (*ing*-Form) sagst du, was gerade jetzt passiert.
Damit beschreibst du auch, was man auf Bildern tut.

Diese Zeitangaben findest du oft in Sätzen im *present progressive:*
now, at the moment, today.

bejahte Sätze Yes

I'm You're He's She's It's We're You're They're	helping.

He isn't feeling good today.

verneinte Sätze No

I'm not You aren't He isn't She isn't It isn't We aren't You aren't They aren't	helping.

Das *present progressive* besteht aus zwei Teilen:

'm oder
're oder
's
\+ Verb + *-ing*

Achtung:
Bei Verben auf *-e* fällt das *-e* bei der *ing*-Form weg:
come – coming
make – making
ride – riding

Fragen ?

Am I Are you Is he Is she Is it Are we Are you Are they	helping?

Bei einigen Verben wird der letzte Buchstabe verdoppelt:
plan – planning
stop – stopping
sit – sitting

LF 3 REVISION Simple past

▸ p.26/27

Yesterday evening I watched TV.
Gestern Abend habe ich ferngesehen / sah ich fern.

Last week I didn't go to football training
Letzte Woche ging ich nicht zum Fußballtraining.

Did you watch the fireworks last night?
Hast du gestern abend das Feuerwerk gesehen?

Mit dem *simple past* sprichst du über Dinge, die in der Vergangenheit geschehen sind. Du verwendest es oft mit Zeitangaben wie *yesterday, last week, last year, last summer, in 2010.*
Die Vergangenheitsform ist für alle Personen gleich. Bei regelmäßigen Verben hängst du *-ed* an das Verb:
walk – walked
look – looked

Bei Verben, die auf *-e* enden, wird nur *-d* angehängt:
arrive – arrived

Unregelmäßige Formen musst du lernen:
buy – bought *find – found*
go – went *have – had*
make – made *meet – met*
Du kannst sie in der zweiten Spalte der *List of irregular verbs* auf S. 200 nachschlagen.

bejahte Sätze Yes

I You He / She / It We They	helped.

Wenn du sagen willst, was nicht geschah, setzt du *didn't* vor das Verb.
Achtung: Das Verb bleibt dann immer in der Grundform:
He didn't watch.
! nicht: *He didn't watched.*

verneinte Sätze No

I You He / She / It We They	didn't help.

Fragen mit did ?

Did	I you he / she / it we they	help?

Fragen im *simple past* bildest du mit *did* und der Grundform des Verbs.

Achtung: Das Verb bleibt immer in der Grundform:
Did he watch?
! nicht: *Did he watched?*

Fragen mit Fragewörtern ?

What	did	she	watch?
When	did	it	finish?
Where	did	they	go?

What did she watch?
– She watched the fireworks.

Manche Fragen beginnen mit Fragewörtern. Auch hier verwendet man *did* bei allen Personen und das Verb in der Grundform:
How did it go?
! nicht: *How did it went?*

Achtung: Bei Fragen im *simple past* ist das Verb in der Grundform. Bei den Antworten musst du das Verb in die Vergangenheitsform setzen.

LF 4 Present perfect

▸ Unit 2, p. 40

I have moved house three times.
Ich bin schon dreimal umgezogen.

My little sister has never been on a plane.
Meine kleine Schwester ist noch nie geflogen.

Have you ever ridden a pony?
Bist du schon einmal geritten?

Mit dem *present perfect* sagst du, dass du etwas schon einmal, öfter oder noch nie gemacht hast.
Du verwendest es oft mit Zeitangaben wie ***ever, never, once, twice, lots of times.***

bejahte Sätze Yes

I You We They	have started early. ('ve started)
He She It	has started early.

Das *present perfect* besteht aus zwei Teilen:

have oder has (Kurzformen: 've oder 's)	+	einer besonderen Verbform, dem *past participle*

verneinte Sätze No

I You We They	haven't started early.
He She It	hasn't started early.

Wie bildest du das *past participle?*
Bei regelmäßigen Verben hängst du *-ed* an das Verb:
walk – walked *look – looked*
Bei Verben die auf *-e* enden, wird nur *-d* angehängt: *arrive – arrived*
Unregelmäßige Verben musst du lernen:
be – been *find – found*
go – gone *have – had*
make – made *meet – met*
Du kannst sie in der dritten Spalte der *List of irregular verbs* auf S. 200 nachschlagen.

Fragen und Kurzantworten ?

Have you started?	– Yes, I have. – No, I haven't.
Has she started?	– Yes, she has. – No, she hasn't.

Jacob has worked a lot today.

LF 5 REVISION *Will*-future

▸ p. 46/47

I think you'll have a great birthday party.
Ich glaube, du wirst eine tolle Geburtstagsparty haben.

Maybe we'll have a barbecue in the garden.
Vielleicht grillen wir im Garten.

I'm sure the weather will be nice.
Ich bin sicher, das Wetter wird schön sein.

Wenn du vermutest, was in der Zukunft geschehen könnte, verwendest du das *will-future*.
Die Sätze beginnen oft mit *I think*, *maybe*, *I'm sure* oder *I hope*.

bejahte Sätze Yes

It	will 'll	be sunny tomorrow.

Du bildest das *will-future*, indem du *will* oder die Kurzform *'ll* vor das Verb setzt.

verneinte Sätze No

It	will not won't	be sunny tomorrow.

Die Kurzform von *will not* ist *won't*.

Fragen und Kurzantworten ?

Will it be sunny tomorrow? – Yes, it will.
– No, it won't.

LF 6 REVISION *Going to*-future

We're going to have a picnic on Sunday.
Wir haben vor, am Sonntag ein Picknick zu machen.

Oh no, he's going to fall!
Oh nein, er fällt gleich herunter!

Mit *going to* … sagst du
- was du vorhast oder für die Zukunft geplant hast,
- was wahrscheinlich bald passieren wird.

bejahte Sätze Yes

I'm You're He's/She's We're They're	going to	watch TV.

Du bildest das *going to-future* mit *'m*, *'re*, *'s* + *going to* + Verb.

Achtung: Das Verb bleibt immer in der Grundform:
I'm going to watch TV.
! nicht: *I'm going to ~~watching~~ TV.*

verneinte Sätze No

I'm not You're not He's/She's not We're not They're not	going to	watch TV.

Fragen und Kurzantworten:
– *Are you going to leave tomorrow?*
– *Yes, I am./No, I'm not.*

LF 7 Have to/can/should

▸ Unit 1, p. 20

Can

I can play the guitar.
Tom can't go to school today – he's ill.
Can I open the window?

Mit *can/can't* sagst du, was jemand (nicht) tun kann oder darf.

Should

You should take your pullover – it's cold.
She shouldn't eat so much chocolate.

Mit *should/shouldn't* rätst du jemandem, etwas zu tun, oder nicht zu tun.

Have to

I have to help me in the kitchen now.
He has to look after his sister today.
You don't have to eat this.
She doesn't have to do chores.

Mit *have to* sagst du, was jemand tun muss. Mit *don't have to* sagst du, was jemand nicht zu tun braucht.

LF 8 Reflexivpronomen

▸ Unit 4, p. 71

It was my mistake so I blame myself.
Es war mein Fehler, also gebe ich mir die Schuld.

He has cut himself.
Er hat sich geschnitten.

We can look after ourselves.
Wir können uns um uns selbst kümmern.

I wash myself.
You wash yourself.
He washes himself.
She washes herself.
We wash ourselves.
You wash yourselves.
They wash themselves.

Reflexivpronomen enden auf *-self* oder *-selves.* Du sagst damit, dass jemand etwas selbst tut. Vergleiche:

She washed the baby.	Sie wusch das Baby.
She washed herself.	Sie wusch sich selbst.

Merke dir diese Ausdrücke:

Help yourself!	Greif zu! Bediene dich.
Enjoy yourself!	Viel Spaß!

LF 9 Adverbien

▸ Unit 2, p. 32

Adverbien sagen, auf welche Weise etwas geschieht.

Don't walk so slowly!
Geh nicht so langsam!

She spoke calmly and clearly.
Sie sprach ruhig und klar.

Drive carefully!
Fahr vorsichtig!

Die meisten Adverbien bildet man durch Anfügen von *-ly* an ein Adjektiv. Manchmal gibt es Unregelmäßigkeiten bei der Schreibung.

clear – clearly	angry – angrily
nervous – nervously	happy – happily
quick – quickly	careful – carefully
slow – slowly	

Es gibt auch Ausnahmen:
! *He worked hard. She did well.*

LF 10 Vergleiche

▸ Unit 3, p. 63

I'm taller than you
Ich bin größer als du.

Mobiles are more expensive than comics.
Handys sind teurer als Comics.

This is the cheapest supermarket in town.
Das ist der billigste Supermarkt in der Stadt.

Today it's as hot as yesterday.
Heute ist es genauso heiß wie gestern.

Personen und Sachen kann man miteinander vergleichen.

Bei kurzen Adjektiven hängst du *-er* bzw. *-est* an das Adjektiv, um die Steigerungsformen zu bilden.

cheap	cheaper	the cheapest
near	nearer	the nearest
tall	taller	the tallest

! Diese Formen sind unregelmäßig:
good – better – best
bad – worse – worst

Bei einigen Adjektiven musst du bei der Schreibung aufpassen.

big	bigger	the biggest
hot	hotter	the hottest
noisy	noisier	the noisiest
happy	happier	the happiest

Bei langen Adjektiven setzt du *more* bzw. *most* vor das Adjektiv.

expensive	more expensive	the most expensive
exciting	more exciting	the most exciting
popular	more popular	the most popular

Wenn du sagen willst, dass zwei Personen oder Dinge genau gleich groß, alt, teuer, etc. sind, verwendest du *as … as*.

Tom is as old as Luca.
The red bike is as expensive as the green bike.

LF 11 *If*-Sätze ▸ *Unit 3, p. 60*

If you wash the car, I'll give you 5 euro.
Wenn du das Auto wäscht, gebe ich dir 10 Euro.

If the shop has the computer game, I'll buy it.
Wenn der Laden das Computerspiel hat, kaufe ich es.

Mit *if*-Sätzen sagst du, was unter bestimmten Bedingungen geschehen wird.

if-Satz	Hauptsatz
If you help me,	I'll be faster.
If it rains,	we'll stay at home.

If-Sätze bestehen aus zwei Teilen:
- einem Nebensatz mit ***if*** im *simple present*
- einem Hauptsatz mit *will* oder *'ll*.

LF 12 Relativsätze ▸ *Unit 4, p. 80*

He's the boy who lives in our street.
Er ist der Junge, der in unserer Straße wohnt.

It's a shop that sells mobiles and TVs.
Es ist ein Laden, der Handys und Fernseher verkauft.

Mit Relativsätzen kannst du zusätzliche Informationen über eine Person oder eine Sache geben.

This is the man who works at the hotel.
Are you the girl who won the first prize?

Nach Personen verwendest du ***who.***

The boy who's playing the guitar is cool.

The game that I got for my birthday is great.
The film that we saw yesterday was boring.

Nach Sachen benutzt du ***that.***

Wordbank 1: My neighbourhood

▸ Unit 1, p. 16

Transport

airport
bus station
bus stop

garage

harbour

petrol station

traffic lights

tram station

train station
underground

Shopping

baker's

butcher's

bookshop
bike shop

chemist's

dry cleaner's

fruit and veg shop
market

newsagent's

pet shop
phone shop
shopping centre
supermarket
video shop

Sport

bowling centre
football field

ice rink

inline skate track

skate park

tennis court

sports club
sports hall
stadium
swimming pool

Other places

bank
cafe

children's playground

cinema
farm

fast food stand

flats
hairdresser's
hospital
houses
museum
park
post office
restaurant
river
school
second-hand shop
theatre

youth centre

Our nearest ... is ... minutes away. That's good/OK/important/terrible/...
There aren't any ... near us. That's OK/no problem/a big problem.
We live near ... You can ... there.
There's a big/new/great/good/cool/nice/expensive ... near our house.
There are lots of ... in my neighbourhood. I think that's great/not so good.

Wordbank 2: City and country

▸ Unit 2, p. 36

In the foreground / In the background you can see ...
On the left / On the right / In the middle of the picture there's a ...
Next to the ... there are some ... Behind / in front of the ... there's a ...
Between the ... and the ... you can see ...

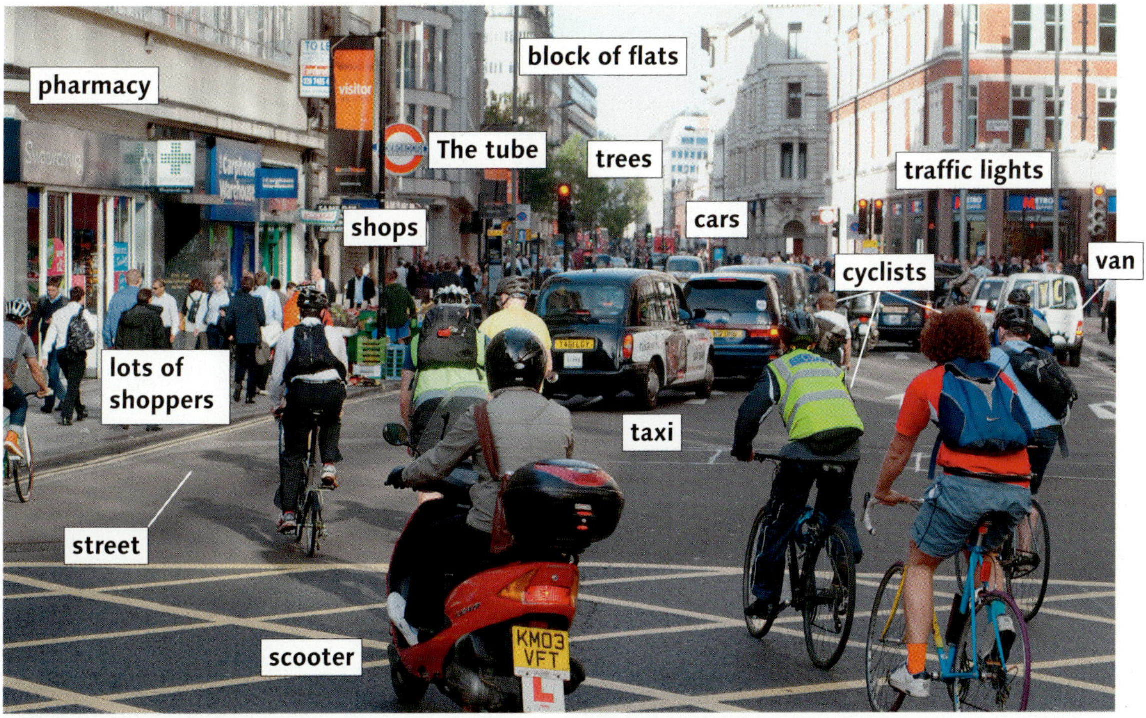

Wordbank 3: Food

▸ Unit 3, p. 51

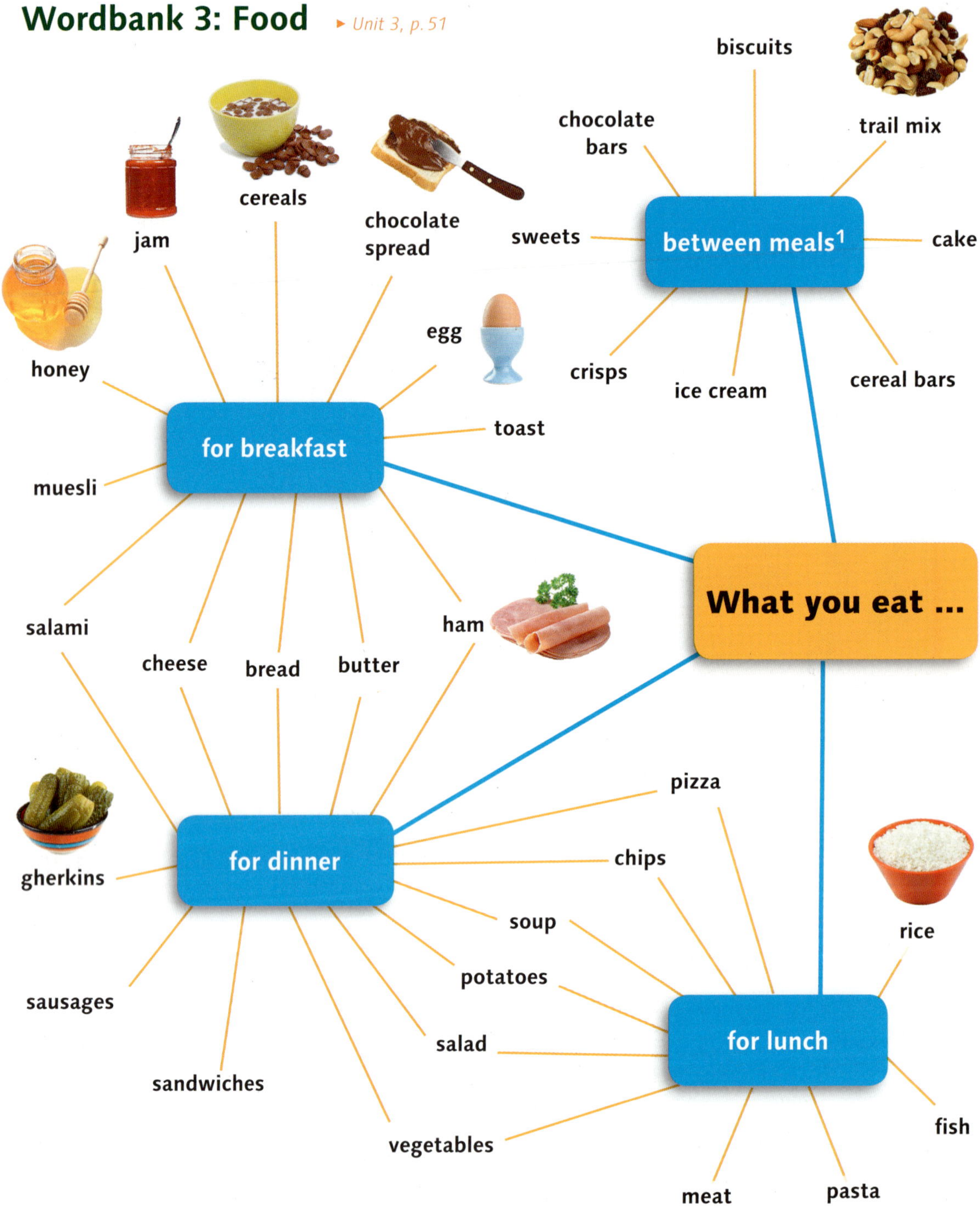

Yesterday I had ... for breakfast.
I ate ... for lunch.
In the evening I had ... for dinner.
Usually we have ... for breakfast / lunch / dinner.

[1] between meals *zwischen den Mahlzeiten*

Wordbank 4: Useful words for tourists ▸ Unit 4, p. 81

At a restaurant

In a hotel

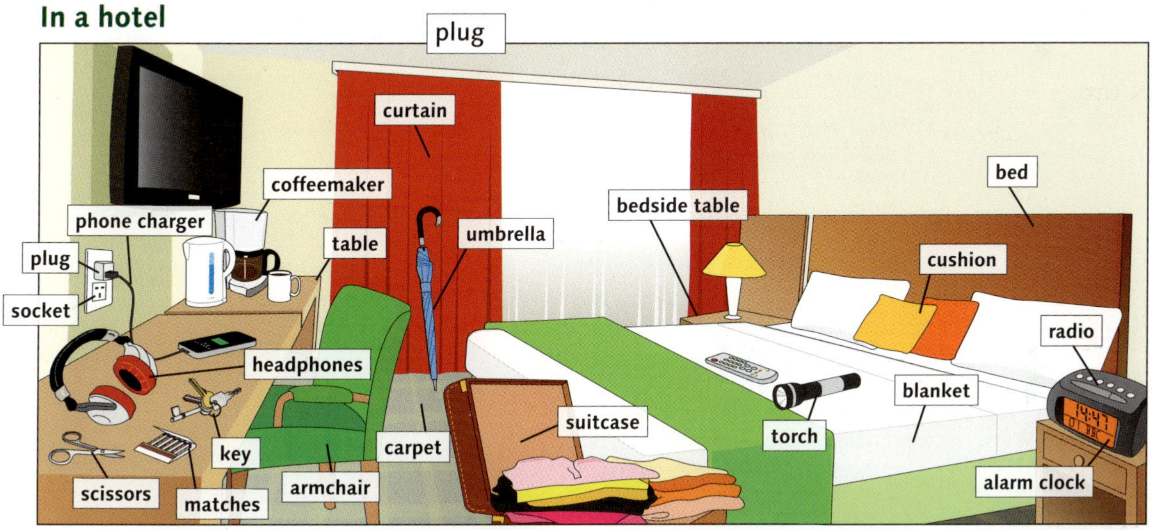

VOCABULARY

Das **Vocabulary** (S. 150–165) enthält alle neuen Wörter und Wendungen des Buches, die du **lernen** musst. Sie stehen in der Reihenfolge, in der sie im Buch zum ersten Mal vorkommen.

Hier siehst du, wie das **Vocabulary** aufgebaut ist:

Diese Zahl gibt die **Seite** an, auf der die Wörter zum ersten Mal vorkommen. p. 10 = Seite 10

Die **blauen Kästen** solltest du dir immer besonders gut ansehen. Dort stehen wichtige Hinweise zu den neuen Wörtern.

	mustn't do	nicht tun dürfen ➔	**must – mustn't** • **must** = **müssen** You **must** do your homework now. • **mustn't** = **nicht dürfen** You **mustn't** wear trainers at school.
p. 19	**Oh dear!**	oje!	
	milkshake	Milchshake	
	lose, *simple past:* **lost**	verlieren	**lose a job** ◄► **get a job** **lose a game** ◄► **win a game**
	act	Theater spielen; schauspielern	
	surprised	überrascht	
	Focus on language		
p. 20	**aunt**	Tante	
	airport	Flughafen	
	diner	(AE) Imbissstube, Lokal	! **(AE)** zeigt dir, dass dieses Wort besonders in Amerika gebräuchlich ist.
	clothes *(pl)*	Kleidung, Kleidungsstücke	! *Deutsch:* Ihre gesamte **Kleidung ist** schwarz. *Englisch:* All her **clothes are** black.
	find, *simple past:* **found**	finden	They **found** a house.
p. 21	**make friends,** *simple past:* **made**	Freunde finden	
	perhaps	vielleicht	I'm not sure, but **perhaps** I can come

Der **blaue Pfeil** heißt: Zu diesem Eintrag gibt es in der rechten Spalte einen blauen Kasten.

Das **rote Ausrufezeichen** bedeutet: Vorsicht, hier macht man leicht Fehler!

Dies ist das „Gegenteil"- Zeichen. **lose** a job ◄► **get** a job bedeutet: „**lose**" ist das Gegenteil von „**get**".

Tipps zum Wörterlernen findest du im **Skills file** auf Seite 124.

Im **Vocabulary** werden folgende **Abkürzungen** verwendet:

p. = page (Seite)
pp. = pages (Seiten)
sb. = somebody (jemand)
sth. = something (etwas)
jn. = jemanden
jm. = jemandem
pl = *plural* (Mehrzahl)
infml = *informal* (umgangssprachlich)

Wenn du **nachschlagen** möchtest, was ein englisches Wort bedeutet oder wie man es ausspricht, dann solltest du das **Dictionary English – German** auf den Seiten 166–182 verwenden.

Und wenn du vergessen hast, wie etwas auf Englisch heißt, dann kann dir das **Dictionary German – English** auf den Seiten 183–196 eine erste Hilfe sein.

Unit 1: I love London

p. 8	**palace** ['pæləs]	Palast	
	king [kɪŋ]	König	
	queen [kwiːn]	Königin	
	president ['prezɪdənt]	Präsident/in	

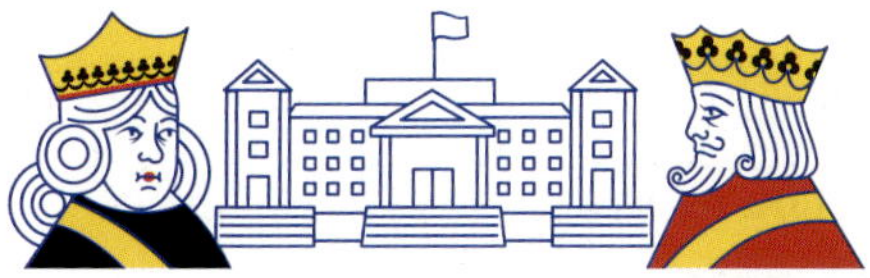

	the Tube [tjuːb]	die U-Bahn *(in London)*	! *English:* **on the Tube** *German:* **in der U-Bahn**
	travel ['trævl]	reisen; fahren, sich fortbewegen	Last year we **travelled** to Italy in the holidays. In big cities we always try to **travel** by bus.

	underground ['ʌndəgraʊnd]	U-Bahn	Another name for the **underground** in London is "the Tube".
	famous (for) ['feɪməs]	berühmt (für, wegen)	London is **famous for** its theatre shows.
	detective [dɪ'tektɪv]	Detektiv/in	
	bell [bel]	Glocke; Klingel	**bells**

> **Lautschrift**
> Wie man englische Wörter ausspricht, das zeigt dir die Lautschrift hinter dem Wort. Sie steht immer in eckigen Klammern. Lautschriftsymbole zeigen dir, wie sich das Wort anhört. Alle diese Symbole findest du in der Liste English sounds auf S. 182. Ein Apostroph in der Lautschrift steht vor der Silbe, die du betonen musst. Zum Beispiel sieht der Name "London" in der Lautschrift so aus: ['lʌndən].
>
> [aɪ] [uː] ['haɪlaɪt] [tjuːb]

p. 9	**tourist** ['tʊərɪst]	Tourist/in	! Betonung auf der 1. Silbe: **<u>tou</u>rist** ['tʊərɪst]
	eye [aɪ]	Auge	
	hour [aʊə]	Stunde	
	tower ['taʊə]	Turm	
	high [haɪ]	hoch	What's the **highest** mountain in Germany?
	window ['wɪndəʊ]	Fenster	

Theme 1

p. 10	**by** Sam Holmes [baɪ]	*(geschrieben)* von Sam Holmes	
	think of/about [θɪŋk], *simple past:* **thought** [θɔːt]	halten von, denken über	
	I've lived here all my life.	Ich wohne hier schon mein ganzes Leben (lang).	
	downside ['daʊnsaɪd]	Kehrseite, Nachteil	
	fashion ['fæʃn]	Mode(trend)	

	also ['ɔːlsəʊ]	auch	I like coffee and I like tea too. = I like coffee and I **also** like tea.
	be allowed to do sth. [ə'laʊd]	etwas tun dürfen	**Are** you **allowed to** use dictionaries in your English tests?
	culture ['kʌltʃə]	Kultur	
	Greek [griːk]	griechisch; Griechisch; Grieche/Griechin	
	Irish ['aɪrɪʃ]	irisch, aus Irland	
	Scottish ['skɒtɪʃ]	schottisch, aus Schottland	
	amazing [ə'meɪzɪŋ]	erstaunlich	
p. 11	two years **ago** [ə'gəʊ]	vor zwei Jahren	The Bakers moved to Bristol six weeks **ago**. ! *English:* **two years/six weeks ago** *German:* **vor zwei Jahren/sechs Wochen**
	its football [ɪts]	sein Fußball / ihr Fußball	→ This is my hamster. **Its** name is Joe.

I – **my** name	**we** – **our** names
you – **your** name	**you** – **your** names
he – **his** name	**they** – **their** names
she – **her** name	
it – **its** name	

Theme 2

p. 12	**advert** ['ædvɜːt]	Anzeige, Werbung	

Story

p. 14	**clever** ['klevə]	schlau, klug	
	call [kɔːl]	rufen; nennen; anrufen	Please **call** your dog. It's in our garden. **Call** me tomorrow. Here's my phone number. Her name is Jessica, but we **call** her Jess.
	geek [giːk]	*jemand, der sich sehr stark für etwas begeistert (und manchmal von anderen deswegen belächelt wird)*	
	museum [mju'ziːəm]	Museum	
	natural ['nætʃrəl]	natürlich, Natur-	
	natural history [nætʃrəl 'hɪstri]	Naturkunde	
	dinosaur ['daɪnəsɔː]	Dinosaurier	! Betonung auf der 1. Silbe **di**nosaur ['daɪnəsɔː]
	answer ['ɑːnsə]	antworten; beantworten	! **answer** = **1.** Antwort; **2.** anworten; beantworten
	disaster [dɪ'zɑːstə]	Katastrophe, Unglück	
	begin [bɪ'gɪn], *simple past:* **began** [bɪ'gæn]	beginnen, anfangen	

	security [sɪ'kjʊərəti]	Sicherheit	 **security men** at the airport
p. 15	**next** [nekst]	als Nächstes	First let's eat something. **Next** we can watch a film.
	drink [drɪŋk], *simple past:* **drank** [dræŋk]	trinken	! **drink** = **1.** Getränk; **2.** trinken
	kick [kɪk]	treten, schießen	
	idiot ['ɪdiət]	Idiot/in	! Betonung auf der 1. Silbe: **i̲diot** ['ɪdiət]
	keep [kiːp], *simple past:* **kept** [kept]	behalten	Thanks for the magazine. Can I **keep** it, or do you want to have it back?
	loud [laʊd]	laut	
	police *(pl)* [pə'liːs]	Polizei	→ **police** ist immer Plural: Where **are** the **police**? We have to call **them**. Wo **ist** die **Polizei**? Wir müssen **sie** rufen.
	like a million dollars	fantastisch	
	at last [ət 'lɑːst]	schließlich, endlich	
	earthquake ['ɜːθkweɪk]	Erdbeben	
	especially [ɪ'speʃəli]	insbesondere	I love team sports, **especially** basketball.

Skills

p. 16	**busy** ['bɪzi]	belebt; verkehrsreich	! the road is **busy** = die Straße ist belebt, hektisch I'm **busy** = ich bin beschäftigt, ich habe (viel) zu tun
	far [fɑː]	weit	
	plane [pleɪn]	Flugzeug	a **plane** 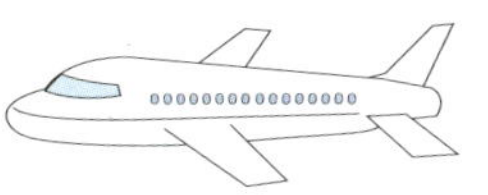
	transport ['trænspɔːt]	Verkehrsmittel; Transport(wesen)	! Betonung auf der 1. Silbe: **tra̲nsport** ['trænspɔːt]
p. 17	**world** [wɜːld]	Welt	
	diver ['daɪvə]	Taucher/in	
	driver ['draɪvə]	Fahrer/in	
	sun [sʌn]	Sonne	**the sun**
	postcard ['pəʊstkɑːd]	Postkarte	
p. 18	**waste** [weɪst]	Verschwendung	What a **waste** of time!
	waste [weɪst]	verschwenden	You're **wasting** so much time!
	spend money/time (on) [spend], *simple past:* **spent** [spent]	Geld ausgeben (für); Zeit verbringen (mit)	Do you **spend** a lot of money **on** fashion? I should **spend** more time with my friends.
	a lot of [ə 'lɒt əv]	viel(e)	= lots of I do **a lot of** / **lots of** sport in my free time.

	be right	Recht haben	Yes, **you're right**. I agree with you.
	be wrong	Unrecht haben	**be right ◄► be wrong**
p. 19	**ringtone** ['rɪŋtəʊn]	Klingelton *(Handy)*	
	a cup of tea [kʌp]	eine Tasse Tee	! *English:* a cup **of** coffee *German:* eine Tasse Kaffee 

Focus on language

p. 20	**safe** [seɪf]	sicher *(gefahrlos)*; in Sicherheit	! *German* **sicher**: Be careful and you'll be **safe**. *(sicher, in Sicherheit)* I'm **sure** you'll be OK. *(sicher(lich))*
	have to do sth. ['hæv tə]	etwas tun müssen	Look, it's late. We **have to** go now. ! *German* **müssen** = **1.** have to; **2.** must (**have to** wird häufiger verwendet als **must**)
	not have to do sth.	etwas nicht tun müssen / brauchen	! You **mustn't** do this. *(darfst nicht)* You **don't need to** do this. *(brauchst nicht)* You **don't have to** do this. *(brauchst nicht unbedingt)*
	subway ['sʌbweɪ]	Unterführung	
	pickpocket ['pɪkpɒkɪt]	Taschendieb/in	
	escalator ['eskəleɪtə]	Rolltreppe	You should stand on the right on British **escalators**. 
p. 21	**pick** sb. **up** [pɪk 'ʌp]	jn. abholen	He's **picking up** Mr Carter. 
	dark [dɑːk]	dunkel	It's too **dark** in here. I can't see anything.
	worry (about) ['wʌri]	sich Sorgen machen (wegen, um)	Mum always **worries about** me when I come home late.

Unit 2: Country life

p. 29	**in the country**	auf dem Land	
	crossroads, *pl* **crossroads** ['krɒsrəʊdz]	(Straßen-)Kreuzung	
	church [tʃɜːtʃ]	Kirche	
	block of flats [blɒk əv'flæts]	Mehrfamilienhaus, Wohnblock	! Plural: **blocks** of flats
	high street ['haɪ striːt]	Hauptstraße; Einkaufsstraße	 **a very busy high street**

gate [geɪt]	Tor	
wood [wʊd]	Wald; Holz	
pub [pʌb]	Kneipe	

Theme 1

p.30 **You're joking!** ['dʒəʊkɪŋ]	Du machst wohl Witze! / Spitzenwitz!	
joke [dʒəʊk]	Witze machen, scherzen	
Come on! [kʌm 'ɒn]	Komm(t) (schon)! / Ach komm!	
buy: we've **bought** [bɔːt]	kaufen: wir haben gekauft	
CCTV [siː siː tiː 'viː]	Überwachungssystem; Überwachungskamera(s)	
business ['bɪznəs]	Geschäft, Betrieb	My mum's new **business** is on Summer Street.
start a business	ein Geschäft aufmachen, einen Betrieb gründen/eröffnen	
start: he has **started**	anfangen: er hat angefangen ➜	**I've** started – I **haven't** started he **has** bought – he **hasn't** bought
van [væn]	Transporter, Lieferwagen	a **van** 
find: she has **found** [faʊnd]	finden: sie hat gefunden	
meet: she has **met** [met]	treffen: sie hat getroffen	
It sucks! *(infml)* [sʌks]	Es nervt/ Es ist Mist!	
believe [bɪ'liːv]	glauben	**Believe** me, he isn't British. He's German.
see: I've **seen** [siːn]	sehen: ich habe gesehen	
speak: I've **spoken** ['spəʊkən]	sprechen: ich habe gesprochen	
not … yet [jet]	noch nicht	I need more time. I have**n't** finished my homework **yet**.
What a pain! *(infml)* [peɪn]	So ein Mist! / Es nervt!	
p.31 **close** [kləʊz]	schließen, zumachen	**open the door** ◂▸ **close the door**
Take it easy! *(infml)*	Reg dich nicht auf. / Bleib mal locker.	

Theme 2

p. 32	**save** [seɪv]	retten	
	brave [breɪv]	mutig	! **brave** = *mutig* / *brav* = **good** — Molly was **brave**. **Good** dog!
	calm [kɑːm]	ruhig, still; besonnen	
	deep [diːp]	tief	He saved his dog from the **deep** water. 
	heavy ['hevi]	schwer *(Gewicht; Regen)*	! **schwer** *(von Gewicht)*: a **heavy** box / **schwer, schwierig:** a **difficult** question
	work **hard** [hɑːd]	hart arbeiten	
	father ['fɑːðə]	Vater	
	speak: he **spoke** [spəʊk]	sprechen: er sprach, er hat gesprochen	
	daughter ['dɔːtə]	Tochter	
	have: we've **had** [hæd], [həd]	haben: wir haben gehabt	
	accident ['æksɪdənt]	Unfall	
	police officer [pə'liːs ɒfɪsə]	Polizeibeamter/-beamtin	an English **police officer** 
	behave dangerously [bɪ'heɪv]	sich gefährlich verhalten	! *English:* **behave** nicely / *German:* **sich** nett **verhalten**
	farmer ['fɑːmə]	Bauer, Bäuerin; Landwirt/in	
	describe [dɪ'skraɪb]	beschreiben	! *English*: **Describe** the picture **to** **him/her**. / *German*: **Beschreibe** **ihm/ihr** das Bild.
p. 33	**message** ['mesɪdʒ]	Nachricht, Mitteilung	
	take a message	etwas ausrichten	
	Is that the Taylors?	Sind da die Taylors? *(am Telefon)*	
	Who's speaking?	Wer spricht (da)? *(am Telefon)*	
	This is Rob Blake.	Hier spricht Rob Blake. *(am Telefon)*	
	right now	gerade jetzt, genau jetzt	

Story

p. 34	**across** the fields [ə'krɒs]	(quer) über die Felder	Birds can fly **across** the sea. 

	smile [smaɪl]	lächeln; *(das)* Lächeln	! **smile** = **1.** lächeln; **2.** *(das/ein)* Lächeln
	bush [bʊʃ]	Busch, Strauch	
	suddenly ['sʌdənli]	plötzlich	
	nose [nəʊz]	Nase	
	full (of …) [fʊl]	voll; voller …	There's too much traffic here. All the streets are **full of** cars.
	catch [kætʃ], **caught** [kɔːt], **caught**	(ein)fangen	 The cat is trying to **catch** the mouse.
	light [laɪt]	Licht; Lampe	
	office ['ɒfɪs]	Büro	
	fox [fɒks]	Fuchs	
	mouth [maʊθ]	Mund; *(Tier)* Schnauze	
p. 35	**quiet** ['kwaɪət]	ruhig, still, leise	**quiet** ◂▸ **loud, noisy**
	park (a car) [pɑːk]	parken	You can't **park** your car here! 
	write down [raɪt 'daʊn], **wrote** [rəʊt], **written** ['rɪtn]	aufschreiben	
	mother ['mʌðə]	Mutter	! **mother** – **father**; **mum** – **dad**
	people **who** leave rubbish	Menschen, die Müll zurücklassen	
	article ['ɑːtɪkl]	Artikel	! Betonung auf der 1. Silbe: **article** ['ɑːtɪkl]
	put: he has **put**	*(etwas wohin)* tun, legen, stellen, stecken: er hat getan, gelegt, gestellt, gesteckt	

Skills

p. 36	**foreground** ['fɔːgraʊnd]	Vordergrund	There are two boys in the **foreground**. In the **background**, you can see a river. 
	background ['bækgraʊnd]	Hintergrund	
	horse [hɔːs]	Pferd	
p. 37	**everywhere** ['evriweə]	überall(hin)	There are London taxis **everywhere** in London.
	usually ['juːʒʊəli]	meistens, normalerweise	
	ideal [aɪ'dɪəl]	ideal	! Betonung auf der 2. Silbe: i**deal** [aɪ'dɪəl]
	move (to) [muːv]	(um)ziehen (nach)	They **moved to** York, **to** a nice flat in town.
	uncle ['ʌŋkl]	Onkel	**aunt** ◂▸ **uncle**
p. 38	**little** ['lɪtl]	klein	Ellie sometimes has to look after her **little** brother.
p. 39	**grandad** ['grædæd]	Opa	

Focus on language

p. 40	**questionnaire** [kwestʃə'neə]	Fragebogen	
	ride: I **rode** [rəʊd], I've **ridden** ['rɪdn]	reiten: ich ritt, ich bin geritten; (Rad) fahren: ich fuhr (Rad), ich bin (Rad) gefahren	
	move house	umziehen *(an einen neuen Wohnort)*	We **moved house** last year. We moved from London to Plymouth.
	once [wʌns]	einmal	
	twice [twaɪs]	zweimal	**once** (1x) – **twice** (2x) – **three times** (3x)
	person ['pɜːsn]	Person	! Nur selten wird der Plural **persons** benutzt. Normalerweise: one **person** – five **people**.

Irregular verbs

buy	**bought**	**bought**	*kaufen*	**put**	**put**	**put**	*legen, stellen*
do	**did**	**done**	*tun, machen*	**ride**	**rode**	**ridden**	*reiten, (Rad) fahren*
catch	**caught**	**caught**	*fangen*	**see**	**saw**	**seen**	*sehen*
find	**found**	**found**	*finden*	**speak**	**spoke**	**spoken**	*sprechen*
have	**had**	**had**	*haben*	**write**	**wrote**	**written**	*schreiben*
meet	**met**	**met**	*(sich) treffen*				

▸ *Unregelmäßige Verben, p. 200*

Unit 3: The world in one city

p. 48	**China** ['tʃaɪnə]	China	
	ship [ʃɪp]	Schiff	
	slave [sleɪv]	Sklave, Sklavin	
	Europe ['jʊərəp]	Europa	
	America [ə'merɪkə]	Amerika	
	Australia [ɒ'streɪliə]	Australien	

Theme 1

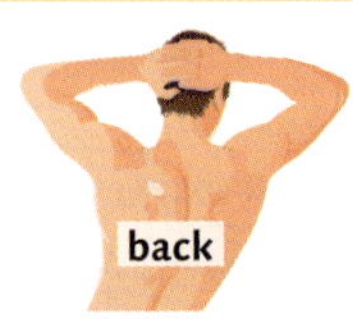

p. 50	**sell** [sel], **sold** [səʊld], **sold**	verkaufen	**buy** ◂▸ **sell**
	packet (of) ['pækɪt]	Packung, Päckchen, Schachtel	! *English:* **a packet of crisps** *German:* **eine Packung Chips**
	cost [kɒst], **cost, cost**	kosten	How much did your new computer **cost**?
	bicycle ['baɪsɪkl]	Fahrrad	**bicycle** = **bike**
	back [bæk]	Rücken; Rückseite	
	chocolate bar ['tʃɒklət bɑː]	Schokoriegel	
p. 51	**more and more**	immer mehr	**more and more** ◂▸ **less and less** immer mehr – immer weniger
	as much **as** [æz], [əz]	so viel wie	Please write **as** many words **as** you can. My photos aren't **as** good **as** Anne's.

possible ['pɒsəbl]	möglich	I'd like to finish this today, if **possible**.
son [sʌn]	Sohn	**daughter ◄► son**
bring: he **brought** [brɔːt]	(mit)bringen: er brachte (mit), er hat (mit)gebracht	
against [ə'genst]	gegen	We're not allowed to use our mobiles at school. It's **against** the school rules.
Yours sincerely [jɔːz sɪn'sɪəli]	Mit freundlichen Grüßen *(Briefschluss)*	
less [les]	weniger	**less ◄► more**
etc. *(aus dem Lateinischen)* [et'setərə]	usw. (und so weiter)	
What sort of ...? [sɔːt]	Welche Art/Sorte (von) ...?	**What sort of** music do you like?
make money, made, made	Geld verdienen	
biscuit ['bɪskɪt]	Keks, Plätzchen	**!** *German:* Keks – *English:* **biscuit** *German:* Kuchen – *English:* **cake**
cereal bar ['sɪəriəl bɑː]	Müsliriegel	
energy ['enədʒi]	Energie	**!** Betonung auf der 1. Silbe: **energy** ['enədʒi]

Theme 2

p. 52 **be good at** sth.	etwas gut können, gut sein in etwas	**!** *English:* I'm **good at** maths. *German:* Ich bin **gut in** Mathematik.
Miss [mɪs]	*Anrede für Lehrerin in GB*	
active ['æktɪv]	aktiv	**!** Betonung auf der 1. Silbe: **active** ['æktɪv]
term [tɜːm]	Trimester	The school year in Britain has three **terms**.
salesperson ['seɪlzpɜːsn], *pl* **salespeople** ['seɪlzpiːpl]	Verkäufer/in	
serious ['sɪəriəs]	ernst(haft)	This is a **serious** problem. *(ernst)* **Seriously**, Ben, you're a good salesperson. *(ernsthaft, im Ernst)*
hear: I've **heard** [hɜːd]	hören: ich habe gehört	
competition [kɒmpə'tɪʃn]	Wettbewerb	
take part in sth. [teɪk 'pɑːt], **took, taken** ['teɪkən]	an etwas teilnehmen, bei etwas mitmachen	More than 200 singers **took part in** the concert.
information (about) *(no pl)* [ɪnfə'meɪʃn]	Information(en) (über)	**!** Das englische Wort **information** hat keinen Plural: *English:* Here**'s** the **information** about ... *German:* Hier **sind** die Information**en** über ...
p. 53 the **most** money [məʊst]	das meiste Geld, am meisten Geld	**!** *Steigerung:* **much/many – more – (the) most**
on TV	im Fernsehen	I saw an interesting programme **on TV** last night. 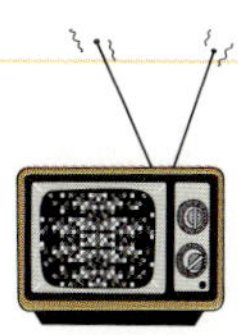
the USA [juː es 'eɪ]	die USA (= die Vereinigten Staaten von Amerika)	

badge [bædʒ]	Anstecknadel, Button	
balloon [bəˈluːn]	Ballon	
plant [plɑːnt]	Pflanze	a **plant**
cost [kɒst]	Kosten, Preis	**!** *English:* **cost** (Singular!) *German:* **Kosten**
euro (€) [ˈjʊərəʊ]	Euro	

Pounds and euros

In **Britain** you pay with **pounds** and **pence**:

You say:	*You write:*
fifty p [piː] / **fifty pence** [pens]	**50 p**
one pound / a pound	**£1**
two pounds fifty	**£2.50**

In **Germany** you pay with **euros** and **cents**:

You say:	*You write:*
fifty cents [sents]	**€0.50**
one euro / a euro	**€1**
two euros fifty	**€2.50**

total [ˈtəʊtl]	Gesamtbetrag, Summe	
per balloon [pɜː], [pə]	pro Ballon	
profit [ˈprɒfɪt]	Gewinn, Profit	I made a **profit** of £ 15 when I sold my bike. **!** Betonung auf der 1 Silbe: **profit** [ˈprɒfɪt]

Story

p. 54	**look around** [lʊk əˈraʊnd]	sich umschauen (in)	Let's go to town and **look around** the shops.
	flour [ˈflaʊə]	Mehl	
	break [breɪk], **broke** [brəʊk], **broken** [ˈbrəʊkən]	(zer)brechen	**!** something is **broken** = etwas ist gebrochen, zerbrochen, kaputt
	egg [eg]	Ei	You need **eggs** and flour to make cupcakes.
	impressed [ɪmˈprest]	beeindruckt	Dad was really **impresse** all the house.
	at 16	mit 16, im Alter von 16	In the USA you can learn to drive **at 16**.
	sit down [sɪt ˈdaʊn], **sat** [sæt], **sat**	sich (hin)setzen	
	grandfather [ˈgrænfɑːðə]	Großvater	**grandfather** = **grandad** = **grandpa**
	negative [ˈnegətɪv]	negativ	
	enough [ɪˈnʌf]	genug	It's not perfect, but it's good **enough**.
	mean [miːn], **meant** [ment], **meant**	meinen, sagen wollen	I don't understand. What do you **mean**?
p. 55	send: they **sent** [sent]	schicken: sie schickten, sie haben geschickt	

	represent [reprɪ'zent]	repräsentieren, vertreten	Teams from six countries took part in the competition. A team from Kiel **represented** Germany.
	fantastic [fæn'tæstɪk]	fantastisch	

Skills

p.56	**useful** ['juːsfl]	nützlich	
	underline [ʌndə'laɪn]	unterstreichen	Please **underline** the new words.
	fact [fækt]	Tatsache; Information	
	task [tɑːsk]	Aufgabe	
p.57	**opinion** [ə'pɪnjən]	Meinung	
	comment ['kɒment]	Kommentar	
	for lots of reasons ['riːznz]	aus vielen Gründen	I want a good job. **For** this **reason** I work hard at school.
	in my opinion [ə'pɪnjən]	meiner Meinung nach	
	role model ['rəʊl mɒdl]	Vorbild	
	boxing ['bɒksɪŋ]	*(das)* Boxen	
	Olympic [ə'lɪmpɪk]	olympisch	the **Olympic** Games = die Olympischen Spiele
	even ['iːvn]	sogar, selbst	Everybody tried to help, **even** the children.
	violent ['vaɪələnt]	gewalttätig; gewaltsam	Do you think judo is a **violent** sport?
	fight [faɪt], **fought** [fɔːt], **fought**	kämpfen	
	prefer sth. **to** sth. [prɪ'fɜː]	etwas lieber mögen als etwas, etwas einer Sache vorziehen	I like team sports, so I **prefer** football **to** jogging.
	strong [strɒŋ]	stark	She's very **strong**. 
p.59	**Get ready. Steady. Go!** [get redi stedi 'gəʊ]	Auf die Plätze, fertig, los!	
	ready ['redi]	bereit, fertig	Are you **ready**? Can we go?
	I guess [ges]	ich glaube, ich nehme an	
	message ['mesɪdʒ]	Botschaft, Aussage	**!** **message** = **1.** Nachricht, Mitteilung; **2.** Botschaft, Aussage
p.61	**be bored** [bɔːd]	Langeweile haben, gelangweilt sein	**!** The play was **boring**. **langweilig** I was **bored**. **gelangweilt**
	jump [dʒʌmp]	springen; *(vor Schreck)* zusammenzucken	Can you **jump** on your chair? Suddenly there was a loud noise. We all **jumped**.

Irregular verbs

bring	**brought**	**brought**	*(mit)bringen*
break	**broke**	**broken**	*(zer)brechen*
cost	**cost**	**cost**	*kosten*
fight	**fought**	**fought**	*kämpfen*
hear	**heard**	**heard**	*hören*
make	**made**	**made**	*machen*
mean	**meant**	**meant**	*meinen, sagen wollen*
sell	**sold**	**sold**	*verkaufen*
send	**sent**	**sent**	*schicken*
sit	**sat**	**sat**	*sitzen*
take	**took**	**taken**	*nehmen*

► *Unregelmäßige Verben, p. 200*

Unit 4: Scotland is different

p.68	**Scotland** ['skɒtlənd]	Schottland	
	castle ['kɑːsl]	Burg	a **castle** 
	lake [leɪk]	(Binnen-)See	a **lake** 
p.69	**throw** [θrəʊ], **threw** [θruː], **thrown** [θrəʊn]	werfen	
	grey [greɪ]	grau	They're **grey**.
	sky [skaɪ]	Himmel	! *English:* clouds **in the sky** *German:* Wolken **am Himmel**
	modern ['mɒdn]	modern	! Betonung auf der 1. Silbe: **modern** ['mɒdn]
	building ['bɪldɪŋ]	Gebäude	
	capital ['kæpɪtl]	Hauptstadt	Berlin is the **capital** of Germany.
	which lake? [wɪtʃ]	welcher See?	
	its **own** flag [əʊn]	seine eigene Fahne	! *English:* Do you have **your own** room? *German:* Hast du **ein eigenes** Zimmer?
	parliament ['pɑːləmənt]	Parlament	! Beachte die Schreibweise: **parliament**
	language ['læŋgwɪdʒ]	Sprache	
	musical ['mjuːzɪkl]	Musik-, musikalisch	The piano is a **musical** instrument.

Theme 1

p.70	**change** [tʃeɪndʒ]	Veränderung, Wechsel	! **change** = **1.** (ver)ändern, sich (ver)ändern; **2.** Veränderung, Wechsel
	for the last time	zum letzten Mal	
	equipment *(no pl)* [ɪ'kwɪpmənt]	Ausrüstung, Ausstattung	walking **equipment** 
	shop [ʃɒp]	(ein)kaufen	! **shop** = **1.** Geschäft, Laden; **2.** (ein)kaufen
	unemployed [ʌnɪm'plɔɪd]	arbeitslos	
	month [mʌnθ]	Monat	
p.71	**meal** [miːl]	Mahlzeit, Essen	Do you eat a hot **meal** at lunchtime? *(warme Mahlzeit)*
	blame sb. **(for)** [bleɪm]	jm. die Schuld geben (an), jm. Vorwürfe machen (wegen)	Don't **blame** me. It wasn't my mistake.
	Don't blame yourself. [jɔː'self], [jə'self]	Mach dir keine Vorwürfe.	

myself, yourself, himself ... (Reflexivpronomen)

I listen to **myself.**	Ich höre **mir** zu	/ **mich** an.	
You listen to **yourself.**	Du ... **dir** ...	/ **dich** ...	
He listens to **himself.**	Er ... **sich** ...	/ **sich** ...	
She listens to **herself.**	Sie ... **sich** ...	/ **sich** ...	! Aussprache und Betonung:
It listens to **itself.**	Es ... **sich** ...	/ **sich** ...	**-self** [-'self]
We listen to **ourselves.**	Wir ... **uns** ...	/ **uns** ...	**-selves** [-'selvz]
You listen to **yourselves.**	Ihr ... **euch** ...	/ **euch** ...	
They listen to **themselves.**	Sie ... **sich** ...	/ **sich** ...	

beautiful ['bju:tɪfl]	(wunder)schön	Your baby sister is a **beautiful** little girl.
Enjoy yourself/yourselves.	Viel Vergnügen! / Viel Spaß!	
bed and breakfast (B&B)	Frühstückspension; Zimmer mit Frühstück	We stayed at a nice **B&B** in York last year. **Bed and breakfast** can be quite expensive.
teach [ti:tʃ], **taught** [tɔ:t], **taught**	unterrichten, lehren	Mr Schwarz is a teacher. He **teaches** English.
get cold, **got**, **got**	kalt werden	It **gets** very hot here in the summer. ! **get** = **1.** bekommen, kriegen; **2.** werden
Help yourselves.	Bedient euch! / Greift zu!	I've made cupcakes. **Help yourselves.** Take as many as you like!

Theme 2

p. 72	**exhibition** [eksɪ'bɪʃn]	Ausstellung	
	guest [gest]	Gast	
	twin room [twɪn 'ru:m]	Zweibettzimmer	
	single room [sɪŋgl 'ru:m]	Einzelzimmer	

a **single room**

a **twin room**

	kettle ['ketl]	Wasserkocher *(elektrisch)*	
	dry [draɪ]	trocknen	
	coat [kəʊt]	Mantel; Jacke	
	Canadian [kə'neɪdiən]	kanadisch, aus Kanada; Kanadier/in	
	book [bʊk]	buchen, reservieren	That restaurant is quite famous. You should **book** a table. ! **book** = **1.** Buch; **2.** buchen, reservieren
p. 73	**confirm** [kən'fɜ:m]	bestätigen	
	reservation [rezə'veɪʃn]	Reservierung	"I'd like to make a **reservation** for two people for this evening, please."
	directions *(pl)* [də'rekʃnz]	Wegbeschreibung(en)	
	just [dʒʌst]	einfach; nur, bloß	**Just** listen to me for five minutes, please. Don't **just** sit there! Get up and help me.
	knife [naɪf], *pl* **knives** [naɪvz]	Messer	! Aussprache – das „k" wird nicht gesprochen: **knife** [naɪf]

sock [sɒk]	Socke	
bagpipes *(pl)* ['bægpaɪps]	Dudelsack	

Story

p.74 **ghost** [gəʊst]	Gespenst	
exist [ɪg'zɪst]	existieren	
down [daʊn]	hinunter, runter, nach unten	**up ◄► down**
wave [weɪv]	winken	
land [lænd]	landen	
hire ['haɪə]	mieten, leihen	
driving licence ['draɪvɪŋ laɪsns]	Führerschein	You need a **driving licence** if you want to drive a car.
mine [maɪn]	meine, meiner, meins	Is that Ryan's pencil? – No, it's **mine**.
hoot [hu:t]	hupen	
luckily ['lʌkɪli]	glücklicherweise	I forgot my homework, but **luckily** our teacher didn't check.
p.75 **finger** ['fɪŋgə]	Finger	! Aussprache: **finger** ['fɪŋgə]
ruin *(oft auch pl:* ruins*)* ['ru:ɪn]	Ruine	Urquhart Castle is now a **ruin**. ! Betonung auf der 1. Silbe: **ruin** ['ru:ɪn]
car park ['kɑ: pɑ:k]	Parkplatz	
narrow ['nærəʊ]	eng, schmal	The road was too **narrow** for the big bus. 
yours [jɔ:z]	deiner, deine, deins; eurer, eure, eures	
not ... either ['eɪðə]	auch nicht	I hate coffee and I do**n't** like tea **either**.
over there [əʊvə 'ðeə]	da drüben; da hinüber	
accent ['æksent]	Akzent	I find it hard to understend people with a strong Scottish **accent**.

Skills

p.76 **fly** [flaɪ], **flew** [flu:], **flown** [fləʊn]	fliegen	
p.77 **pride** [praɪd]	Stolz	you're very **proud** – you're full of **pride**
born [bɔ:n]	geboren	When's your birthday? When were you **born**?
bass guitar [beɪs gɪ'tɑ:]	E-Bass	
p.78 **skim** a text [skɪm]	einen Text überfliegen *(um den Inhalt grob zu erfassen)*	
region ['ri:dʒən]	Region	! Betonung auf der 1. Silbe: **region** ['ri:dʒən]
p.79 **salt** [sɔ:lt]	Salz	
sugar ['ʃʊgə]	Zucker	

Focus on language

p. 80	a thing **that** we use …	ein Ding, das wir … benutzen
	shower [ˈʃaʊə]	Dusche; Schauer
	What do you call …?	Wie nennt man …?
	waiter [ˈweɪtə], **waitress** [ˈweɪtrəs]	Kellner, Kellnerin
	mechanic [mɪˈkænɪk]	Mechaniker/in
	mirror [ˈmɪrə]	Spiegel
	towel [ˈtaʊəl]	Handtuch
p. 81	**machine** [məˈʃiːn]	Maschine, Gerät

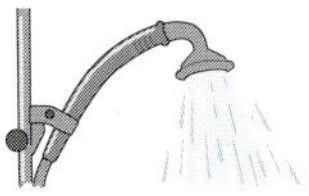

She looked at herself in the **mirror**.

Irregular verbs

fly	**flew**	**flown**	*fliegen*	**teach**	**taught**	**taught**	*unterrichten, lehren*
get	**got**	**got**	*bekommen; werden*	**throw**	**threw**	**thrown**	*werfen*

▸ *Unregelmäßige Verben, p. 200*

Grammatical terms (Grammatische Fachbegriffe)

adjective	[ˈædʒɪktɪv]	Adjektiv	*good, red, new, boring, …*
adverb	[ˈædvɜːb]	Adverb	*slowly, happily, well, …*
comparison	[kəmˈpærɪsn]	Steigerung	*old – older – oldest*
conditional sentence	[kənˈdɪʃənl ˈsentəns]	Bedingungssatz	*If we win, we'll go to London.*
future	[ˈfjuːtʃə]	Zukunft, Futur	*Wait, I'll help you!*
infinitive	[ɪnˈfɪnətɪv]	Grundform des Verbs, Infinitiv	*go, open, see, read*
irregular verb	[ɪˈregjələ ˈvɜːb]	unregelmäßiges Verb	*go – went – gone*
linker, linking word	[ˈlɪŋkɪŋ wɜːd]	Bindewort (Konjunktion)	*and, because, but, so*
noun	[naʊn]	Nomen, Hauptwort, Substantiv	*Alfie, boy, mother, time, …*
opposite	[ɒpəzɪt]	Gegenteil	*hot – cold; start – stop*
past participle	[pɑːst ˈpɑːtɪsɪpl]	Partizip Perfekt, 3. Form des Verbs	*happened, eaten, gone, …*
present perfect	[preznt ˈpɜːfɪkt]	*present perfect*	*He **has drunk** your water.*
present progressive	[preznt prəˈgresɪv]	Verlaufsform der Gegenwart	*They**'re having** lunch.*
question word	[ˈkwestʃən wɜːd]	Fragewort	*what?, when?, where?, how?, …*
reflexive pronoun	[rɪˌfleksɪv ˈprəʊnaʊn]	Reflexivpronomen	*myself, yourself, himself, …*
relative pronoun	[ˌrelətɪv ˈprəʊnaʊn]	Relativpronomen	*who, that*
regular verb	[ˈregjələ ˈvɜːb]	regelmäßiges Verb	*help – helped – helped*
simple past	[sɪmpl ˈpɑːst]	einfache Form der Vergangenheit	*I **loved** the holidays.*
simple present	[sɪmpl ˈpreznt]	einfache Form der Gegenwart	*I always **go** to school by bike.*
time phrase	[ˈtaɪm freɪz]	Zeitangabe	*yesterday, after school*
***will*-future**	[ˈwɪl fjuːtʃə]	Futur mit *will*	*I think our trip **will be** fun.*
word building	[ˈwɜːd bɪldɪŋ]	Wortbildung	*sleep – sleepy; run – runner*

Das **DICTIONARY** besteht aus **zwei alphabetischen Wörterlisten**:
English – German (S. 166–182) und **German – English** (S. 183–196)

Das **English – German dictionary** enthält den Wortschatz der Bände 1–3 von *Highlight*. Wenn du wissen möchtest, was ein englisches Wort bedeutet, wie man es ausspricht oder wie es genau geschrieben wird, dann kannst du hier nachschlagen.

Im **Dictionary** werden folgende **Abkürzungen und Symbole** verwendet:

sb. = somebody sth. = something *pl* = *plural* (Mehrzahl)
infml = *informal* (umgangssprachlich) *AE* = American English

° Mit diesem Kringel sind Wörter markiert, die nicht zum Lernwortschatz gehören.

Die **Fundstellenangaben** zeigen, wo ein Wort zum ersten Mal vorkommt.
Die Ziffern in Klammern bezeichnen Seitenzahlen:

I = *Highlight* Band 1
III 1 (17) = *Highlight* Band 3, Unit 1, Seite 17

Tipps zur Arbeit mit einem Wörterbuch findest du im Skills file auf Seite 126.

A

a [ə] ein/e I **£10 a week** 10 Pfund pro Woche II
°ability [ə'bɪləti] Fähigkeit, Können
about [ə'baʊt]:
1. ungefähr I
2. über I
What about you? Und du? / Was ist mit dir? I **What's special about him?** Was ist das Besondere an ihm? II **write about** schreiben über I
°abseil ['æbseɪl] sich abseilen
accent ['æksent] Akzent III 4 (75)
accident ['æksɪdənt] Unfall III 2 (32)
°accommodation [əkɒmə'deɪʃn] Unterkunft; Wohnung, Zimmer
across the fields [ə'krɒs] (quer) über die Felder III 2 (34)
act [ækt] Theater spielen; schauspielern II
°action ['ækʃn] Aktion, Handlung
active ['æktɪv] aktiv III 3 (52)
activity [æk'tɪvəti] Aktivität, Beschäftigung I
°actor ['æktə] Schauspieler/in
°add [æd] hinzufügen, addieren
address [ə'dres] Adresse I
°adrenaline-filled [ə'drenəlɪn fɪld] voller Adrenalin *(sehr aufregend)*
adult ['ædʌlt] Erwachsene/r II
adventure [əd'ventʃə] Abenteuer II
advert ['ædvɜːt] Anzeige, Werbung III 1 (12)
°advertise sth ['ædvətaɪz] Werbung machen für etwas
Africa ['æfrɪkə] Afrika I
after school [ɑːftə 'skuːl] nach der Schule I
afternoon [ɑːftə'nuːn] Nachmittag I
again [ə'gen] wieder, noch einmal I
against [ə'genst] gegen III 3 (51)
ago [ə'gəʊ]: **two years ago** vor zwei Jahren III 1 (11)
agree [ə'griː]: **agree with sb.** jm. zustimmen II **°agree on** sich einigen auf
airport ['eəpɔːt] Flughafen II
°alarm clock [ə'lɑːm klɒk] Wecker
°alcohol ['ælkəhɒl] Alkohol
all [ɔːl] alle(s) I **all day** den ganzen Tag (lang) II
allowed [ə'laʊd]: **be allowed to do sth.** etwas tun dürfen III 1 (10)
alone [ə'ləʊn] allein(e) II
along the street [ə'lɒŋ] die Straße entlang II
alphabet ['ælfəbət] Alphabet I
°already [ɔːl'redi] schon
also ['ɔːlsəʊ] auch III 1 (10)
always ['ɔːlweɪz] immer I
am [æm]: **I'm (= I am)** ich bin I
am [eɪ'em]: **5 am** 5 Uhr morgens/vormittags I
amazed [ə'meɪzd] erstaunt, verwundert II
amazing [ə'meɪzɪŋ] erstaunlich III 1 (10)
America [ə'merɪkə] Amerika III 3 (48)
°American [ə'merɪkən] amerikanisch
an [ən] ein/e *(vor Vokalen)* I
and [ænd], [ənd] und I
angry ['æŋgri] wütend, ärgerlich I
animal ['ænɪml] Tier I
another [ə'nʌðə] ein/e andere(r, s); noch ein/e II
answer ['ɑːnsə]:
1. Antwort I
2. antworten; beantworten III 1 (14)
°answer the phone ans Telefon gehen
any ['eni]: **there aren't any trees** es gibt keine Bäume II
anything ['eniθɪŋ]: **Anything else?** Sonst noch etwas? I **not (…) anything** nichts II
°appetite ['æpɪtaɪt] Appetit
apple ['æpl] Apfel II
°appointment [ə'pɔɪntmənt] Verabredung
April ['eɪprəl] April I
are [ɑː] bist; seid; sind I
The mobiles are £ 10. Die Handys kosten 10 Pfund. I
°arena [ə'riːnə] Arena
°argument ['ɑːgjumənt] Argument
arm [ɑːm] Arm II
around [ə'raʊnd]: **look around** sich umschauen (in) III 3 (54)
°around 7 um ca. 7 Uhr
°around London durch London, in London umher
arrive [ə'raɪv] ankommen II
art [ɑːt] Kunst I
article ['ɑːtɪkl] Artikel III 2 (35)
as [æz], [əz]: **as much as** so viel wie III 3 (51) **°as a footballer** als Fußballer/in **°as many as you can** so viele (wie) du kannst
ask [ɑːsk] fragen I **ask for sth.** um etwas bitten II

at [æt], [ət]: **at a restaurant** in einem Restaurant I **at Eggbuckland** auf der Eggbuckland-Schule I **at Ellie's house** bei Ellie daheim, bei Ellie zu Hause I **at home** zu Hause I **at MARTINS** bei MARTINS I **at school** in der Schule I **at the cinema** im Kino I **at the top (of)** oben, am oberen Ende (von); an der Spitze (von) II °**at least** mindestens, wenigstens
ate [eɪt], [et] *siehe* **eat**
°**athletics** [æθ'letɪks] Sport, Leichtathletik
August ['ɔːgəst] August I
aunt [ɑːnt] Tante II
Australia [ɒ'streɪliə] Australien III 3 (48)
°**available** [ə'veɪləbl] verfügbar; erhältlich; möglich
away [ə'weɪ] weg, fort I

B

baby ['beɪbi] Baby I
babysitter ['beɪbisɪtə] Babysitter I
back [bæk]:
1. Rücken; Rückseite III 3 (50)
2. zurück I
°**3.** hinteres Ende
background ['bækgraʊnd] Hintergrund III 2 (36)
bad [bæd] schlecht; schlimm I
badge [bædʒ] Anstecknadel, Button III 3 (53)
badminton ['bædmɪntən] Badminton, Federball II
bag [bæg] Tasche I
bagpipes *(pl)* ['bægpaɪps] Dudelsack III 4 (73)
ball [bɔːl] Ball I
balloon [bə'luːn] Ballon III 3 (53)
banana [bə'nɑːnə] Banane I **banana skin** Bananenschale I
band [bænd] Band, Musikgruppe II
bank [bæŋk] Bank *(Geldinstitut)* II
baseball ['beɪsbɔːl] Baseball II
basketball ['bɑːskɪtbɔːl] Basketball I
bass guitar [beɪs gɪ'tɑː] E-Bass III 4 (77)
bathroom ['bɑːθruːm] Bad(ezimmer) I
battle ['bætl] Wettstreit, Battle *(im Rap)* I
be [biː], **was/were, been** sein I
beach [biːtʃ] Strand I
°**bean** [biːn] Bohne
bear [beə] Bär I
°**Beatlemania** [biːtl'meɪniə] *extreme Begeisterung für die Beatles*
beautiful ['bjuːtɪfl] (wunder-)schön III 4 (71)
because [bɪ'kɒz] weil I
bed [bed] Bett I
bed and breakfast (B&B) [bed ən 'brekfəst] Frühstückspension; Zimmer mit Frühstück III 4 (71)
bedroom ['bedruːm] Schlafzimmer I
been [biːn], [bɪn] *siehe* **be**
before [bɪ'fɔː] vor *(zeitlich)* I
before you read bevor du liest I
began [bɪ'gæn] *siehe* **begin**
begin [bɪ'gɪn], **began, begun** beginnen, anfangen III 1 (14)
behave [bɪ'heɪv] sich verhalten III 2 (32) **behave dangerously** sich gefährlich verhalten III 2 (32)
behind [bɪ'haɪnd] hinter I
believe [bɪ'liːv] glauben III 2 (30)
bell [bel] Glocke; Klingel III 1 (8)
°**below** [bɪ'ləʊ] unten; unter(halb von)
best [best] beste(r, s); am besten I
Best wishes Viele Grüße, … *(Briefschluss)* I **like sth. best** etwas am liebsten mögen II
better ['betə] besser II **do better** besser abschneiden II **like sth. better** etwas lieber mögen II
between [bɪ'twiːn] zwischen II
°**beware of** [bɪ'weər əv] sich in Acht nehmen vor
bicycle ['baɪsɪkl] Fahrrad III 3 (50)
big [bɪg] groß I
bike [baɪk] Fahrrad I **ride a bike** Rad fahren I
bird [bɜːd] Vogel I
birdhouse ['bɜːdhaʊs] Nistkasten *(für Vögel)* II
birthday ['bɜːθdeɪ] Geburtstag I
Happy birthday! Herzlichen Glückwunsch zum Geburtstag! I
It's her birthday. Sie hat Geburtstag. I
biscuit ['bɪskɪt] Keks, Plätzchen III 3 (51)
bit [bɪt]: **a bit** ein bisschen II
black [blæk] schwarz I
blame sb. (for) [bleɪm] jm. die Schuld geben (an), jm. Vorwürfe machen (wegen) III 4 (71)
blazer ['bleɪzə] Blazer *(Jackett, oft Teil der Schuluniform)* III 1 (20)
block of flats [blɒk əv 'flæts] Mehrfamilienhaus, Wohnblock III 2 (29)
°**blog** [blɒg] Blog *(Internet-Tagebuch)*
°**blow** [bləʊ] wehen
blue [bluː] blau I
°**board** [bɔːd] Tafel *(im Klassenraum)*
boat [bəʊt] Boot; Schiff I
°**bold** [bəʊld] fett (gedruckt)
bonfire ['bɒnfaɪə] *(Freuden-)*Feuer II
book [bʊk]:
1. Buch I
2. buchen, reservieren III 4 (72)
bookshop ['bʊkʃɒp] Buchladen II
boot [buːt] Stiefel II
bored [bɔːd]: **be bored** Langeweile haben, gelangweilt sein III 3 (61)
boring ['bɔːrɪŋ] langweilig I
born [bɔːn] geboren III 4 (77)
°**she was born** sie wurde geboren
borrow ['bɒrəʊ] (aus)leihen, sich borgen I
boss [bɒs] Boss, Chef/in III 4 (70)
bossy ['bɒsi] herrisch I
°**both** [bəʊθ] beide
bottle ['bɒtl] Flasche I
bought [bɔːt] *siehe* **buy**
bowling ['bəʊlɪŋ]: **go bowling** Bowling spielen gehen I
box [bɒks]
1. Box, Kasten I
°**2.** boxen
°**boxer** ['bɒksə] Boxer/in
boxing *(das)* Boxen III 3 (57)
boy [bɔɪ] Junge I
°**boyband** ['bɔɪbænd] Boyband
boyfriend ['bɔɪfrend] (fester) Freund II
brave [breɪv] mutig III 2 (32)
bread [bred] Brot II
break [breɪk] Pause I
break [breɪk], **broke, broken** (zer)brechen III 3 (54)
breakfast ['brekfəst] Frühstück I
bridge [brɪdʒ] Brücke II
°**bright** [braɪt] hell
bring [brɪŋ], **brought, brought** bringen, mitbringen I
Britain ['brɪtn] Großbritannien II
British ['brɪtɪʃ] britisch I
brochure ['brəʊʃə] Broschüre, Prospekt I
broke [brəʊk] *siehe* **break**
broken ['brəʊkən]:
1. *siehe* **break**
2. zerbrochen, kaputt III 3 (54)
brother ['brʌðə] Bruder I
brought [brɔːt] *siehe* **bring**
brown [braʊn] braun I
°**browse** [braʊz] stöbern in, sich umschauen in, durchstöbern
building ['bɪldɪŋ] Gebäude III 4 (69)

bull [bʊl] Bulle I
burger ['bɜːgə] Hamburger *(Frikadelle)* II
bus [bʌs] Bus I
bus stop ['bʌs stɒp] Bushaltestelle II
bush [bʊʃ] Busch, Strauch III 2 (34)
business ['bɪznəs] Geschäft, Betrieb III 2 (30) **start a business** ein Geschäft aufmachen, einen Betrieb gründen/eröffnen III 2 (30)
°**business studies** *(pl)* ['bɪznəs stʌdiːz] Wirtschaftskunde
busy ['bɪzi]:
1. belebt; verkehrsreich III 1 (16)
2. **be busy** beschäftigt sein, (viel) zu tun haben II
but [bʌt] aber I
buy [baɪ], **bought, bought** kaufen I
by [baɪ]: **by Sam Holmes** *(geschrieben)* von Sam Holmes III 1 (10) **go by bus** mit dem Bus fahren I
Bye. [baɪ] Tschüs. I

C

cafe ['kæfeɪ] Café I
cake [keɪk] Kuchen II
calculator ['kælkjuleɪtə] Taschenrechner I
calendar ['kælɪndə] Kalender I
call [kɔːl]:
1. rufen; nennen; anrufen III 1 (14)
2. *(kurz für:* **phone call)** (Telefon-)Anruf II
calm [kɑːm] ruhig, still; besonnen III 2 (32)
came [keɪm] *siehe* **come**
camera ['kæmərə] Fotoapparat; Kamera I
°**camping** ['kæmpɪŋ]: **go camping** zelten gehen, campen gehen
can [kæn], [kən] können I **can't (= cannot)** nicht können I
Canadian [kə'neɪdiən] kanadisch, aus Kanada; Kanadier/in III 4 (72)
°**canoe** [kə'nuː] Kanu, Paddelboot
°**canoeing** [kə'nuːɪŋ] Paddeln, Kanusport
canteen [kæn'tiːn] (Schul-)Mensa, Kantine I
°**canyoning** ['kænjənɪŋ] Canyoning *(in Schluchten springen oder sich abseilen)*
capital ['kæpɪtl] Hauptstadt III 4 (69)
°**captain** ['kæptɪn] Kapitän/in
°**caption** ['kæpʃn] Bildunterschrift
car [kɑː] Auto I
car park ['kɑː pɑːk] Parkplatz III 4 (75)
card [kɑːd] Karte I
careful ['keəfl] vorsichtig; sorgfältig II
carefully ['keəfəli]: **drive carefully** vorsichtig fahren II
°**carriage** ['kærɪdʒ] (Eisenbahn-)Wagen
carrot ['kærət] Möhre, Karotte II
°**carry out** [kæri 'aʊt] durchführen
cartoon [kɑː'tuːn] Zeichentrickfilm; Comic II
castle ['kɑːsl] Burg III 4 (68)
cat [kæt] Katze I
catch [kætʃ], **caught, caught** (ein)fangen III 2 (34)
caught [kɔːt] *siehe* **catch**
°**'cause** [kɔːz] weil *(= because)*
CCTV [siː siː tiː 'viː] Überwachungssystem; Überwachungskamera(s) III 2 (30)
CD [siː'diː] CD I
CD player [siː'diː pleɪə] CD-Spieler II
celebrate ['selɪbreɪt] feiern II
cent [sent] Cent III 3 (53)
centre ['sentə] Zentrum, (Stadt-)Mitte II
cereal bar ['sɪəriəl bɑː] Müsliriegel III 3 (51)
°**ceremony** ['serəməni] Zeremonie
chair [tʃeə] Stuhl I
champion ['tʃæmpiən] Meister/in *(Sport)* III 3 (59)
change [tʃeɪndʒ]:
1. (ver)ändern, sich (ver)ändern II
2. Veränderung, Wechsel III 4 (70)
°3. wechseln
charity ['tʃærəti] wohltätige Organisation II **charity shop** *Geschäft, das gespendete Waren für wohltätige Zwecke verkauft* II
chat [tʃæt]:
1. Gespräch, Unterhaltung; Chat II
2. **chat (with)** plaudern (mit); „chatten" (mit) II
cheap [tʃiːp] billig, preiswert II **It's cheaper than that.** So viel kostet das nicht. II
check [tʃek] (über)prüfen, kontrollieren II
cheese [tʃiːz] Käse I
chicken ['tʃɪkɪn] Huhn; (Brat-)Hähnchen I
child, *(pl)* **children** [tʃaɪld], ['tʃɪldrən] Kind I
chill [tʃɪl] *(infml)* relaxen, sich ausruhen II
China ['tʃaɪnə] China III 3 (48)
chipmunk ['tʃɪpmʌŋk] Streifenhörnchen I
chips *(pl)* [tʃɪps] Pommes frites I °**fish and chips** Backfisch mit Pommes frites
chocolate ['tʃɒklət] Schokolade; Praline II
chocolate bar ['tʃɒklət bɑː] Schokoriegel III 3 (50)
°**choose** [tʃuːz] (aus)wählen
chores [tʃɔːz]: **do chores** (Haus-)Arbeiten erledigen II
°**chorus** ['kɔːrəs] Refrain *(in einem Lied)*
°**Christmas** ['krɪsməs] Weihnachten **Christmas Day** 1. Weihnachtstag (25. 12.) **Christmas pantomime** *(GB) Theaterstück zur Weihnachtszeit*
church [tʃɜːtʃ] Kirche III 2 (29)
cinema ['sɪnəmə] Kino I
°**circle** ['sɜːkl] Kreis
circus ['sɜːkəs] Zirkus II
city ['sɪti] (Groß-)Stadt I
class [klɑːs] (Schul-)Klasse I
class teacher ['klɑːs tiːtʃə] Klassenlehrer/in I
classroom ['klɑːsruːm] Klassenraum I
clear [klɪə] deutlich, klar II
clearly ['klɪəli]: **talk clearly** deutlich sprechen II
clever ['klevə] schlau, klug III 1 (14)
°**click** [klɪk] klicken
°**cliff** [klɪf] Klippe, Felsen
climb [klaɪm] klettern (auf) II **climbing** *(das)* Klettern *(Sport)* II
clock [klɒk] Uhr I
close [kləʊz] schließen, zumachen III 2 (31) °**close sth. down** etwas schließen, stillegen *(Fabrik, Geschäft)*
closed [kləʊzd]: **be closed** geschlossen sein, zu sein II
clothes *(pl)* [kləʊðz] Kleidung, Kleidungsstücke II
cloud [klaʊd] Wolke II
cloudy ['klaʊdi] wolkig, bewölkt II
club [klʌb] Klub, Verein I
coat [kəʊt] Mantel; Jacke III 4 (72)
coffee ['kɒfi] Kaffee I
cold [kəʊld] kalt II
collect [kə'lekt] sammeln II
°**collection** [kə'lekʃn] Abholung, Abhol-
colour ['kʌlə] Farbe I
coloured ['kʌləd] bunt, farbig II
°**colourful** ['kʌləfl] farbenfroh, bunt

°column ['kɒləm] Spalte *(in einem gedruckten Text)*
come [kʌm], **came, come** (mit) kommen I **Come on!** Komm(t) (schon)! / Ach komm! III 2 (30)
comedy ['kɒmədi] Comedyshow; Komödie II
comfortable ['kʌmftəbl] bequem, gemütlich II **make yourself comfortable** es sich gemütlich machen III 4 (74)
comic ['kɒmɪk] Comic(heft) II
comment ['kɒment] Kommentar III 3 (57)
°community [kə'mju:nəti] Gemeinde(-), Lokal-
°compare [kəm'peə] vergleichen
°comparison [kəm'pærɪsn] Vergleich
competition [kɒmpə'tɪʃn] Wettbewerb III 3 (52)
°complete [kəm'pli:t]:
1. vervollständigen
2. vollständig
computer [kəm'pju:tə] Computer I
concert ['kɒnsət] Konzert I
confirm [kən'fɜ:m] bestätigen III 4 (73)
Congratulations (on ...)! [kəngrætʃu'leɪʃnz] Herzlichen Glückwunsch (zu ...)! I
cook [kʊk] kochen I
°cooker ['kʊkə] Herd
cool [ku:l] cool I
°copy ['kɒpi] kopieren, abschreiben
corner ['kɔ:nə] Ecke I
correct [kə'rekt]:
1. korrigieren, berichtigen II
°2. korrekt
cost [kɒst] Kosten, Preis III 3 (53)
cost [kɒst], **cost, cost** kosten III 3 (50)
cottage ['kɒtɪdʒ] Häuschen, Hütte II
could [kʊd]:
1. **she could** sie konnte II
2. **you could** du könntest II
country ['kʌntri] Land I **in the country** auf dem Land III 2 (28)
°course [kɔ:s] Kurs(us)
°cousin ['kʌzn] Cousin, Cousine
°cover ['kʌvə] abdecken, zudecken
cow [kaʊ] Kuh I
crab [kræb] Krebs I
cream [kri:m] Sahne I
°cream tea [kri:m 'ti:] *Tee mit scones, Marmelade und Sahne*
cricket ['krɪkɪt] Cricket *(Mannschaftssportart)* II
crime series, *(pl)* **crime series** ['kraɪm sɪəri:z] Krimiserie II
crisps *(pl)* [krɪsps] (Kartoffel-)Chips II
crocodile ['krɒkədaɪl] Krokodil I
cross [krɒs] überqueren II
crossroads, *(pl)* **crossroads** ['krɒsrəʊdz] (Straßen-)Kreuzung III 2 (29)
°cruise [kru:z] Kreuzfahrt, Schiffsreise
cry [kraɪ] weinen II
°cubic metre [kju:bɪk 'mi:tə] Kubikmeter
culture ['kʌltʃə] Kultur III 1 (10)
cup [kʌp] Tasse III 1 (19) **a cup of tea** eine Tasse Tee III 1 (19)
cupcake ['kʌpkeɪk] Cupcake *(kleiner runder Kuchen)* III 3 (54)
cushion ['kʊʃn] Kissen I
customer ['kʌstəmə] Kunde, Kundin I
cut [kʌt], **cut, cut** schneiden; *(Rasen)* mähen II
cute [kju:t] niedlich, süß I
cycle ['saɪkl] Rad fahren II

D

dad [dæd] Papa, Vati I
dance [dɑ:ns] tanzen II
dancer ['dɑ:nsə] Tänzer/in III 1 (17)
dancing ['dɑ:nsɪŋ] *(das)* Tanzen I
dangerous ['deɪndʒərəs] gefährlich I
dark [dɑ:k] dunkel III 1 (21)
date [deɪt] Datum I
daughter ['dɔ:tə] Tochter III 2 (32)
day [deɪ] Tag I **day out** (Tages-)Ausflug II
deal [di:l] Geschäft; Vereinbarung II **It's a deal!** Abgemacht! II **make a deal** ein Geschäft abschließen, vereinbaren II
dear [dɪə]: **Oh dear!** oje! II
Dear ... [dɪə] Liebe ... / Lieber ... I
December [dɪ'sembə] Dezember I
°decide [dɪ'saɪd] sich entscheiden, beschließen
deep [di:p] tief III 2 (32)
°delivery [dɪ'lɪvəri] Lieferung; Lieferer-
Denmark ['denmɑ:k] Dänemark II
°departure [dɪ'pɑ:tʃə] Abfahrt
describe [dɪ'skraɪb] beschreiben III 2 (32)
desk [desk] Schreibtisch II
°detail ['di:teɪl] Detail, Einzelheit
detective [dɪ'tektɪv] Detektiv/in III 1 (8)
°diagram ['daɪəgræm] Diagramm
°dialogue ['daɪəlɒg] Dialog
°diary ['daɪəri] Tagebuch; Kalender
dictionary ['dɪkʃənri] Wörterbuch, (alphabetisches) Wörterverzeichnis I
did [dɪd] *siehe* **do** **Did they go?** Gingen sie?/Sind sie gegangen? II **we didn't have a ...** wir hatten kein/keine ... II
die [daɪ] sterben II
difference ['dɪfrəns] Unterschied I **make a difference** etwas bewirken, etwas ausmachen I
different ['dɪfrənt] unterschiedlich, verschieden, anders I
difficult ['dɪfɪkəlt] schwierig, schwer I
diner ['daɪnə] *(AE)* Imbissstube, Lokal II
dinner ['dɪnə] Abendessen I
dinosaur ['daɪnəsɔ:] Dinosaurier III 1 (14)
directions *(pl)* [də'rekʃnz] Wegbeschreibung(en) III 4 (73)
°disagree [dɪsə'gri:] nicht zustimmen, widersprechen
disappointed [dɪsə'pɔɪntɪd] enttäuscht II
disaster [dɪ'zɑ:stə] Katastrophe, Unglück III 1 (14)
°discover [dɪ'skʌvə] entdecken
dishwasher ['dɪʃwɒʃə] Geschirrspülmaschine II
dive [daɪv] einen Kopfsprung machen I
°diver ['daɪvə] Kunst-/Turmspringer/in
diving ['daɪvɪŋ] *(das)* Tauchen *(Sport)* II
do [du:], **did, done** machen, tun I **50p will do** 50 Pence reichen (auch) II **do a trip** einen Ausflug/eine Reise machen II **I do my homework** ich mache (meine) Hausaufgaben I
doctor ['dɒktə] Arzt/Ärztin, Doktor/in II
dog [dɒg] Hund I **dogs' home** Hundeheim II
dollar ($) ['dɒlə] Dollar III 1 (15) **like a million dollars** fantastisch III 1 (15)
done [dʌn] *siehe* **do**
donkey ['dɒŋki] Esel I
door [dɔ:] Tür II
°dormitory ['dɔ:mətri] Schlafsaal
°dossier ['dɒsieɪ] Mappe, Dossier
°double room [dʌbl 'ru:m] Doppelzimmer

down [daʊn] hinunter, runter, nach unten III 4 (74)
downside ['daʊnsaɪd] Kehrseite, Nachteil III 1 (10)
°**draft** [drɑːft] Entwurf
drama ['drɑːmə] Schauspiel, darstellende Kunst I
drank [dræŋk] *siehe* **drink**
°**draw** [drɔː], **drew, drawn** zeichnen
dream [driːm] Traum II
dress [dres] Kleid II
°**dressing room** ['dresɪŋ ruːm] Umkleide(kabine)
°**drew** [druː] *siehe* **draw**
drink [drɪŋk] Getränk I
drink [drɪŋk], **drank, drunk** trinken III 1 (15)
°**drip** [drɪp] tropfen
drive [draɪv], **drove, driven** *(mit dem Auto)* fahren II
driver ['draɪvə] Fahrer/in III 1 (17)
driving licence ['draɪvɪŋ laɪsns] Führerschein III 4 (74)
drove [drəʊv] *siehe* **drive**
drums [drʌmz] Schlagzeug; Trommeln I
dry [draɪ] trocknen III 4 (72)
duck [dʌk] Ente I
DVD [diːviː'diː] DVD I
DVD player [diːviː'diː pleɪə] DVD-Player III 4 (72)

E

°**each** [iːtʃ] jede(r, s) (einzelne)
ear [ɪə] Ohr II
early ['ɜːli] früh I
earthquake ['ɜːθkweɪk] Erdbeben III 1 (15)
east [iːst] Osten; östlich; Ost- II
easy ['iːzi] einfach, leicht II **Take it easy!** *(infml)* Reg dich nicht auf. / Bleib mal locker. III 2 (31)
eat [iːt], **ate, eaten** essen; fressen I
egg [eg] Ei III 3 (54)
eight [eɪt] acht I
either ['eɪðə]: **not ... either** auch nicht III 4 (75)
elephant ['elɪfənt] Elefant I
eleven [ɪ'levən] elf I
else [els]: **Anything else?** Sonst noch etwas? I
email ['iːmeɪl] E-Mail I
empty ['empti]:
1. leer II
2. leeren II

end [end] Ende, Schluss I **in the end** schließlich, zum Schluss II
ending ['endɪŋ] Ende *(Text, Geschichte)* II **happy ending** Happy End II
energy ['enədʒi] Energie III 3 (51)
energy drink ['enədʒi drɪŋk] Energiegetränk III 3 (51)
England ['ɪŋglənd] England I
English ['ɪŋglɪʃ] Englisch; englisch I
enjoy [ɪn'dʒɔɪ] genießen II **Enjoy yourself/yourselves.** Viel Vergnügen! / Viel Spaß! III 4 (71) °**Enjoy your meal.** Guten Appetit!
enough [ɪ'nʌf] genug III 3 (54)
°**entertainment** [entə'teɪnmənt] Unterhaltung
°**entry** ['entri] Eintritt, Zutritt
equipment [ɪ'kwɪpmənt] Ausrüstung, Ausstattung III 4 (70)
e-reader ['iː riːdə] E-Book-Reader II
escalator ['eskəleɪtə] Rolltreppe III 1 (20)
especially [ɪ'speʃəli] insbesondere III 1 (15)
etc. [et'setərə] *(aus dem Lateinischen)* usw. (und so weiter) III 3 (51)
euro (€) ['jʊərəʊ] Euro III 3 (53)
Europe ['jʊərəp] Europa III 3 (48)
even ['iːvn] sogar, selbst III 3 (57)
evening ['iːvnɪŋ] Abend I
°**event** [ɪ'vent] Ereignis
ever ['evə] je(mals) II **Have you ever been ...?** Warst du schon mal ...? / Bist du schon mal ... gewesen? II
every ['evri] jede(r, s) II °**every 3 minutes** alle 3 Minuten
everybody ['evribɒdi] jeder; alle I
everyone ['evriwʌn] jeder; alle II
°**everything** ['evriθɪŋ] alles
everywhere ['evriweə] überall(hin) III 2 (37)
example [ɪg'zɑːmpl] Beispiel I **for example** zum Beispiel I
excited [ɪk'saɪtɪd] aufgeregt, gespannt I
exciting [ɪk'saɪtɪŋ] aufregend II
Excuse me, ... [ɪks'kjuːz mi] Entschuldigung, ... II
exercise ['eksəsaɪz] Übung, Aufgabe I **exercise book** Schulheft, Übungsheft I **do exercises** Übungen machen II
exhibition [eksɪ'bɪʃn] Ausstellung III 4 (72)
exist [ɪg'zɪst] existieren III 4 (74)
expensive [ɪk'spensɪv] teuer I
°**experience** [ɪk'spɪəriəns]:
1. erfahren, erleben
2. Erfahrung, Erlebnis

°**expert** ['ekspɜːt] fachmännisch, ausgezeichnet
°**explain** [ɪk'spleɪn] erklären
°**explore** [ɪk'splɔː] erforschen, erkunden
°**explorer** [ɪk'splɔːrə] Forschungsreisende/r, Entdecker/in
°**express** [ɪk'spres] ausdrücken, zum Ausdruck bringen
°**expression** [ɪk'spreʃn] Ausdruck
eye [aɪ] Auge III 1 (9)

F

face [feɪs] Gesicht I
fact [fækt] Tatsache; Information III 3 (56)
fall [fɔːl], **fell, fallen** fallen; hinfallen I
false [fɔːls] falsch, unrichtig II
family ['fæməli] Familie I **family tree** (Familien-)Stammbaum I **family-friendly** familienfreundlich III 4 (72)
famous (for) ['feɪməs] berühmt (für, wegen) III 1 (8)
fan [fæn] Fan III 1 (11)
°**fancy** ['fænsi] Lust haben auf
fantastic [fæn'tæstɪk] fantastisch III 3 (55)
far [fɑː] weit III 1 (16)
farm [fɑːm] Bauernhof I
farmer ['fɑːmə] Bauer, Bäuerin; Landwirt/in III 2 (32)
fashion ['fæʃn] Mode(trend) III 1 (10)
°**fast** [fɑːst] schnell
father ['fɑːðə] Vater III 2 (32)
favourite ['feɪvərɪt] Lieblings- I **favourite thing** Lieblingssache I
February ['februəri] Februar I
fed up [fed 'ʌp]: **feel fed up** genervt sein, sauer sein; die Nase voll haben I
feed [fiːd] füttern I
feel [fiːl], **felt, felt** sich fühlen; fühlen I
°**feeling** ['fiːlɪŋ] Gefühl
fell [fel] *siehe* **fall**
felt [felt] *siehe* **feel**
°**female** ['fiːmeɪl] weiblich; Frau
ferry ['feri] Fähre I
festival ['festɪvl] Fest II
°**few** [fjuː]: **a few** ein paar, einige
field [fiːld] Feld; Weide I
fifty ['fɪfti] fünfzig I

fight [faɪt], **fought, fought** kämpfen III 3 (57)
°**file** [faɪl] Datei
fill [fɪl] füllen II
film [fɪlm] Film I
film star ['fɪlm stɑː] Filmstar III 1 (8)
find [faɪnd], **found, found** finden II **find out** herausfinden II
fine [faɪn] gut, schön I **I'm fine.** Es geht mir gut. I
finger ['fɪŋgə] Finger III 4 (75)
finish ['fɪnɪʃ]:
1. beenden, enden II
°2. Ende, Ziel
fire ['faɪə] Feuer II
firefighter ['faɪəfaɪtə] Feuerwehrmann, Feuerwehrfrau I
firework ['faɪewɜːk] Feuerwerkskörper II **fireworks** *(pl)* Feuerwerk
first [fɜːst]:
1. zuerst I
2. **first (= 1st)** erste, erster, erstes I
first aid [fɜːst 'eɪd] Erste Hilfe II
first-aid kit [fɜːst 'eɪd kɪt] Erste-Hilfe-Set, Verbandkasten II
fish, *(pl)* **fish** [fɪʃ] Fisch I °**fish and chips** Backfisch mit Pommes frites
fit [fɪt] fit III 3 (57)
five [faɪv] fünf I **Give me five!** Gib mir fünf! *(Aufforderung, gegen die erhobene Hand des Gegenübers zu klatschen, Geste der Freude/Begrüßung)* II
flag [flæg] Fahne, Flagge II
flat [flæt] Wohnung I **block of flats** Mehrfamilienhaus, Wohnblock III 2 (29)
flat-screen TV ['flæt skriːn tiː viː] Flachbildfernseher I
flew [fluː] *siehe* **fly**
flour ['flaʊə] Mehl III 3 (54)
flown [fləʊn] *siehe* **fly**
fly [flaɪ], **flew, flown** fliegen III 4 (76)
°**focus** ['fəʊkəs] Schwerpunkt **focus on language** *(etwa)* Schwerpunkt: Sprache
fog [fɒg] Nebel II
foggy ['fɒgi] nebelig II
°**follow** ['fɒləʊ] folgen **follow in sb.'s footsteps** in js. Fußstapfen treten
food [fuːd] Essen, Lebensmittel; Futter I
°**foot,** *(pl)* **feet** [fʊt], [fiːt] Fuß **on foot** zu Fuß
football ['fʊtbɔːl] Fußball I **football club (FC)** Fußballverein III 1 (11) **playing football** Fußballspielen I
footballer ['fʊtbɔːlə] Fußballspieler/in III 1 (17)
°**footstep** ['fʊtstep]: **follow in sb.'s footsteps** in js. Fußstapfen treten
for [fɔː], [fə] für I **for 100 metres** 100 Meter weit II **for lots of reasons** aus vielen Gründen III 3 (57) **for the last time** zum letzten Mal III 4 (70) °**for miles and miles** meilenweit
°**forecast** ['fɔːkɑːst]: **(weather) forecast** (Wetter-)Vorhersage
foreground ['fɔːgraʊnd] Vordergrund III 2 (36)
forget [fə'get], **forgot, forgotten** vergessen II
forgot [fə'gɒt] *siehe* **forget**
I forgot my homework. Ich habe meine Hausaufgaben vergessen. I
°**form** [fɔːm] Form
°**forum** ['fɔːrəm] Forum
fought [fɔːt] *siehe* **fight**
found [faʊnd] *siehe* **find**
four [fɔː] vier I
fox [fɒks] Fuchs III 2 (34)
France [frɑːns] Frankreich I
free [friː]:
1. frei III 4 (72)
Are you free at one o'clock? Hast du um ein Uhr Zeit? I
2. kostenlos I
French [frentʃ] Französisch; französisch I
°**fresh** [freʃ] frisch
°**freshwater** ['freʃwɔːtə] Süßwasser-
Friday ['fraɪdeɪ], ['fraɪdi] Freitag I
friend [frend] Freund/in I **make friends** Freunde finden II
friendly ['frendli] freundlich, nett II
from [frɒm] aus I **from Monday to Friday** von Montag bis Freitag I **a text from mum** eine SMS von Mama I
front [frʌnt]: **in front of** vor I
fruit [fruːt] Früchte, Obst; Frucht II
full [fʊl] voll III 2 (34) **full of ...** voller ... III 2 (34) °**(half-)full** (halb)voll
°**fully guided** [fʊli 'gaɪdɪd] geführt
fun [fʌn]: **they're fun** es macht Spaß, mit ihnen zusammen zu sein I
°**fun run** ['fʌn rʌn] Spaß(wett)lauf
funny ['fʌni] lustig I
future ['fjuːtʃə] Zukunft II

G

game [geɪm] Spiel I
garage ['gærɑːʒ] Garage I **garage sale** Garagenflohmarkt *(privater Flohmarkt)* I
garden ['gɑːdn] Garten I
gate [geɪt] Tor III 2 (29)
gave [geɪv] *siehe* **give**
geek [giːk] *jemand, der sich sehr stark für etwas begeistert (und manchmal von anderen deswegen belächelt wird)* III 1 (14)
°**general** ['dʒenrəl] allgemein
geography [dʒi'ɒgrəfi] Geografie, Erdkunde I
German ['dʒɜːmən]:
1. Deutsch; deutsch I
2. Deutsche/r II
Germany ['dʒɜːməni] Deutschland I
get [get], **got, got**:
1. bekommen, kriegen I
get the bus den Bus nehmen I
get up aufstehen I
2. **get cold** kalt werden III 4 (71)
ghost [gəʊst] Gespenst III 4 (74)
ginger ['dʒɪndʒə] Ingwer; rotblond *(Haare)* II
girl [gɜːl] Mädchen I
girlfriend ['gɜːlfrend] (feste) Freundin II
give [gɪv], **gave, given** geben II **give a talk** einen Vortrag halten II **Give me five!** Gib mir fünf! *(Aufforderung, gegen die erhobene Hand des Gegenübers zu klatschen, Geste der Freude/Begrüßung)* II
glad [glæd]: **I'm glad** ich bin froh II
glasses *(pl)* ['glɑːsɪz] Brille II
glove [glʌv] Handschuh II
go [gəʊ], **went, gone** gehen; fahren I **go away** weggehen I **go out** ausgehen; hinausgehen II **I'm going to ask ...** ich werde ... fragen/bitten II
°**goal** [gəʊl] Tor *(Sport)*
good [gʊd] gut I **Good luck.** Viel Glück! I **Good morning.** Guten Morgen. I **be good at sth.** etwas gut können, gut sein in etwas III 3 (52) **Have a good day.** Ich wünsche dir einen schönen Tag. / Schönen Tag noch. I
Goodbye. [gʊd'baɪ] Auf Wiedersehen. I
got [gɒt] *siehe* **get**
GPS [dʒiː piː 'es] GPS III 4 (73)
grandad ['grændæd] Opa III 2 (39)

grandfather ['grænfɑːðə] Großvater III 3 (54)
grandma ['grænmɑː] Oma I
grandpa ['grænpɑː] Opa I
grass [grɑːs] Gras II
great [greɪt] großartig, toll I
Great Britain [grəɪt 'brɪtn] Großbritannien II
Greek [griːk] griechisch; Griechisch; Grieche/Griechin III 1 (10)
green [griːn] grün I
grey [greɪ] grau III 4 (69)
ground [graʊnd] Erde *(Erdboden)* II
group [gruːp] Gruppe I **group work** Gruppenarbeit I
guess [ges]:
1. I guess ich glaube, ich nehme an III 3 (59)
°**2.** (er)raten
guest [gest] Gast III 4 (72)
°**guide** [gaɪd] Reiseleiter/in, Fremdenführer/in
guitar [gɪ'tɑː] Gitarre I
°**guitarist** [gɪ'tɑːrɪst] Gitarrist/in
guy [gaɪ] Guy-Fawkes-Puppe II **guys** Leute *(als Anrede verwendet)* II
gymnastics [dʒɪm'næstɪks] Turnen, Gymnastik II

H

had [hæd], [həd] *siehe* **have**
hair [heə] Haar, Haare II
hairdresser ['heədresə] Frisör/in II
hairdryer ['heədraɪə] Föhn, Haartrockner II
°**half, *(pl)* halves** [hɑːf], [hɑːvz] Hälfte **half the class** die halbe Klasse
Halloween [hæləʊ'iːn] Halloween *(Abend des 31. 10.)* II
hamster ['hæmstə] Hamster I
hand [hænd] Hand II
hang-gliding ['hæŋ glaɪdɪŋ] Drachenfliegen II
happen ['hæpən] geschehen, passieren II
happy ['hæpi] glücklich, froh I **Happy birthday!** Herzlichen Glückwunsch zum Geburtstag! I **happy ending** Happy End II
harbour ['hɑːbə] Hafen I
hard [hɑːd] schwer; schwierig; hart I **work hard** hart arbeiten III 2 (32)
has [hæz], [həz]: **he/she/it has** er/sie/es hat I
hat [hæt] Hut, Mütze II
have [hæv], **had, had** haben I **Have a good day.** Ich wünsche dir einen schönen Tag. / Schönen Tag noch. I **have a salad** einen Salat nehmen, essen II **have to do sth.** etwas tun müssen III 1 (20) **I've lived here all my life.** Ich wohne hier schon mein ganzes Leben (lang). III 1 (10) **not have to do sth.** etwas nicht tun müssen / brauchen III 1 (20)
he [hiː] er I
headache ['hedeɪk]: **have a headache** Kopfschmerzen haben II
°**heading** ['hedɪŋ] Überschrift
°**headline** ['hedlaɪn] Überschrift
healthy ['helθi] gesund II
hear [hɪə], **heard, heard** hören I
heard [hɜːd] *siehe* **hear**
°**heart** [hɑːt] Herz
heavy ['hevi] schwer *(Gewicht; Regen)* III 2 (32)
Hello. [hə'ləʊ] Hallo. I
help [help]:
1. helfen I **Help yourselves.** Bedient euch! / Greift zu! III 4 (71)
2. Hilfe I
helper ['helpə] Helfer/in II
her [hɜː]:
1. her dad ihr Vater I
2. with her mit ihr II
3. for her für sie *(weibliche Person)* II
here [hɪə] hier; hierher I **Here you are.** Bitte schön. / Hier, bitte. I
herself [hɜː'self] sie/sich selbst *(weibliche Person)* III 4 (71)
Hi! [haɪ] Hallo. I
high [haɪ] hoch III 1 (9)
high school ['haɪ skuːl] *(GB etwa:)* Gesamtschule I
high street ['haɪ striːt] Hauptstraße; Einkaufsstraße III 2 (29)
°**highlight** ['haɪlaɪt] Höhepunkt, Schlaglicht
hiking ['haɪkɪŋ] *(das)* Wandern II
hill [hɪl] Hügel II
hilly ['hɪli] hügelig III 1 (17)
him [hɪm] ihn; ihm I
himself [hɪm'self] er/sich selbst III 4 (71)
hip hop ['hɪp hɒp] Hip-Hop I
hire ['haɪə] mieten, leihen III 4 (74) °**for hire** zum Mieten, Miet-
his [hɪz] sein/e I
history ['hɪstri] Geschichte I
hit [hɪt] Hit III 4 (77)
hobby ['hɒbi] Hobby I **do a hobby** einem Hobby nachgehen II
hockey ['hɒki] (Feld-)Hockey II
°**hold: hold it together** durchhalten **hold sth. back** etwas zurückhalten
holiday ['hɒlədeɪ] Urlaub II **a week's / six weeks' holiday** eine Woche / sechs Wochen Urlaub II
holidays ['hɒlədeɪz] Ferien I
home [həʊm]:
1. nach Hause I **at home** zu Hause I
2. Heim, Zuhause II **dogs' home** Hundeheim II
homework ['həʊmwɜːk] Hausaufgabe/n I **I do my homework** ich mache (meine) Hausaufgaben I
°**honest** ['ɒnɪst] ehrlich
hoodie ['hʊdi] Kapuzenpullover I
°**Hooray!** [hu'reɪ] Hurra!
hoot [huːt] hupen III 4 (74)
hoover ['huːvə] staubsaugen II
hope [həʊp] hoffen I
horse [hɔːs] Pferd III 2 (36)
hospital ['hɒspɪtl] Krankenhaus I
°**host** [həʊst] Gastgeber/in **host family** Gastfamilie **host mother** Gastmutter
hot [hɒt]:
1. heiß, warm II
°**2.** cool, (brand)heiß
°**hot chocolate** [hɒt 'tʃɒklət] Kakao, heiße (Trink-)Schokolade
hot dog ['hɒt dɒg] Hot Dog *(heißes Würstchen in einem Brötchen)* III 3 (51)
hotel [həʊ'tel] Hotel III 4 (71)
hour [aʊə] Stunde III 1 (9)
house [haʊs] Haus I
how [haʊ] wie I **How are you?** Wie geht's? / Wie geht es dir/euch? I
hundred ['hʌndrəd]: **a hundred, one hundred** (ein)hundert I
hungry ['hʌŋgri]: **be hungry** Hunger haben, hungrig sein II
°**hurt** [hɜːt]: **be hurt** verletzt sein **get hurt** sich verletzen

I

I [aɪ] ich I **I'm (= I am)** ich bin I
°**ice** [aɪs] Eis *(gefrorenes Wasser)*
ice cream [aɪs 'kriːm] (Speise-)Eis II
°**ice hockey** ['aɪs hɒki] Eishockey
ice skating ['aɪs skeɪtɪŋ] Schlittschuhlaufen II

°**iceberg** ['aɪsbɜːg] Eisberg
ICT (information and communication technology) [aɪ siː 'tiː], [ɪnfəmeɪʃn ənd kəmjuːnɪkeɪʃn tek'nɒlədʒi] Informations- und Kommunikationstechnologie I
idea [aɪ'dɪə] Idee I
ideal [aɪ'dɪəl] ideal III 2 (37)
idiot ['ɪdiət] Idiot/in III 1 (15)
if [ɪf] wenn, falls II
ill [ɪl] krank II
°**imagine sth.** [ɪ'mædʒɪn] sich etwas vorstellen
important [ɪm'pɔːtənt] wichtig I
impressed [ɪm'prest] beeindruckt III 3 (54)
in [ɪn] in I **in English** auf Englisch I **in my opinion** meiner Meinung nach III 3 (57) **in the country** auf dem Land III 2 (28) **in the morning/afternoon/evening** am Morgen/Nachmittag/Abend I °**in a word** mit einem Wort °**in other words** mit anderen Worten
°**include** [ɪn'kluːd] einschließen
°**including** [ɪn'kluːdɪŋ] einschließlich, inklusive
information (about) [ɪnfə'meɪʃn] Information(en) (über) III 3 (52)
inside [ɪn'saɪd] (nach) drinnen II
instrument ['ɪnstrəmənt] Instrument I
interested ['ɪntrəstɪd]: **be interested in** sich interessieren für, interessiert sein an II °**if interested** falls man interessiert ist, bei Interesse
interesting ['ɪntrəstɪŋ] interessant II
°**international** [ɪntə'næʃnəl] international
internet ['ɪntənet] Internet II
interview ['ɪntəvjuː]:
1. Interview I
°2. befragen, interviewen
into ['ɪntu], ['ɪntə] in (... hinein) II **into the classroom** in den Klassenraum (hinein) II
invitation (to) [ɪnvɪ'teɪʃn] Einladung (zu, nach) I
Irish ['aɪrɪʃ] irisch, aus Irland III 1 (10)
is [ɪz] *(er/sie/es)* ist I **The calculator is £ 1.** Der Taschenrechner kostet 1 Pfund. I
it [ɪt] es, *(bei Dingen und Tieren)* er, sie I **it's (= it is)** es ist *(bei Dingen und Tieren auch:* er ist, sie ist) I

°**Italian** [ɪ'tæliən] Italiener/in; italienisch
its [ɪts] sein/e; ihr/e *(bei Dingen und Tieren)* III 1 (11)
itself [ɪt'self] es/sich selbst III 4 (71)

J

jacket ['dʒækɪt] Jacke, Jackett II
jam [dʒæm] Marmelade I
January ['dʒænjuəri] Januar I
jeans [dʒiːnz] Jeans I
°**jewel** ['dʒuːəl] Juwel
jigsaw ['dʒɪgsɔː] Puzzle II
job [dʒɒb] Job II
jogging ['dʒɒgɪŋ] Jogging II
join [dʒɔɪn] mitmachen (bei); *(einem Klub)* beitreten II
joke [dʒəʊk]:
1. Witz, Scherz II
2. Witze machen, scherzen III 2 (30)
You're joking! Du machst wohl Witze! / Spitzenwitz! III 2 (30)
judo ['dʒuːdəʊ] Judo II
juice [dʒuːs] Saft I
July [dʒu'laɪ] Juli I
jump [dʒʌmp] springen, *(vor Schreck)* zusammenzucken III 3 (61)
June [dʒuːn] Juni I
junk food ['dʒʌŋk fuːd] Junkfood *(ungesundes Essen)* II
just [dʒʌst]:
1. einfach; nur, bloß III 4 (73)
°2. gerade (eben)
3. **just like Berry** genau wie Berry II

K

°**kangaroo** [kæŋgə'ruː] Känguru
karate [kə'rɑːti] Karate II
keep [kiːp], **kept, kept** behalten III 1 (15)
kept [kept] *siehe* **keep**
kettle ['ketl] Wasserkocher *(elektrisch)* III 4 (72)
kick [kɪk] treten, schießen III 1 (15)
kid [kɪd] Kind, Jugendliche/r I
kilometre (km) ['kɪləmiːtə] Kilometer II
kilt [kɪlt] Kilt *(Schottenrock)* III 4 (73)
kind [kaɪnd] freundlich, nett II
°**kind (of)** [kaɪnd]: **all kinds of ...** alle Arten/Sorten (von) ...
king [kɪŋ] König III 1 (8)
kiss [kɪs] Kuss I
kitchen ['kɪtʃɪn] Küche I
kitten ['kɪtn] Kätzchen, junge Katze II
°**knee** [niː] Knie

°**knew** [njuː] *siehe* **know**
knife, *(pl)* **knives** [naɪf], [naɪvz] Messer III 4 (73)
know [nəʊ], **knew, known** wissen; kennen I

L

lake [leɪk] (Binnen-)See III 4 (68)
lamp [læmp] Lampe I
land [lænd] landen III 4 (74)
°**landmark** ['lændmɑːk] Wahrzeichen
language ['læŋgwɪdʒ] Sprache III 4 (69) °**language file** Anhang zum Thema Sprache
lantern ['læntən] Laterne II
laptop ['læptɒp] Laptop I
lasagne [lə'zænjə] Lasagne II
last [lɑːst] letzte(r, s) I **last week** vorige Woche II **at last** schließlich, endlich III 1 (15)
late [leɪt] (zu) spät I **my bus is late** mein Bus hat Verspätung I °**sleep late** lange schlafen
later ['leɪtə] später II
laugh [lɑːf] lachen I
leader ['liːdə] Leiter/in, (An-)Führer/in II
learn [lɜːn] lernen II
°**learner log** ['lɜːnə lɒg] Lern-Tagebuch
leave [liːv], **left, left** (jn.) verlassen; weggehen; abfahren; zurücklassen II
left [left]:
1. *siehe* **leave**
2. links; nach links I
on the left links, auf der linken Seite I
leg [leg] Bein I
°**legend** ['ledʒənd] Legende, Sage
lemonade [lemə'neɪd] Limonade II
less [les] weniger III 3 (51) **less and less** immer weniger III 3 (51)
lesson ['lesn] (Unterrichts-)Stunde I
let's (= let us) [lets], ['let əs] lass(t) uns I **Let's see.** Lass(t) uns (mal) sehen. II
letter ['letə] Brief I
life, *(pl)* **lives** [laɪf], [laɪvz] Leben I
lifestyle ['laɪfstaɪl] Lebensstil II
light [laɪt] Licht; Lampe III 2 (34)
like [laɪk] mögen I **I'd like (= I would like)** ich hätte gern, ich möchte (...) haben I **I'd like to (= I would like to) join** ich würde / möchte gern mitmachen II °**she likes living in ...** sie lebt/wohnt gern in ...

like [laɪk] wie II **I don't feel like it.** Mir ist nicht danach. II **just like Berry** genau wie Berry II **What's the weather like?** Wie ist das Wetter? II
line [laɪn]:
1. Zeile I
°2. Reihe
°**lion** ['laɪən] Löwe
°**list** [lɪst] Liste
listen ['lɪsn] zuhören I **listen for sth.** auf etwas horchen, *(beim Zuhören)* auf etwas achten II **listen to** *(sich etwas)* anhören I
listener ['lɪsənə] Zuhörer/in III 1 (17)
little ['lɪtl] klein III 2 (38)
°**little-known** [lɪtl 'nəʊn] wenig bekannt
live [lɪv] leben, wohnen I
living room ['lɪvɪŋ ru:m] Wohnzimmer I
°**local** ['ləʊkəl] einheimisch, am/vom Ort
°**located** [ləʊ'keɪtɪd]: **be located in ...** in ... liegen
°**lodge** [lɒdʒ] (Berg., Ski-)Hütte
Londoner ['lʌndənə] Londoner/in III 1 (10)
lonely ['ləʊnli] einsam II
long [lɒŋ] lang II
look [lʊk]:
1. aussehen II
2. sehen, schauen I
look after sich kümmern um; aufpassen auf I **look at** anschauen I **look for** suchen II
lose [lu:z], **lost, lost** verlieren II
°**loser** ['lu:zə] Verlierer/in
lost [lɒst] *siehe* **lose**
lot [lɒt]:
1. **lots (of); a lot of** viel(e) I; III 1 (18)
2. **I worry a lot** ich mache mir große Sorgen, ich bin sehr besorgt III 1 (21)
loud [laʊd] laut III 1 (15)
love [lʌv] lieben, sehr mögen I **I'd love to come. (= I would love to come.)** Ich komme sehr gern. / Ich würde sehr gern kommen. I
°**lovely** ['lʌvli] wunderschön, herrlich
luck [lʌk]: **Good luck.** Viel Glück! I
luckily ['lʌkɪli] glücklicherweise III 4 (74)
lucky ['lʌki]: **Lucky you!** Du Glückliche/r! II **you're lucky** du hast Glück I
lunch [lʌntʃ] Mittagessen I **have lunch** (zu) Mittag essen I
lunchtime ['lʌntʃtaɪm]: **at lunchtime** mittags, zur Mittagszeit II

M

machine [mə'ʃi:n] Maschine, Gerät III 4 (81)
made [meɪd] *siehe* **make**
madhouse ['mædhaʊs] Irrenhaus I
magazine [mægə'zi:n] Zeitschrift II
°**main** [meɪn] Haupt-
make [meɪk], **made, made** machen, herstellen I **make a deal** ein Geschäft abschließen, vereinbaren II **make friends** Freunde finden II **make money** Geld verdienen III 3 (51) **What makes a perfect weekend?** Was macht ein perfektes Wochenende aus? II °**make sth. up** etwas erfinden, sich etwas ausdenken
make-up ['meɪkʌp] Make-up II
man, (pl) men [mæn], [men] Mann I
°**manage (to do sth.)** ['mænɪdʒ] (es) schaffen (etwas zu tun)
manager ['mænɪdʒə] Geschäftsführer/in, Manager/in III 4 (70)
many ['mæni] viele II **How many ...?** Wie viele ...? II
map [mæp] Landkarte, Stadtplan II
March [mɑ:tʃ] März I
°**maritime** ['mærɪtaɪm] See-, Schifffahrts-
market ['mɑ:kɪt] Markt I
mask [mɑ:sk] Maske II
°**match with** ['mætʃ wɪð] zuordnen
°**match** [mætʃ] Spiel *(z.B. Fußball)*
maths [mæθs] Mathematik I
May [meɪ] Mai I
maybe ['meɪbi:] vielleicht II
°**mayonnaise** [meɪə'neɪz] Mayonnaise
me [mi] mir; mich I **It's me.** Ich bin's. I
meal [mi:l] Mahlzeit, Essen III 4 (71)
mean [mi:n]:
1. geizig II
2. gemein, fies I
mean [mi:n], **meant, meant** meinen, sagen wollen III 3 (54)
°**meaning** ['mi:nɪŋ] Bedeutung
meant [ment] *siehe* **mean**
meat [mi:t] Fleisch II
mechanic [mɪ'kænɪk] Mechaniker/in III 4 (80)
°**mediation** [mi:di'eɪʃn] Vermittlung, Sprachmittlung
meet [mi:t], **met, met** kennenlernen; (sich) treffen I
men [men] *Plural von* **man** I
menu ['menju:] Speisekarte I
message ['mesɪdʒ]:
1. Botschaft, Aussage III 3 (59)
2. Nachricht, Mitteilung III 2 (33)
take a message etwas ausrichten III 2 (33)
messy ['mesi] unordentlich I
met [met] *siehe* **meet**
metre ['mi:tə] Meter II
°**mice** [maɪs] *Plural von* **mouse**
middle ['mɪdl] Mitte I **in the middle** in der Mitte I
mile [maɪl] Meile *(ca. 1,6 km)* II
milk [mɪlk] Milch II
milkshake ['mɪlkʃeɪk] Milchshake II
million ['mɪljən] Million III 1 (15)
like a million dollars fantastisch III 1 (15)
mine [maɪn] meine, meiner, meins III 4 (74)
minute ['mɪnɪt] Minute I
mirror ['mɪrə] Spiegel III 4 (80)
miss [mɪs] vermissen I
Miss Borowski [mɪs] Frau Borowski I
Miss [mɪs] *Anrede für Lehrerin in GB* III 3 (52)
missing ['mɪsɪŋ] vermisst II
°**mistake** [mɪ'steɪk] Fehler
°**mobile** ['məʊbaɪl] mobil
mobile (phone) [məʊbaɪl 'fəʊn] Handy I
model ['mɒdl] Modell **model car** [mɒdl 'kɑ:] Modellauto II
modern ['mɒdn] modern III 4 (69)
Monday ['mʌndeɪ], ['mʌndi] Montag I
money ['mʌni] Geld I **make money** Geld verdienen III 3 (51)
monitor ['mɒnɪtə] Monitor III 2 (34)
monkey ['mʌŋki] Affe I
monster ['mɒnstə] Monster III 4 (69)
month [mʌnθ] Monat III 4 (70)
more [mɔ:]:
1. mehr, weitere II
more and more immer mehr III 3 (51)
2. **more popular** beliebter, populärer II
morning ['mɔ:nɪŋ] Morgen I
Good morning. Guten Morgen. I
most [məʊst]:
1. **the most money** das meiste Geld, am meisten Geld III 3 (53)
°**most students** die meisten Schüler/innen

2. **most popular** der/die/das beliebteste/populärste, am beliebtesten/populärsten II
mother ['mʌðə] Mutter III 2 (35/157)
°**motto** ['mɒtəʊ] Motto
mountain ['maʊntən] Berg II
°**mountain biker** ['maʊntən baɪkə] Mountainbiker/in
°**mountain biking** ['maʊntən baɪkɪŋ] *(das)* Mountainbikefahren
°**mouse,** *(pl)* **mice** [maʊs], [maɪs] Maus
mouth [maʊθ] Mund; *(Tier)* Schnauze III 2 (34)
move (to) [muːv] (um)ziehen (nach) III 2 (37) **move house** umziehen *(an einen neuen Wohnort)* III 2 (40)
Mr Smith ['mɪstə] Herr Smith I
Mrs Smith ['mɪsɪz] Frau Smith I
Ms Lee [mɪz] Frau Lee I
much [mʌtʃ] viel II **miss/like/love sb. so much** jn. so sehr vermissen/mögen/lieben II **Thanks very much.** Vielen Dank. II
mud [mʌd] Matsch, Schlamm II
°**muddy** ['mʌdi] matschig
muffin ['mʌfɪn] Muffin *(kleiner runder Kuchen)* II
mum [mʌm] Mama, Mutti I
museum [mju'ziːəm] Museum III 1 (14)
music ['mjuːzɪk] Musik I
musical ['mjuːzɪkl]:
1. Musik-, musikalisch III 4 (69)
°2. Musical
°**musician** [mju'zɪʃn] Musiker/in
must [mʌst] müssen I
mustn't do ['mʌsnt] nicht tun dürfen II
my [maɪ] mein/e I
myself [maɪ'self] ich/mich/mir selbst III 4 (71)
°**mystery** ['mɪstri] Geheimnis

N

name [neɪm] Name I **What's your name?** Wie heißt du? I
narrow ['nærəʊ] eng, schmal III 4 (75)
national ['næʃnəl] national II
national park [næʃnəl 'pɑːk] Nationalpark *(staatliches Naturschutzgebiet)* II
natural ['nætʃrəl] natürlich, Natur- III 1 (14)
natural history [nætʃrəl 'hɪstri] Naturkunde III 1 (14)
near [nɪə] in der Nähe von, nahe (bei) II
need [niːd] brauchen I
negative ['negətɪv] negativ III 3 (54)
neighbour ['neɪbə] Nachbar/in II
neighbourhood ['neɪbəhʊd] Nachbarschaft, Viertel, Gegend II
nervous ['nɜːvəs] nervös, aufgeregt I
°**net** [net] Netz *(Sport)*
network ['netwɜːk] Netz; Wortnetz I
never ['nevə] nie, niemals I
new [njuː] neu I
news [njuːz] Nachrichten I
newsletter ['njuːzletə] Mitteilungsblatt, Informationsblatt II
newspaper ['njuːzpeɪpə] (Tages-) Zeitung II
next [nekst]:
1. als Nächstes III 1 (15)
2. nächste(r, s) I
next to ['nekst tə] neben I
nice [naɪs] nett, schön I **Nice to be together again.** Schön, wieder zusammenzusein. II
night [naɪt] Nacht I **at night** nachts, in der Nacht I
nine [naɪn] neun I
nineties ['naɪntiz]: **the 90s** die Neunzigerjahre II
no [nəʊ] kein/e I
no [nəʊ] nein I
nobody ['nəʊbədi] niemand II
noise [nɔɪz] Geräusch; Lärm I
noisy ['nɔɪzi] laut, voller Lärm I
normal ['nɔːml] normal I
north [nɔːθ] Norden; nördlich; Nord- II **north-east** Nordosten, nordöstlich II **north-west** Nordwesten, nordwestlich II
nose [nəʊz] Nase III 2 (34)
not [nɒt] nicht; kein/e I
°**note** [nəʊt] notieren
°**notepad** ['nəʊtpæd] Notizblock
°**notes** [nəʊts] Notizen **take notes** (sich) Notizen machen
°**note-taking** ['nəʊt teɪkɪŋ] sich Notizen machen
nothing ['nʌθɪŋ] nichts I
°**notice** ['nəʊtɪs] Anschlag, Bekanntmachung *(an einem Schwarzen Brett)*
November [nəʊ'vembə] November I
now [naʊ] nun, jetzt I **right now** gerade jetzt, genau jetzt III 2 (33)
°**nowhere** ['nəʊweə] nirgendwo(hin)
number ['nʌmbə]:
1. Anzahl III 4 (72)
2. Nummer I

O

o'clock [ə'klɒk]: **at one o'clock** um 1 Uhr / um 13 Uhr I
October [ɒk'təʊbə] Oktober I
of [ɒv], [əv] von I **the last day of the holidays** der letzte Tag der Ferien I
of course [əv 'kɔːs] natürlich, selbstverständlich I
°**offer** ['ɒfə] anbieten
office ['ɒfɪs] Büro III 2 (34)
°**off-road** ['ɒf rəʊd] abseits der Straße
often ['ɒfn], ['ɒftən] oft I
oh [əʊ] Null *(im gesprochenen Englisch)* I
OK [əʊ'keɪ]: **I'm OK.** Es geht mir gut. I
old [əʊld] alt I
Olympic [ə'lɪmpɪk] olympisch III 3 (57) **Olympic Games** Olympische Spiele III 3 (57) °**the Olympics** die olympischen Spiele
on [ɒn] auf I **on Monday** am Montag I **on my birthday** an meinem Geburtstag I **on the bus** im Bus I **on TV** im Fernsehen III 3 (53) °**work on sth.** an etwas arbeiten
once [wʌns] einmal III 2 (40)
one [wʌn] eins I
online [ɒn'laɪn] online, Online- II
only ['əʊnli]:
1. nur, bloß I
2. **the only student** der einzige Schüler / die einzige Schülerin I
°**onto** ['ɒntu] auf (... hinauf)
open ['əʊpən]:
1. öffnen, aufmachen II
2. sich öffnen, aufgehen III 1 (9)
3. offen, geöffnet II
opinion [ə'pɪnjən] Meinung III 3 (57) **in my opinion** meiner Meinung nach III 3 (57)
°**option** ['ɒpʃn] Wahl(möglichkeit), Option
or [ɔː] oder I
orange ['ɒrɪndʒ]:
1. Orange I
2. orange(farben) I
°**order** ['ɔːdə] Reihenfolge
°**organic eggs** [ɔː'gænɪk] **Bio-Eier**
°**organised** ['ɔːgənaɪzd] organisiert
other ['ʌðə] andere(r, s) I
our ['aʊə], [ɑː] unser/e I
ourselves [aʊə'selvz] wir/uns selbst III 4 (71)

out [aʊt] hinaus, heraus, raus II **go out** ausgehen; hinausgehen II
°**outdoor sport** ['aʊtdɔː] Sport für draußen / der draußen stattfindet
outside [aʊt'saɪd] draußen; nach draußen I
°**over 16** ['əʊvə] über 16
over there [əʊvə 'ðeə] da drüben; da hinüber III 4 (75)
own [əʊn]: **its own flag** seine eigene Fahne III 4 (69)
°**owner** ['əʊnə] Besitzer/in

P

p [piː]: **50p** 50 Pence I
pack [pæk] packen, einpacken II
°**packed lunch** [pækt 'lʌntʃ] Lunchpaket
packet (of) ['pækɪt] Packung, Päckchen, Schachtel III 3 (50)
page (= p.) [peɪdʒ] (Buch-, Heft-) Seite I
paid [peɪd] *siehe* **pay**
pain [peɪn]: **What a pain!** *(infml)* So ein Mist! / Es nervt! III 2 (30)
°**painting** ['peɪntɪŋ] Gemälde, *(gemaltes)* Bild
°**pair** [peə] Paar
palace ['pæləs] Palast III 1 (8)
paper ['peɪpə] Zeitung II **do a paper round** Zeitungen austragen II
°**paragraph** ['pærəgrɑːf] (Text-) Abschnitt
parents ['peərənts] Eltern I
park [pɑːk] Park I
park (a car) [pɑːk] parken III 2 (35)
parliament ['pɑːləmənt] Parlament III 4 (69)
part [pɑːt] Teil II **take part in sth.** an etwas teilnehmen, bei etwas mitmachen III 3 (52)
partner ['pɑːtnə] Partner/in I **partner work** Partnerarbeit I
party ['pɑːti] Party I **have a party** eine Party feiern I
past the shop [pɑːst] am Geschäft vorbei II
pasty ['pæsti] Pastete *(mit Fleisch- oder Gemüsefüllung)* II
pay [peɪ], **paid, paid** (be)zahlen II
PE (physical education) [piː 'iː], [fɪzɪkl edʒu'keɪʃn] (Schul-)Sport I
pen [pen] Kugelschreiber, Stift; Füller I
pence [pens] Pence III 3 (53)
pencil ['pensl] Bleistift I
pencil case ['pensl keɪs] Federmäppchen I
pencil sharpener ['pensl ʃɑːpnə] Bleistiftanspitzer I
penny ['peni] Penny *(kleinste britische Münze)* II
people ['piːpl] Leute, Menschen I
per balloon [pɜː], [pə] pro Ballon III 3 (53)
perfect ['pɜːfɪkt] perfekt II
perhaps [pə'hæps] vielleicht II
person ['pɜːsn] Person III 2 (40)
pet [pet] Haustier I **pets corner** Streichelzoo I
phone [fəʊn]:
1. anrufen I
2. Telefon I
°**answer the phone** ans Telefon gehen
phone call ['fəʊn kɔːl] (Telefon-) Anruf II
phone number ['fəʊn nʌmbə] Telefonnummer I
photo ['fəʊtəʊ] Foto I **take a photo** ein Foto machen I
phrase [freɪz] Ausdruck, (Rede-) Wendung I
piano [pi'ænəʊ] Klavier I
pick [pɪk] (aus)wählen, aussuchen II **pick sb. up** jn. abholen III 1 (21)
pickpocket ['pɪkpɒkɪt] Taschendieb/in III 1 (20)
picnic ['pɪknɪk] Picknick II **have a picnic** ein Picknick machen II
picture ['pɪktʃə] Bild I
°**piece** [piːs] Stück
pig [pɪg] Schwein I
°**pilates** [pɪ'lɑːtiːz] Pilates *(Fitnessprogramm)*
pink [pɪŋk] rosa I
place [pleɪs] Ort, Platz, Stelle I
°**placemat** ['pleɪsmæt] Platzdeckchen
plan [plæn]:
1. Plan II
2. planen II
plane [pleɪn] Flugzeug III 1 (16)
°**plankton** ['plæŋktən] Plankton *(Kleinstlebewesen im Wasser)*
plant [plɑːnt] Pflanze III 3 (53)
plastic ['plæstɪk] Plastik, Kunststoff II **plastic bag** Plastiktüte II
platform ['plætfɔːm] Bahnsteig II
play [pleɪ]:
1. spielen I
playing football Fußballspielen I
playing games Spiele spielen I
2. Theaterstück II
°**player** ['pleɪə] Spieler/in
please [pliːz] bitte I
pm [piː'em]: **5 pm** 5 Uhr nachmittags/abends / 17 Uhr I
pocket ['pɒkɪt] Tasche *(an Kleidungsstücken)* II
pocket money ['pɒkɪt mʌni] Taschengeld II
poem ['pəʊɪm] Gedicht I
°**poet** ['pəʊɪt] Dichter/in
°**point** [pɔɪnt] Punkt
police *(pl)* [pə'liːs] Polizei III 1 (15)
police officer [pə'liːs ɒfɪsə] Polizeibeamter/-beamtin III 2 (32)
pony ['pəʊni] Pony I
°**pony-trekking** ['pəʊni trekɪŋ] Wanderreiten
poor [pʊə] arm II **poor Mrs Trent** (die) arme Mrs Trent II **Poor you!** Du Arme/r! II
°**pop (music)** ['pɒp mjuːzɪk] Pop(musik)
popular ['pɒpjələ] beliebt, populär II
possible ['pɒsəbl] möglich III 3 (51)
post [pəʊst] Post *(Briefe etc.)* III 1 (17)
post office ['pəʊst ɒfɪs] Post(amt) II
postcard ['pəʊstkɑːd] Postkarte III 1 (17)
poster ['pəʊstə] Poster I
postman, *(pl)* **postmen** ['pəʊstmən] Briefträger III 1 (17)
postwoman, *(pl)* **postwomen** ['pəʊstwʊmən], ['pəʊstwɪmɪn] Briefträgerin III 1 (17)
°**pot** [pɒt] Topf
potato, *(pl)* **potatoes** [pə'teɪtəʊ] Kartoffel II
pound (£) [paʊnd] Pfund *(britische Währung)* I
°**practice** ['præktɪs] Übung; Training
practise ['præktɪs] üben I
prefer sth. to sth. [prɪ'fɜː] etwas lieber mögen als etwas, etwas einer Sache vorziehen III 3 (57)
°**prepare (for)** [prɪ'peə] vorbereiten; sich vorbereiten (auf)
present ['preznt]:
1. Geschenk I
°2. präsentieren, vorstellen
°**presentation** [prezn'teɪʃn] Referat, Präsentation
president ['prezɪdənt] Präsident/in III 1 (8)
price [praɪs] (Kauf-)Preis I
pride [praɪd] Stolz III 4 (77)
prince [prɪns] Prinz I
principal ['prɪnsəpl] Schulleiter/in I
prize [praɪz] Preis *(Gewinn)* I

problem ['prɒbləm] Problem I
°**profile** ['prəʊfaɪl] Profil; Beschreibung, Portrait
profit ['prɒfɪt] Gewinn, Profit III 3 (53)
programme ['prəʊgræm] (Fernseh-)Sendung I
proud (of) [praʊd] stolz (auf) I
°**provide** [prə'vaɪd] (an)bieten, zur Verfügung stellen
pub [pʌb] Kneipe III 2 (29)
pullover ['pʊləʊvə] Pullover I
put [pʊt], **put**, **put** *(etwas wohin)* tun, legen, stellen II **He puts it with the other things.** Er legt sie zu den anderen Dingen. II
put on trousers eine Hose anziehen II

Q

°**quad bike** ['kwɒd baɪk] Quad *(vierrädriges Motorrad)*
°**quad biking** ['kwɒd baɪkɪŋ] Quad fahren
queen [kwi:n] Königin III 1 (8)
question ['kwestʃən] Frage I
questionnaire [kwestʃə'neə] Fragebogen III 2 (40)
quick [kwɪk] schnell II
quiet ['kwaɪət] ruhig, still, leise III 2 (35)
quiz [kwɪz] Quiz I

R

rabbit ['ræbɪt] Kaninchen I
°**radio** ['reɪdiəʊ] Radio
°**rafting** ['rɑ:ftɪŋ]: **(white-water) rafting** Rafting, Wildwasserfahren
rain [reɪn]:
1. Regen II
2. regnen II
rain jacket ['reɪn dʒækɪt] Regenjacke II
rain trousers *(pl)* ['reɪn traʊzəz] Regenhose II
rainy ['reɪni] regnerisch II
ran [ræn] *siehe* **run**
rang [ræŋ] *siehe* **ring**
ranger ['reɪndʒə] *Aufseher/in in einem Nationalpark* II
rap [ræp]:
1. Rap I
2. rappen I
rat [ræt] Ratte I
°**rather** ['rɑ:ðə]: **I'd rather be ...** ich wäre lieber ...
read [ri:d], **read**, **read** lesen I
reading *(das)* Lesen I
read [red] *siehe* **read**
reader ['ri:də] Leser/in III 1 (17)
ready ['redi] bereit, fertig III 3 (59)
Get ready. Steady. Go! Auf die Plätze, fertig, los! III 3 (59)
real [rɪəl] echt, wirklich I
reality [ri'æləti] Realität, Wirklichkeit II
really nice ['rɪəli] wirklich nett I
reason ['ri:zn] Grund, Begründung III 3 (57) **for lots of reasons** aus vielen Gründen III 3 (57)
recipe ['resəpi] (Koch-)Rezept II
red [red] rot I
region ['ri:dʒən] Region III 4 (78)
remember [rɪ'membə] daran denken, nicht vergessen; sich erinnern an I
°**repair** [rɪ'peə] Reparatur
°**repeat** [rɪ'pi:t] wiederholen
°**report** [rɪ'pɔ:t] Bericht
reporter [rɪ'pɔ:tə] Reporter/in III 1 (10)
represent [reprɪ'zent] repräsentieren, vertreten III 3 (55)
reservation [rezə'veɪʃn] Reservierung III 4 (73)
°**respect** [rɪ'spekt] respektieren
°**rest** [rest] Rest
restaurant ['restrɒnt] Restaurant I
°**revision** [rɪ'vɪʒn] Wiederholung *(von Lernstoff)*
reward [rɪ'wɔ:d] Belohnung II
°**rewrite** [ri:'raɪt] noch einmal schreiben, neu schreiben
°**rhyme** [raɪm] Reim
°**rice** [raɪs] Reis
ridden ['rɪdn] *siehe* **ride**
°**ride** [raɪd] Fahrt
ride [raɪd], **rode**, **ridden**:
1. reiten I
ride a pony auf einem Pony/ein Pony reiten I **riding** *(das)* Reiten I
2. fahren I
ride a bike Rad fahren I
right [raɪt]:
1. richtig I
be right Recht haben III 1 (18)
that's right das stimmt, das ist richtig I
2. rechts I
on the right rechts, auf der rechten Seite I
3. **right now** gerade jetzt, genau jetzt III 2 (33)
ring [rɪŋ], **rang**, **rung** läuten, klingeln II
ringtone ['rɪŋtəʊn] Klingelton *(Handy)* III 1 (19)
river ['rɪvə] Fluss II
road [rəʊd] Straße *(Landstraße zwischen Orten / Straße in Orten)* I
rock (music) ['rɒk mju:zɪk] Rock(musik) I
rode [rəʊd] *siehe* **ride**
°**role** [rəʊl] Rolle (Theater, Rollenspiel)
role model ['rəʊl mɒdl] Vorbild III 3 (57)
room [ru:m] Raum, Zimmer I
°**route** [ru:t] Route, Weg
°**royal** ['rɔɪəl] königlich
rubber ['rʌbə] Radiergummi I
rubbish ['rʌbɪʃ]:
1. Müll, Abfall II
2. Unsinn, dummes Zeug III 1 (18)
rubbish bin ['rʌbɪʃ bɪn] Mülleimer II
rucksack ['rʌksæk] Rucksack II
rugby ['rʌgbi] Rugby *(Ballsportart)* II
ruins *(oft auch pl:* ruins*)* ['ru:ɪn] Ruine III 4 (75)
rule [ru:l] Regel, Vorschrift II
ruler ['ru:lə] Lineal I
run [rʌn], **ran**, **run** rennen II
runner ['rʌnə] Läufer/in III 1 (17)

S

sad [sæd] traurig II
safe [seɪf] sicher *(gefahrlos)*; in Sicherheit III 1 (20)
said [sed] *siehe* **say**
salad ['sæləd] Salat *(als Gericht oder Beilage)* I
sale [seɪl] Verkauf; Schlussverkauf I
salesperson, (pl) salespeople ['seɪlzpɜ:sn], ['seɪlzpi:pl] Verkäufer/in III 3 (52)
salt [sɔ:lt] Salz III 4 (79)
same [seɪm]: **the same** dasselbe / das gleiche; gleich II
sandwich ['sænwɪtʃ] Sandwich I
sang [sæŋ] *siehe* **sing**
sat [sæt] *siehe* **sit**
Saturday ['sætədeɪ], ['sætədi] Samstag I
sausage ['sɒsɪdʒ] Wurst, Würstchen II
save [seɪv] retten III 2 (32)
saw [sɔ:] *siehe* **see**
say [seɪ], **said**, **said** sagen I
scared [skeəd]: **be scared (of)** Angst haben (vor) II
scary ['skeəri] unheimlich, gruselig II

scene [siːn]:
1. Szene I
°2. Schauplatz

school [skuːl] Schule I
science ['saɪəns] Naturwissenschaft I
°**scientist** ['saɪəntɪst] (Natur-)Wissenschaftler/in
scone [skɒn] *Milchbrötchen, leicht süß, oft mit Rosinen* I
°**Scot** [skɒt] Schotte/Schottin
Scotland ['skɒtlənd] Schottland III 4 (68)
Scottish ['skɒtɪʃ] schottisch, aus Schottland III 1 (10)
scream [skriːm] schreien II
sea [siː] Meer II
°**seafaring** ['siːfeərɪŋ] Seefahrer-
seaside ['siːsaɪd]: **at the seaside** am Meer II
second ['sekənd] zweite(r, s) I
second-hand shop [sekənd 'hænd] Second-Hand-Laden II
security [sɪ'kjʊərəti] Sicherheit III 1 (14)
see [siː], **saw, seen** sehen I
See you. Bis dann. / Tschüs. I
seen [siːn] *siehe* **see**
°**self-catering** [self 'keɪtərɪŋ] Selbstversorgung, für Selbstversorger
sell [sel], **sold, sold** verkaufen III 3 (50)
send [send] **sent, sent** schicken, senden I
sent [sent] *siehe* **send**
sentence ['sentəns] Satz I
September [sep'tembə] September I
serious ['sɪəriəs] ernst(haft) II 3 (52)
seriously im Ernst III 3 (52)
°**serve** [sɜːv] servieren
°**service** ['sɜːvɪs] Service; *(bei Fahrzeugen etc.)* Wartung, Inspektion
°**setting** ['setɪŋ] Umgebung; Schauplatz
seven ['sevn] sieben I
°**several** ['sevrəl] mehrere, einige
°**share** [ʃeə] teilen; austauschen
sharpener ['ʃɑːpnə] Anspitzer I
she [ʃiː] sie *(weibliche Person)* I
she's (= she is) sie ist I
sheep, *(pl)* **sheep** [ʃiːp] Schaf I
°**shine** [ʃaɪn] leuchten, glänzen, strahlen
ship [ʃɪp] Schiff III 3 (48)
°**shipping** ['ʃɪpɪŋ] Schifffahrt(s-)
shirt [ʃɜːt] Hemd I
°**shock** [ʃɒk] Schock, Schreck
°**shocked** [ʃɒkt] schockiert

shoe [ʃuː] Schuh I
shop [ʃɒp]:
1. (ein)kaufen III 4 (70)
2. Geschäft, Laden I

°**shopper** ['ʃɒpə] Käufer/in
shopping ['ʃɒpɪŋ]: **go shopping** einkaufen gehen I
shopping centre ['ʃɒpɪŋ sentə] Einkaufszentrum III 1 (10)
short [ʃɔːt] kurz; klein *(Person)* II
should [ʃʊd]: **you should** du solltest II
shoulder ['ʃəʊldə] Schulter I
shout [ʃaʊt] rufen II
show [ʃəʊ]:
1. Show, Vorführung, Aufführung I
2. zeigen II

shower ['ʃaʊə] Dusche; Schauer III 4 (80)
Shut up! [ʃʌt 'ʌp] Halt den Mund! I
°**sightseeing** ['saɪtsiːɪŋ] Besichtigungen *(von Sehenswürdigkeiten)*
sign [saɪn] Schild; Zeichen I
silly ['sɪli] albern, dumm, blöd I
sincerely [sɪn'sɪəli]: **Yours sincerely** Mit freundlichen Grüßen *(Briefschluss)* III 3 (51)
sing [sɪŋ], **sang, sung** singen I
singer ['sɪŋə] Sänger/in I
single room [sɪŋgl 'ruːm] Einzelzimmer III 4 (72)
sister ['sɪstə] Schwester I
sit [sɪt], **sat, sat** sitzen; sich (hin) setzen II **sit down** sich (hin) setzen III 3 (54)
°**site** [saɪt]: **on site** vor Ort, an Ort und Stelle
six [sɪks] sechs I
skateboard ['skeɪtbɔːd] Skateboard II
skateboarding ['skeɪtbɔːdɪŋ] *(das)* Skateboardfahren I
skiing [skiːɪŋ] *(das)* Skilaufen II
°**skill** [skɪl] Fähigkeit, Fertigkeit; Lern- und Arbeitstechnik **skills file** Anhang mit Lern- und Arbeitstechniken
skim a text [skɪm] einen Text überfliegen *(um den Inhalt grob zu erfassen)* III 4 (78)
°**skipping** ['skɪpɪŋ] *(das)* Seilspringen
skirt [skɜːt] Rock II
skive [skaɪv] *(infml)* schwänzen *(Schule)* II
skiver ['skaɪvə] (Schul-)Schwänzer/in III 1 (17)
sky [skaɪ] Himmel III 4 (69)
slave [sleɪv] Sklave, Sklavin III 3 (48)
°**slavery** ['sleɪvəri] Sklaverei

sleep [sliːp] Schlaf II
sleep [sliːp], **slept, slept** schlafen II °**sleep late** lange schlafen
sleeping bag ['sliːpɪŋ bæg] Schlafsack II
sleepover ['sliːpəʊvə] Schlafparty I
°**sleepwalker** ['sliːpwɔːkə] Schlafwandler/in
sleepy ['sliːpi] verschlafen, müde III 1 (17)
slept [slept] *siehe* **sleep**
°**slice** [slaɪs] Scheibe *(z.B. Brot)*; Stück *(z.B. Kuchen)*
slow [sləʊ] langsam II
small [smɔːl] klein I
°**smell** [smel] riechen, duften
smile [smaɪl] lächeln; *(das)* Lächeln III 2 (34)
°**smoothie** ['smuːði] cremiges Fruchtgetränk
snack [snæk] Snack, kleine Mahlzeit I
snake [sneɪk] Schlange I
so [səʊ]:
1. also II
2. so II

so much so sehr II
soap [səʊp] Seife; *(infml auch:)* Seifenoper II
sock [sɒk] Socke III 4 (73)
sofa ['səʊfə] Sofa II
°**soft drink** ['sɒft drɪŋk] alkoholfreies Getränk
sold [səʊld] *siehe* **sell**
some [sʌm], [səm] einige, ein paar; etwas I
somebody ['sʌmbədi] jemand II
someone ['sʌmwʌn] jemand II
something ['sʌmθɪŋ] etwas I
sometimes ['sʌmtaɪmz] manchmal I
son [sʌn] Sohn III 3 (51)
song [sɒŋ] Lied I
soon [suːn] bald I
sore [sɔː] schmerzhaft II **a sore throat** Halsschmerzen II **Her leg was sore.** Ihr Bein tat weh. II
sorry ['sɒri]: **Sorry. / I'm sorry.** Tut mir leid. / Entschuldigung. I **be/feel sorry for sb.** Mitleid mit jm. haben II
sort [sɔːt]: **What sort of ...?** Welche Art/Sorte (von) ...? III 3 (51)
sound [saʊnd] klingen, sich anhören I **Sounds fun.** Hört sich gut an. / Klingt, als ob es Spaß macht. I
°**sound file** ['saʊnd faɪl] Tondatei
soup [suːp] Suppe I
south [saʊθ] Süden; südlich; Süd- II
south-east Südosten, südöstlich II

south-west Südwesten, südwestlich II
space [speɪs] Platz II
Spain [speɪn] Spanien II
speak [spiːk], **spoke, spoken** sprechen I **speak to** sprechen mit I **Who's speaking?** Wer spricht (da)? *(am Telefon)* III 2 (33)
special ['speʃl] besondere(r, s) II
°**spectacular** [spek'tækjələ] spektakulär
°**speech bubble** ['spiːtʃ bʌbl] Sprechblase
spell [spel] buchstabieren I
spend money/time (on) [spend], **spent, spent** Geld ausgeben (für); Zeit verbringen (mit) III 1 (18)
spent [spent] *siehe* **spend**
°**spine** [spaɪn] Wirbelsäule, Rückgrat
spoke [spəʊk] *siehe* **speak**
spoken ['spəʊkən] *siehe* **speak**
sport [spɔːt] Sport; Sportart I
sports shop Sportgeschäft I
°**sportswoman,** *(pl)* **sportswomen** ['spɔːtswʊmən], ['spɔːtswɪmɪn] Sportlerin
sporty ['spɔːti] sportlich II
spot [spɒt]:
1. Tupfen *(Leopard)*; Pickel II
°2. Stelle, Fleck
stadium ['steɪdiəm] Stadion II
°**stall** [stɔːl] (Markt-)Stand, Bude
stand [stænd], **stood, stood** stehen II **stand up** aufstehen II
star [stɑː] Star III 1 (8)
start [stɑːt] anfangen I
°**statement** ['steɪtmənt] Aussage
station ['steɪʃn] Bahnhof II
°**statue** ['stætʃuː] Statue
stay [steɪ] bleiben I
steady ['stedi]: **Get ready. Steady. Go!** Auf die Plätze, fertig, los! III 3 (59)
°**steam** [stiːm] Dampf
°**step** [step] Schritt; Stufe
stepbrother ['stepbrʌðə] Stiefbruder I
stepdad ['stepdæd] Stiefvater I
stepmum ['stepmʌm] Stiefmutter I
stepsister ['stepsɪstə] Stiefschwester I
still [stɪl] (immer) noch; trotzdem II
stood [stʊd] *siehe* **stand**
stop [stɒp] anhalten; stehen bleiben; aufhören (mit) II
°**store** [stɔː] Geschäft
story ['stɔːri] Geschichte I
straight [streɪt]: **Go straight on.** Geh geradeaus (weiter). II
street [striːt] Straße *(in Ortschaften)* I
street surfing ['striːt sɜːfɪŋ] Waveboarden II
strict [strɪkt] streng, strikt II
strong [strɒŋ] stark III 3 (57)
student ['stjuːdnt] Schüler/in; Student/in I
stuff [stʌf] *(infml)* Zeug, Kram II
°**stumble** [stʌmbl] stolpern
stupid ['stjuːpɪd] dumm, blöd; albern I
subway ['sʌbweɪ] Unterführung III 1 (20)
suck [sʌk]: **It sucks!** *(infml)* Es nervt / Es ist Mist! III 2 (30)
suddenly ['sʌdənli] plötzlich III 2 (34)
sugar ['ʃʊgə] Zucker III 4 (79)
°**summary** ['sʌməri] Zusammenfassung
summer ['sʌmə] Sommer I
sun [sʌn] Sonne III 1 (17)
Sunday ['sʌndeɪ], ['sʌndi] Sonntag I
sunglasses *(pl)* ['sʌnglɑːsɪz] Sonnenbrille II
sunny ['sʌni] sonnig II
supermarket ['suːpəmɑːkɪt] Supermarkt II
sure [ʃʊə] sicher I
surprise [sə'praɪz] Überraschung I
surprised [sə'praɪzd] überrascht II
°**swap** [swɒp] tauschen
°**sweat** [swet] Schweiß
sweets [swiːts] Bonbons, Süßigkeiten I
°**swim** [swɪm] schwimmen (durch)
swimming ['swɪmɪŋ]: **go swimming** schwimmen gehen I
swimming pool ['swɪmɪŋ puːl] Schwimmbad II

T

table ['teɪbl] Tisch I
table tennis ['teɪbl tenɪs] Tischtennis II
tae kwon do [taɪ kwɒn 'dəʊ] Taekwondo II
tag rugby ['tæg rʌgbi] Tag Rugby *(kontaktlose Rugby-Variante)* II
tail [teɪl] Schwanz II
take [teɪk], **took, taken** nehmen II **take a photo** ein Foto machen II **take part in sth.** an etwas teilnehmen, bei etwas mitmachen III 3 (52)
taken ['teɪkən] *siehe* **take**
°**talent** ['tælənt] Talent
talk about [tɔːk] sprechen über I
talk [tɔːk] Vortrag, Rede; Gespräch II **give a talk** einen Vortrag halten II **talk show** Talkshow II
talker ['tɔːkə] Redner/in III 1 (17)
tall [tɔːl] groß *(Person)*; hoch *(Gebäude)* II
task [tɑːsk] Aufgabe III 3 (56)
taught [tɔːt] *siehe* **teach**
taxi ['tæksi] Taxi III 1 (9)
tea [tiː] Tee I
teach [tiːtʃ], **taught, taught** unterrichten, lehren III 4 (71)
teacher ['tiːtʃə] Lehrer/in I
team [tiːm] Team, Mannschaft II
technology [tek'nɒlədʒi] Technik, Technologie I
teen [tiːn] Teenager II
teenage kids ['tiːneɪdʒ] Kinder im Teenageralter III 4 (72)
teenager ['tiːneɪdʒə] Teenager I
telephone ['telɪfəʊn] Telefon III 4 (72)
tell [tel], **told, told** erzählen, berichten II **tell about** erzählen von, berichten über II **tell sb. the way** jm. den Weg beschreiben II
temperature ['temprətʃə] Temperatur; Fieber II **I have a temperature.** Ich habe Fieber. II
ten [ten] zehn I
tennis ['tenɪs] Tennis II
tent [tent] Zelt II
term [tɜːm] Trimester III 3 (52)
terrible ['terəbl] schrecklich I
test [test] Test; Klassenarbeit II
text (message) ['tekst mesɪdʒ] SMS I
text [tekst] eine SMS schicken I
than [ðæn]: **It's cheaper than that.** So viel kostet das nicht. II **older than me** älter als ich II
thank you ['θæŋk juː] danke (schön) I
thanks [θæŋks] danke I
that [ðæt]:
1. das (da) I
Is that the Taylors? Sind da die Taylors? *(am Telefon)* III 2 (33)
2. der, die, das *(Relativpronomen)* III 4 (80)
a thing that we use ... ein Ding, das wir ... benutzen III 4 (80)
3. dass II
they think that ... sie denken, dass ... II
the [ðə] der, die, das I

theatre ['θɪətə] Theater I
their [ðeə] ihr/e *(Plural)* II
them [ðem], [ðəm] sie, ihnen *(Plural)* II
°**theme** [θi:m] Thema
themselves [ðəm'selvz] sie/sich selbst *(Plural)* III 4 (71)
then [ðen] dann I
there [ðeə] da, dort; dahin, dorthin I **there are ...** es sind ... / es gibt ... I **there's** es ist ... / es gibt ... I
these people [ði:z] diese Menschen (hier) II
they [ðeɪ] sie *(Plural)* I **they're (= they are)** sie sind I
thing [θɪŋ] Ding, Sache I
think [θɪŋk], **thought, thought** denken, meinen, glauben I **think of/about** halten von, denken über III 1 (10)
third [θɜ:d] dritte(r, s) I
this [ðɪs] diese(r, s) I **This is Rob Blake.** Hier spricht Rob Blake. *(am Telefon)* III 2 (33) **This is ...** Dies ist ... I **this morning/afternoon/evening** heute Morgen/Nachmittag/Abend II
those CDs [ðəʊz] die CDs dort, jene CDs II
thought [θɔ:t] *siehe* **think**
°**thousand** ['θaʊznd] tausend
three [θri:] drei I
threw [θru:] *siehe* **throw**
throat [θrəʊt] Hals II **a sore throat** Halsschmerzen II
through [θru:] durch I °**all through the match** das ganze Spiel hindurch
throw [θrəʊ], **threw, thrown** werfen III 4 (69)
thrown [θrəʊn] *siehe* **throw**
Thursday ['θɜ:zdeɪ], ['θɜ:zdi] Donnerstag I
ticket ['tɪkɪt] Eintrittskarte, Fahrkarte I
tidy ['taɪdi]:
1. aufräumen II
2. ordentlich II
tie [taɪ] Krawatte I
tiger ['taɪgə] Tiger I
time [taɪm]:
1. Zeit; Uhrzeit I
on time pünktlich II **What's the time?** Wie spät ist es? I
2. Mal II
next time nächstes Mal II
timetable ['taɪmteɪbl] Stundenplan I
°**tip** [tɪp] Tipp
tired ['taɪəd] müde I
to [tu], [tə] zu, nach, in I **to the country** aufs Land I **from Monday to Friday** von Montag bis Freitag I **go to dad's flat** in Papas Wohnung gehen I **Have you ever been to London?** Warst du schon mal in London? II **time to eat** Zeit zu essen I **write to** schreiben an I °**ideas what to do** Ideen, was man tun könnte
toast [təʊst] Toast(brot) II
today [tə'deɪ] heute I
together [tə'geðə] zusammen II
toilet ['tɔɪlət] Toilette I
toilet roll ['tɔɪlət rəʊl] Rolle Toilettenpapier II
told [təʊld] *siehe* **tell**
°**tomato,** *(pl)* **tomatoes** [tə'mɑ:təʊ] Tomate
tomorrow [tə'mɒrəʊ] morgen I
too [tu:] auch I
too small [tu:] zu klein I
took [tʊk] *siehe* **take**
top [tɒp]: **at the top (of)** oben, am oberen Ende (von); an der Spitze (von) II
°**torch** [tɔ:tʃ] Fackel
total ['təʊtl] Gesamtbetrag, Summe III 3 (53)
tour [tʊə] Tour; Rundfahrt III 1 (9) °**tour guide** Reiseleiter/in, Fremdenführer/in
tourist ['tʊərɪst] Tourist/in III 1 (9)
towel ['taʊəl] Handtuch III 4 (80)
tower ['taʊə] Turm III 1 (9)
town [taʊn] Stadt I **in town** in der Stadt I
toy [tɔɪ] Spielzeug II
toy animal [tɔɪ 'ænɪml] Kuscheltier II
track [træk] Pfad, (Feld-)Weg II
°**tractor** ['træktə] Traktor
°**tradition** [trə'dɪʃn] Tradition
°**traditional** [trə'dɪʃənl] traditionell
traffic lights *(pl)* ['træfɪk laɪts] Verkehrsampel II
°**trail** [treɪl] Weg, Pfad, Route
train [treɪn] Zug, Eisenbahn II
train station ['treɪn steɪʃn] Bahnhof II
trainer ['treɪnə] Sportschuh I
°**training** ['treɪnɪŋ] Training
trampoline ['træmpəli:n] Trampolin I
transport ['trænspɔ:t] Verkehrsmittel; Transport(wesen) III 1 (16)
travel ['trævl] reisen; fahren, sich fortbewegen III 1 (8)
°**travelcard** ['trævlkɑ:d] Ein- oder Mehrtagesfahrkarte *(London)*
travel-sick ['trævlsɪk] reisekrank III 1 (17)
tree [tri:] Baum I
trick [trɪk] Trick, Kunststück II
trip [trɪp] Ausflug, Reise II
trouble ['trʌbl] Ärger, Schwierigkeit(en) I
trousers *(pl)* ['traʊzəz] Hose II
true [tru:] wahr II
°**truth** [tru:θ] Wahrheit
try [traɪ] versuchen, (aus)probieren II
T-shirt ['ti:ʃɜ:t] T-Shirt I
Tube [tju:b]: **the Tube** die U-Bahn *(in London)* III 1 (8)
Tuesday ['tju:zdeɪ], ['tju:zdi] Dienstag I
°**tunnel** ['tʌnl] Tunnel
Turkey ['tɜ:ki] die Türkei II
°**Turkish** ['tɜ:kɪʃ] türkisch; Türkisch
turn right/left [tɜ:n] (nach) rechts/links abbiegen II
TV [ti:'vi:] Fernseher I
twelve [twelv] zwölf I
twice [twaɪs] zweimal III 2 (40)
twin room [twɪn 'ru:m] Zweibettzimmer III 4 (72)
two [tu:] zwei I

U

uncle ['ʌŋkl] Onkel III 2 (37)
uncool [ʌn'ku:l] uncool II
under ['ʌndə] unter I
underground ['ʌndəgraʊnd] U-Bahn III 1 (8)
underline [ʌndə'laɪn] unterstreichen III 3 (56) °**underlined** unterstrichen
understand [ʌndə'stænd], **understood, understood** verstehen II
understood [ʌndə'stʊd] *siehe* **understand**
unemployed [ʌnɪm'plɔɪd] arbeitslos III 4 (70)
°**unfair** [ʌn'feə] unfair
unfriendly [ʌn'frendli] unfreundlich II
unhappy [ʌn'hæpi] unglücklich I
unhealthy [ʌn'helθi] ungesund II
uniform ['ju:nɪfɔ:m] (Schul-)Uniform I
uninteresting [ʌn'ɪntrəstɪŋ] uninteressant II
°**unique** [ju'ni:k] einmalig
unit ['ju:nɪt] Unit I
unsure [ʌn'ʃʊə] unsicher II

until [ən'tɪl] bis *(zeitlich)* II **not (...) until they're 13** erst, wenn sie 13 sind II
°**untold** [ʌn'təʊld] (noch) nicht erzählt, unbekannt
up [ʌp] hinauf, hoch II
upstairs [ʌp'steəz] oben; nach oben I
°**up-to-the-minute** [ʌp tə ðə 'mɪnɪt] brandaktuell, allerneueste(r, s)
us [ʌs], [əs] uns I
USA [juː es 'eɪ]: **the USA** die USA (= die Vereinigten Staaten von Amerika) III 3 (53)
use [juːz] benutzen I °**they were used** sie wurden benutzt
useful ['juːsfl] nützlich III 3 (56)
usual ['juːʒʊəl] normal, üblich III 3 (54)
usually ['juːʒʊəli] meistens, normalerweise III 2 (37)

V

van [væn] Transporter, Lieferwagen III 2 (30)
°**variety (of)** [və'raɪəti] Auswahl (an)
°**various** ['veəriəs] (mehrere) verschiedene
vegetables, *infml auch* **veg** ['vedʒtəblz], [vedʒ] Gemüse I
°**verse** [vɜːs] Vers, Strophe *(Lied)*
°**version** ['vɜːʃn] Version
very ['veri] sehr I **Thanks very much.** Vielen Dank. II
°**viaduct** ['vaɪədʌkt] Viadukt *(Talbrücke)*
video ['vɪdiəʊ] Video II
video chat ['vɪdiəʊ tʃæt] Videochat, „Cammen" *(Internet-Telefongespräch mit Bildübertragung)* II
°**viewing** ['vjuːɪŋ] *(das)* Anschauen *(von DVDs, Filmen usw.)*
village ['vɪlɪdʒ] Dorf I
°**village hall** ['vɪlɪdʒ hɔːl] Gemeindesaal
violent ['vaɪələnt] gewalttätig; gewaltsam III 3 (57)
visit ['vɪzɪt]:
1. besuchen II
°**2.** zu Besuch kommen
visitor ['vɪzɪtə] Besucher/in, Gast I
°**voice** [vɔɪs] Stimme
volleyball ['vɒlibɔːl] Volleyball II
vote for sb. [vəʊt] für jn. stimmen II

W

wait (for) [weɪt] warten (auf) II **Wait for this.** *(infml)* Stell dir nur vor! / Du wirst es kaum glauben! II
waiter ['weɪtə] Kellner/in III 4 (80)
waitress ['weɪtrəs] Kellnerin III 4 (80)
wake [weɪk] wecken I
°**wake-up call** ['weɪk ʌp kɔːl] Weckruf
walk [wɔːk] (zu Fuß) gehen, wandern I
walker ['wɔːkə] Wanderer/Wanderin, Fußgänger/in III 1 (17)
wall [wɔːl] Wand; Mauer II
want [wɒnt] wollen I **want to buy** kaufen wollen I
wardrobe ['wɔːdrəʊb] Kleiderschrank I
warm [wɔːm] warm II
°**warning** ['wɔːnɪŋ] Warnung
was [wɒz], [wəz]: **he/she/it was** *Vergangenheitsform von* **be** I
°**wash** [wɒʃ] (sich) waschen
wash up [wɒʃ 'ʌp] abwaschen I
waste [weɪst]:
1. verschwenden III 1 (18/153)
2. Verschwendung III 1 (18)
watch [wɒtʃ] *sich etwas* anschauen; beobachten I **watching TV** Fernsehen I
water ['wɔːtə] Wasser I
°**waterfall** ['wɔːtəfɔːl] Wasserfall
wave [weɪv] winken III 4 (74)
way [weɪ] Weg II **ask sb. the way** jn. nach dem Weg fragen II **tell sb. the way** jm. den Weg beschreiben II °**a long way (from)** weit entfernt (von)
we [wiː] wir I **we're (= we are)** wir sind I
°**weak** [wiːk] schwach
wear [weə], **wore, worn** tragen, anhaben *(Kleidung)* II
weather ['weðə] Wetter II
website ['websaɪt] Website III 4 (72)
Wednesday ['wenzdeɪ], ['wenzdi] Mittwoch I
°**wee** [wiː] klein *(schottisches Englisch)*
week [wiːk] Woche I
weekday ['wiːkdeɪ] Werktag, Wochentag I
weekend [wiːk'end] Wochenende I
welcome ['welkʌm]:
1. Welcome to Plymouth. Willkommen in Plymouth! I
2. You're welcome. Bitte, gern geschehen. / Nichts zu danken. I
well [wel] gut (Adv.) II **Well done.** Gut gemacht! I **do well** es gut machen; gut abschneiden, erfolgreich sein III 3 (52) **she can't walk well** sie kann nicht gut gehen/laufen II
°**well-known** [wel 'nəʊn] bekannt
went [went] *siehe* **go**
were [wɜː], [wə]: **we/you/they were** *Vergangenheitsform von* **be** I
west [west] Westen; westlich; West- II
wet [wet] nass I
what [wɒt]:
1. was I
2. welche(r, s) I
What about you? Und du? / Was ist mit dir? I **What do you call ...?** Wie nennt man ...? III 4 (80) **What's the time?** Wie spät ist es? I **What's your name?** Wie heißt du? I
wheelchair ['wiːltʃeə] Rollstuhl I
when [wen]:
1. wann I
When's (= when is) your birthday? Wann hast du Geburtstag? I
2. wenn I
3. als II
where [weə] wo(hin) I
which [wɪtʃ]:
1. which lake? welcher See? III 4 (69)
°**2. a magazine which ...** eine Zeitschrift, die ...
whistle ['wɪsl] (Triller-)Pfeife II
white [waɪt] weiß I
who [huː]:
1. wer I
Who are you? Wer bist du? / Wer seid ihr? I
2. wem?; wen? I
Who did Adam meet? Wen hat Adam getroffen? / Wen traf Adam? II
3. der, die *(Relativpronomen, Person)* III 2 (35)
people who leave rubbish Menschen, die Müll zurücklassen III 2 (35)
°**whole** [həʊl] ganze(r, s)
why [waɪ] warum I
Wi-fi ['waɪ faɪ] WLAN, kabellose Datenübertragung III 4 (72)
wild [waɪld] wild; wild lebend I
will [wɪl]: **50p will do** 50 Pence reichen (auch) II **the weather will be good** das Wetter wird gut sein II
°**win** [wɪn] Gewinn
win [wɪn], **won, won** gewinnen II
wind [wɪnd] Wind II
window ['wɪndəʊ] Fenster III 1 (9)

windy ['wɪndi] windig II
winner ['wɪnə] Gewinner/in III 1 (17)
winter ['wɪntə] Winter II
wish [wɪʃ]: **Best wishes** Viele Grüße, … *(Briefschluss)* I
with [wɪð] mit I **with Ellie** bei Ellie I **He puts it with the other things.** Er legt sie zu den anderen Dingen. II
without [wɪ'ðaʊt] ohne II
woman, *(pl)* **women** ['wʊmən], ['wɪmɪn] Frau I
won [wʌn] *siehe* **win**
won't [wəʊnt]: **it won't rain** es wird nicht regnen II
wood [wʊd] Wald; Holz III 2 (29)
word [wɜːd] Wort I °**in a word** mit einem Wort °**in other words** mit anderen Worten
°**wordbank** ['wɜːdbæŋk] Wortbank *(Sammlung von Wörtern zu einem Thema)*
wore [wɔː] *siehe* **wear**
work [wɜːk]:
1. Arbeit I
at work bei der Arbeit, am Arbeitsplatz I
2. arbeiten I
°**work on sth.** an etwas arbeiten
3. funktionieren I
worker ['wɜːkə] Arbeiter/in; Arbeitskraft III 1 (17)
world [wɜːld] Welt III 1 (17)
worried ['wʌrid]: **be worried (about)** beunruhigt sein, besorgt sein (wegen) II
worry (about) ['wʌri] sich Sorgen machen (wegen, um) III 1 (21)
would [wʊd]: **I'd love to come. (= I would love to come.)** Ich komme sehr gern. / Ich würde sehr gern kommen. I **I'd like (= I would like)** ich hätte gern, ich möchte (…) haben I **I'd like to (= I would like to) join** ich würde / möchte gern mitmachen II
write [raɪt], **wrote, written** schreiben I **write down** aufschreiben III 2 (35)
writer ['raɪtə] Autor/in, Verfasser/in III 1 (17)
written ['rɪtn] *siehe* **write**
wrong [rɒŋ] falsch I **be wrong** Unrecht haben III 1 (18) **that's wrong** das stimmt nicht, das ist falsch I **What's wrong with …?** Was stimmt nicht mit …? II
wrote [rəʊt] *siehe* **write**

Y

yeah [jeə] ja *(infml für „yes")* I
year [jɪə] Jahr(gang) II
yellow ['jeləʊ] gelb I
yes [jes] ja I
yesterday ['jestədeɪ] gestern II
yet [jet]: **not … yet** noch nicht III 2 (30)
yippee [jɪ'piː] hurra I
°**yoga** ['jəʊgə] Yoga
yogurt ['jɒgət] Joghurt II
you [juː]:
1. du; ihr; Sie I
you're (= you are) du bist, ihr seid, Sie sind I **Lucky you! / Poor you!** Du Glückliche/r! / Du Arme/r! II
2. dich; dir; euch; Sie; Ihnen I
3. man III 4 (80)
young [jʌŋ] jung II
your [jɔː] dein/e, euer/eure I
yours [jɔːz] deine, deiner, deins; eurer, eure, eures III 4 (75)
yourself [jɔː'self] du/dir/dich selbst III 4 (71) **Don't blame yourself.** Mach dir keine Vorwürfe. III 4 (71)
yourselves [jɔː'selvz] ihr/euch selbst; Sie/sich selbst III 4 (71)
°**youth** [juːθ] Jugend
°**youth club** ['juːθ klʌb] Jugendklub
yum! [jʌm] lecker! II

Z

zip wire ['zɪp waɪə] Seilrutsche I
zoo [zuː] Zoo I
°**zumba** ['zʊmbə] Zumba

English sounds

[iː]	green, he, sea
[ɑː]	ask, class, car, park
[ɔː]	or, ball, door, four, morning
[uː]	ruler, blue, too, two, you
[ɜː]	early, her, girl, work, T-shirt
[ɪ]	in, big, expensive
[e]	yes, bed, again, breakfast
[æ]	animal, apple, black, cat
[ʌ]	mum, bus, colour
[ɒ]	song, on, dog, what
[ʊ]	book, good, pullover
[ə]	again, today, a sister
[i]	happy, monkey
[eɪ]	name, eight, play, great
[aɪ]	I, time, right, my
[ɔɪ]	boy, toilet, noise
[əʊ]	old, no, road, yellow
[aʊ]	now, house
[eə]	where, pair, share, their
[ʊə]	tour
[ɪə]	here, dear
[b]	bike, table, verb
[p]	pen, paper, shop
[d]	day, window, good
[t]	ten, letter, at
[g]	go, again, bag
[k]	kitchen, car, back
[m]	man, remember, mum
[n]	no, one, ten
[ŋ]	wrong, young, uncle, thanks
[l]	like, old, small
[r]	ruler, friend, sorry
[w]	we, where, one
[j]	yes, you, uniform
[f]	family, after, laugh
[v]	very, seven, have
[s]	six, poster, yes
[z]	zoo, quiz, his, music, please
[ʃ]	she, station, English
[ʒ]	ususally, revision, garage
[tʃ]	child, teacher, watch
[dʒ]	job, German, project, orange
[θ]	thing, three, bathroom, both
[ð]	the, father, with
[h]	house, who, behind

Am besten kannst du dir die Aussprache der einzelnen Lautzeichen einprägen, wenn du dir zu jedem Zeichen ein einfaches Wort merkst – das [iː] ist der **green**-Laut, das [eɪ] ist der **name**-Laut usw.

Das **German – English dictionary** enthält den **Lernwortschatz** der Bände 1 und 2 von *Highlight*. Es kann dir eine erste Hilfe sein, wenn du vergessen hast, wie etwas auf Englisch heißt.

Wenn du wissen möchtest, wo das englische Wort zum ersten Mal in *Highlight* vorkommt, dann kannst du im **English – German dictionary** (S. 166–182) nachschlagen.

Es werden folgende **Abkürzungen** verwendet:

sb. = somebody sth. = something jn. = jemanden jm. = jemandem
pl = *plural* (Mehrzahl) *infml* = *informal* (umgangssprachlich)

A

abbiegen: (nach) rechts/links abbiegen turn right/left [tɜːn]
Abend evening ['iːvnɪŋ]
Abendessen dinner ['dɪnə]
Abenteuer adventure [əd'ventʃə]
aber but [bʌt]
abfahren leave [liːv]
Abfall rubbish ['rʌbɪʃ]
abholen: jn. abholen pick sb. up [pɪk 'ʌp]
abschneiden: gut abschneiden do well [wel] **besser abschneiden** do better ['betə]
abwaschen wash up [wɒʃ 'ʌp]
acht eight [eɪt]
achten: auf etwas achten *(beim Zuhören)* listen for sth. ['lɪsn fə]
Adresse address [ə'dres]
Affe monkey ['mʌŋki]
Afrika Africa ['æfrɪkə]
aktiv active ['æktɪv]
Aktivität activity [æk'tɪvəti]
Akzent accent ['æksent]
albern silly ['sɪli]; stupid ['stjuːpɪd]
alle *(jeder)* everybody ['evribɒdi]; everyone ['evriwʌn] **alle(s)** all [ɔːl]
allein(e) alone [ə'ləʊn]
Alphabet alphabet ['ælfəbət]
alphabetisches Wörterverzeichnis dictionary ['dɪkʃənri]
als
1. *(zeitlich)* when [wen]
2. älter als ich older than me [ðən]
also so [səʊ]
alt old [əʊld]
Alter: im Alter von 16 at 16
am: am Arbeitsplatz at work **am besten** best [best] **am Montag** on Monday **am Morgen/Nachmittag/Abend** in the morning/afternoon/evening
Amerika America [ə'merɪkə]
an: an meinem Geburtstag on my birthday **schreiben an** write to
andere(r, s) other ['ʌðə] **ein/e andere(r, s)** another [ə'nʌðə]
ändern; sich ändern change [tʃeɪndʒ]
anders different ['dɪfrənt]
anfangen start [stɑːt]; begin [bɪ'gɪn]
Anführer/in leader ['liːdə]
Angst haben (vor) be scared (of) [skeəd]
anhaben *(Kleidung)* wear [weə]
anhalten stop [stɒp]
anhören: *(sich etwas)* **anhören** listen to ['lɪsn] **sich anhören** sound [saʊnd] **Hört sich gut an.** Sounds fun.
ankommen arrive [ə'raɪv]
annehmen: ich nehme an I guess [ges]
Anruf *(Telefon)* (phone) call ['fəʊn kɔːl]
anrufen phone [fəʊn]; call [kɔːl]
anschauen look at ['lʊk ət] **sich etwas anschauen** *(beobachten)* watch [wɒtʃ]
Anspitzer sharpener ['ʃɑːpnə]
Anstecknadel badge [bædʒ]
Antwort answer ['ɑːnsə]
antworten answer ['ɑːnsə]
Anzahl number ['nʌmbə]
Anzeige advert ['ædvɜːt]
anziehen: eine Hose anziehen put on trousers [pʊt 'ɒn]
Apfel apple ['æpl]
April April ['eɪprəl]
Arbeit work [wɜːk]
arbeiten work [wɜːk]
Arbeiten erledigen *(im Haus)* do chores [tʃɔːz]
Arbeiter/in worker ['wɜːkə]
Arbeitskraft worker ['wɜːkə]
arbeitslos unemployed [ʌnɪm'plɔɪd]
Arbeitsplatz: am Arbeitsplatz at work [wɜːk]
Ärger trouble ['trʌbl]
ärgerlich angry ['æŋgri]
Arm arm [ɑːm]
arm poor [pʊə] **(die) arme Mrs Trent** poor Mrs Trent **Du Arme/r!** Poor you!
Art: Welche Art (von) ...? What sort of ...? [sɔːt]
Artikel article ['ɑːtɪkl]
Arzt/Ärztin doctor ['dɒktə]
auch also ['ɔːlsəʊ]; too [tuː] **auch nicht** not ... either ['eɪðə]
auf on [ɒn] **auf dem Foto** in the photo **auf dem Land** in the country **auf der Eggbuckland-Schule** at Eggbuckland **auf Englisch** in English **aufs Land** to the country **Auf Wiedersehen.** Goodbye. [gʊd'baɪ]
Aufführung show [ʃəʊ]
Aufgabe task [tɑːsk]; exercise ['eksəsaɪz]
aufgehen *(sich öffnen)* open ['əʊpən]
aufgeregt *(gespannt)* excited [ɪk'saɪtɪd]; *(nervös)* nervous ['nɜːvəs]
aufhören (mit) stop [stɒp]
aufmachen open ['əʊpən]
aufpassen auf look after [lʊk 'ɑːftə]
aufräumen tidy ['taɪdi]
aufregen: Reg dich nicht auf. Take it easy!
aufregend exciting [ɪk'saɪtɪŋ]
aufschreiben write down [raɪt 'daʊn]
Aufseher/in *(in einem Nationalpark)* ranger ['reɪndʒə]
aufstehen *(aus dem Bett)* get up [get 'ʌp]; *(sich hinstellen)* stand up [stænd 'ʌp]
Auge eye [aɪ]
August August ['ɔːgəst]
aus from [frɒm]
Ausdruck phrase [freɪz]
Ausflug trip [trɪp]; *(Tagesausflug)* day out [deɪ 'aʊt] **einen Ausflug machen** do a trip
ausgeben: Geld ausgeben (für) spend money (on) [spend]
ausgehen go out [gəʊ 'aʊt]
ausleihen: sich etwas (aus)leihen borrow sth. ['bɒrəʊ]

ausmachen: etwas ausmachen make a difference ['dɪfrəns] **Was macht ein perfektes Wochenende aus?** What makes a perfect weekend?
ausprobieren try [traɪ]
ausrichten: etwas ausrichten take a message ['mesɪdʒ]
ausruhen: sich ausruhen chill [tʃɪl]
Ausrüstung equipment [ɪ'kwɪpmənt]
Aussage *(Botschaft)* message ['mesɪdʒ]
aussehen look [lʊk]
Ausstattung equipment [ɪ'kwɪpmənt]
Ausstellung exhibition [eksɪ'bɪʃn]
aussuchen pick [pɪk]
austragen: Zeitungen austragen do a paper round ['peɪpə raʊnd]
Australien Australia [ɒ'streɪliə]
auswählen pick [pɪk]
Auto car [kɑː]
Autor/in writer ['raɪtə]

B

Baby baby ['beɪbi]
Babysitter babysitter ['beɪbisɪtə]
Bad(ezimmer) bathroom ['bɑːθruːm]
Badminton badminton ['bædmɪntən]
Bahnhof (train) station ['treɪn steɪʃn]
Bahnsteig platform ['plætfɔːm]
bald soon [suːn]
Ball ball [bɔːl]
Ballon balloon [bə'luːn]
Banane banana [bə'nɑːnə]
Bananenschale banana skin [bə'nɑːnə skɪn]
Band *(Musikgruppe)* band [bænd]
Bank *(Geldinstitut)* bank [bæŋk]
Bär bear [beə]
Baseball baseball ['beɪsbɔːl]
Basketball basketball ['bɑːskɪtbɔːl]
Battle *(im Rap)* battle ['bætl]
Bauer, Bäuerin farmer ['fɑːmə]
Bauernhof farm [fɑːm]
Baum tree [triː]
beantworten answer ['ɑːnsə]
Bedient euch! *(Greift zu!)* Help yourselves. [jɔː'selvz]
beeindruckt impressed [ɪm'prest]
beenden finish ['fɪnɪʃ]
beginnen begin [bɪ'gɪn]
behalten keep [kiːp]
bei with [wɪð] **bei der Arbeit** at work **bei Ellie daheim/zu Hause** at Ellie's house **bei MARTINS** at MARTINS
Bein leg [leg]
Beispiel example [ɪg'zɑːmpl] **zum Beispiel** for example
beitreten *(einem Klub)* join [dʒɔɪn]
bekommen get [get]
belebt busy ['bɪzi]
beliebt popular ['pɒpjələ]
Belohnung reward [rɪ'wɔːd]
benutzen use [juːz]
beobachten watch [wɒtʃ]
bequem comfortable ['kʌmftəbl]
bereit ready ['redi]
Berg mountain ['maʊntən]
berichten tell (about) [tel]
berichtigen correct [kə'rekt]
berühmt (für, wegen) famous (for) ['feɪməs]
beschäftigt sein be busy ['bɪzi]
Beschäftigung activity [æk'tɪvəti]
beschreiben describe [dɪ'skraɪb] **jm. den Weg beschreiben** tell sb. the way
besondere(r, s) special ['speʃl] **Was ist das Besondere an ihm?** What's special about him?
besonnen calm [kɑːm]
besorgt sein (wegen) be worried (about) ['wʌrid]
besser better ['betə] **besser abschneiden** do better
bestätigen confirm [kən'fɜːm]
beste(r, s), am besten best [best]
besuchen visit ['vɪzɪt]
Besucher/in visitor ['vɪzɪtə]
Betrieb *(Geschäft)* business ['bɪznəs] **einen Betrieb gründen/eröffnen** start a business
Bett bed [bed]
beunruhigt sein (wegen) be worried (about) ['wʌrid]
bevor before [bɪ'fɔː]
bewirken: etwas bewirken make a difference ['dɪfrəns]
bewölkt cloudy ['klaʊdi]
bezahlen pay [peɪ]
Bild picture ['pɪktʃə]
billig *(preiswert)* cheap [tʃiːp]
Binnensee lake [leɪk]
bis *(zeitlich)* until [ən'tɪl] **Bis dann.** See you. **von Montag bis Freitag** from Monday to Friday
bisschen: ein bisschen a bit [bɪt]
bitte
1. *(in Fragen und Aufforderungen)* please [pliːz]
2. Bitte schön. / Hier, bitte. Here you are.
3. *(Nichts zu danken.)* You're welcome. ['welkʌm]
bitten um ask for [ɑːsk]
blau blue [bluː]
Blazer *(Jackett, oft Teil der Schuluniform)* blazer ['bleɪzə]
bleiben stay [steɪ]
Bleistift pencil ['pensl]
Bleistiftanspitzer pencil sharpener ['pensl ʃɑːpnə]
blöd silly ['sɪli]; stupid ['stjuːpɪd]
bloß just [dʒʌst]; only ['əʊnli]
Bonbon sweet [swiːt]
Boot boat [bəʊt]
borgen: sich etwas borgen borrow sth. ['bɒrəʊ]
Boss boss [bɒs]
Botschaft *(Aussage)* message ['mesɪdʒ]
Bowling spielen gehen go bowling ['bəʊlɪŋ]
Box box [bɒks]
Boxen *(Boxsport)* boxing ['bɒksɪŋ]
Brathähnchen chicken ['tʃɪkɪn]
brauchen need [niːd] **etwas nicht (zu) tun brauchen** not have to do sth.
braun brown [braʊn]
brechen break [breɪk]
Brief letter ['letə]
Briefträger postman, *(pl)* postmen ['pəʊstmən]
Briefträgerin postwoman, *(pl)* postwomen ['pəʊstwʊmən], ['pəʊstwɪmɪn]
Brille glasses *(pl)* ['glɑːsɪz]
bringen bring [brɪŋ]
britisch British ['brɪtɪʃ]
Broschüre brochure ['brəʊʃə]
Brot bread [bred]
Brücke bridge [brɪdʒ]
Bruder brother ['brʌðə]
Buch book [bʊk]
buchen book [bʊk]
Buchladen bookshop ['bʊkʃɒp]
Buchseite page [peɪdʒ]
buchstabieren spell [spel]
Bulle bull [bʊl]
bunt coloured ['kʌləd]
Burg castle ['kɑːsl]
Büro office ['ɒfɪs]
Bus bus [bʌs] **den Bus nehmen** get the bus **im Bus** on the bus
Busch bush [bʊʃ]
Bushaltestelle bus stop ['bʌs stɒp]
Button *(Anstecknadel)* badge [bædʒ]

C

Café cafe ['kæfeɪ]
Cammen *(Internet-Telefongespräch mit Bildübertragung)* video chat ['vɪdiəʊ tʃæt]
CD CD [siː'diː]
CD-Spieler CD player [siː'diː pleɪə]
Cent cent [sent]
Champion champion ['tʃæmpiən]
Chat chat [tʃæt]
chatten (mit) chat (with) [tʃæt]
Chef/in boss [bɒs]
chillen chill [tʃɪl]
China China ['tʃaɪnə]
Chips crisps *(pl)* [krɪsps]
Comedyshow comedy ['kɒmədi]
Comic cartoon [kɑː'tuːn]
Comic(heft) comic ['kɒmɪk]
Computer computer [kəm'pjuːtə]
cool cool [kuːl]
Cricket *(Mannschaftssportart)* cricket ['krɪkɪt]
Cupcake *(kleiner runder Kuchen)* cupcake ['kʌpkeɪk]

D

da *(dort)* there [ðeə] **Sind da die Taylors?** *(am Telefon)* Is that the Taylors?
daheim: bei Ellie daheim at Ellie's house
daheim: bei Ellie daheim at Ellie's house
dahin there [ðeə]
danach: Mir ist nicht danach. I don't feel like it.
Dänemark Denmark ['denmɑːk]
Dank: Vielen Dank. Thanks very much.
danke thanks [θæŋks] **danke (schön)** thank you ['θæŋk juː]
danken: Nichts zu danken. *(Gern geschehen.)* You're welcome. ['welkʌm]
dann then [ðen]
darstellende Kunst drama ['drɑːmə]
das *(Artikel)* the [ðə]
das (da) that [ðæt]
das *(Relativpronomen)* that [ðæt]
dass that [ðæt]
dasselbe the same [seɪm]
Datum date [deɪt]
dein/e your [jɔː]
deine, deiner, deins yours [jɔːz]
denken think [θɪŋk] **denken über** think of/about **daran denken** remember [rɪ'membə]
der *(Artikel)* the [ðə]
der *(Relativpronomen)* that [ðæt] *(Person)* who [huː]
Detektiv/in detective [dɪ'tektɪv]
deutlich clear [klɪə] **deutlich sprechen** talk clearly ['klɪəli]
Deutsch; deutsch German ['dʒɜːmən]
Deutsche/r German ['dʒɜːmən]
Deutschland Germany ['dʒɜːməni]
Dezember December [dɪ'sembə]
dich you [juː] **dich selbst** yourself [jɔː'self]
die *(Artikel)* the [ðə]
die *(Relativpronomen)* that [ðæt] *(Person)* who [huː]
Dienstag Tuesday ['tjuːzdeɪ], ['tjuːzdi]
diese(r, s) this [ðɪs] **diese Menschen (hier)** these people [ðiːz] **Dies ist …** This is …
Ding thing [θɪŋ]
Dinosaurier dinosaur ['daɪnəsɔː]
dir you [juː] **dir selbst** yourself [jɔː'self]
Doktor/in doctor ['dɒktə]
Dollar dollar ($) ['dɒlə]
Donnerstag Thursday ['θɜːzdeɪ], ['θɜːzdi]
Dorf village ['vɪlɪdʒ]
dort there [ðeə] **die (CDs) dort** those (CDs) [ðəʊz]
dorthin there [ðeə]
Drachenfliegen hang-gliding ['hæŋ glaɪdɪŋ]
draußen, nach draußen outside [aʊt'saɪd]
drei three [θriː]
drinnen; nach drinnen inside [ɪn'saɪd]
dritte(r, s) third [θɜːd]
drüben: da drüben over there [əʊvə 'ðeə]
du you [juː] **du selbst** yourself [jɔː'self]
Dudelsack bagpipes *(pl)* ['bægpaɪps]
dumm silly ['sɪli]; stupid ['stjuːpɪd]
dunkel dark [dɑːk]
durch through [θruː]
dürfen: etwas tun dürfen be allowed to do sth. [ə'laʊd] **nicht tun dürfen** mustn't do ['mʌsnt]
Dusche shower ['ʃaʊə]
DVD DVD [diːviː'diː]
DVD-Player DVD player [diːviː'diː pleɪə]

E

E-Bass bass guitar [beɪs gɪ'tɑː]
E-Book-Reader e-reader ['iː riːdə]
echt real [rɪəl]
Ecke corner ['kɔːnə]
Ei egg [eg]
eigene(r, s): seine eigene Fahne its own flag [əʊn]
ein/e a [ə]; *(vor Vokalen)* an [ən]
einfach *(nicht schwierig)* easy ['iːzi] **Tu es einfach!** Just do it! [dʒʌst]
einfangen catch [kætʃ]
einhundert a hundred, one hundred ['hʌndrəd]
einige some [sʌm], [səm]
einkaufen shop [ʃɒp] **einkaufen gehen** go shopping
Einkaufsstraße high street ['haɪ striːt]
Einkaufszentrum shopping centre ['ʃɒpɪŋ sentə]
Einladung (zu, nach) invitation (to) [ɪnvɪ'teɪʃn]
einmal once [wʌns]
einpacken pack [pæk]
eins one [wʌn]
einsam lonely ['ləʊnli]
Eintrittskarte ticket ['tɪkɪt]
Einzelzimmer single room [sɪŋgl 'ruːm]
einzige(r, s) only ['əʊnli]
Eis ice cream [aɪs 'kriːm]
Eisenbahn train [treɪn]
Elefant elephant ['elɪfənt]
elf eleven [ɪ'levən]
Eltern parents ['peərənts]
E-Mail email ['iːmeɪl]
Ende end [end]; *(Text, Geschichte)* ending ['endɪŋ] **am oberen Ende (von)** at the top (of) [tɒp]
enden finish ['fɪnɪʃ]
endlich at last [ət 'lɑːst]
Energie energy ['enədʒi]
Energiegetränk energy drink ['enədʒi drɪŋk]
eng narrow ['nærəʊ]
England England ['ɪŋglənd]
Englisch; englisch English ['ɪŋglɪʃ]
Ente duck [dʌk]
entlang: die Straße entlang along the street [ə'lɒŋ]
Entschuldigung. *(Darf ich mal stören?)* Excuse me, … [ɪks'kjuːz mi]; *(Tut mir leid.)* Sorry. / I'm sorry. ['sɒri]
enttäuscht disappointed [dɪsə'pɔɪntɪd]

er
1. he [hiː] **er/sich selbst** himself [hɪm'self]
2. *(bei Dingen und Tieren)* it [ɪt] **er/sich selbst** itself [ɪt'self]
Erdbeben earthquake ['ɜːθkweɪk]
Erde *(Erdboden)* ground [graʊnd]
Erdkunde geography [dʒi'ɒgrəfi]
erfolgreich sein do well [wel]
erinnern: sich erinnern an remember [rɪ'membə]
Ernst: im Ernst seriously ['sɪəriəsli]
ernst(haft) serious ['sɪəriəs]
erst, wenn sie 13 sind not (…) until they're 13 [ən'tɪl]
erstaunlich amazing [ə'meɪzɪŋ]
erstaunt amazed [ə'meɪzd]
Erste Hilfe first aid [fɜːst 'eɪd] **Erste-Hilfe-Set** first-aid kit [fɜːst 'eɪd kɪt]
erste(r, s) first (= 1st) [fɜːst]
Erwachsene/r adult ['ædʌlt]
erzählen (von) tell (about) [tel]
es it [ɪt] **es/sich selbst** itself [ɪt'self]
Esel donkey ['dɒŋki]
Essen food [fuːd]
essen eat [iːt] **einen Salat essen** have a salad
Essen *(Mahlzeit)* meal [miːl]
etwas something ['sʌmθɪŋ]; *(ein bisschen)* some [sʌm], [səm] **Sonst noch etwas?** Anything else? ['eniθɪŋ]
euch you [juː] **euch selbst** yourselves [jɔː'selvz]
euer/eure your [jɔː]
Euro euro (€) ['jʊərəʊ]
Europa Europe ['jʊərəp]
existieren exist [ɪg'zɪst]

F

Fahne flag [flæg]
Fähre ferry ['feri]
fahren go [gəʊ]; *(mit dem Auto)* drive [draɪv]; *(reisen)* travel ['trævl] **mit dem Bus fahren** go by bus **Rad fahren** cycle ['saɪkl]; ride a bike
Fahrer/in driver ['draɪvə]
Fahrkarte ticket ['tɪkɪt]
Fahrrad bicycle ['baɪsɪkl]; bike [baɪk]
fallen fall [fɔːl]
falls if [ɪf]
falsch wrong [rɒŋ]; false [fɔːls] **das ist falsch** that's wrong
Familie family ['fæməli]
familienfreundlich family-friendly
Familienstammbaum family tree
Fan fan [fæn]
fangen catch [kætʃ]
fantastisch fantastic [fæn'tæstɪk]; like a million dollars
Farbe colour ['kʌlə]
farbig coloured ['kʌləd]
Februar February ['februəri]
Federball badminton ['bædmɪntən]
Federmäppchen pencil case ['pensl keɪs]
feiern celebrate ['selɪbreɪt] **eine Party feiern** have a party
Feld field [fiːld]
Fenster window ['wɪndəʊ]
Ferien holidays ['hɒlədeɪz]
Fernsehen, Fernsehgerät TV [tiː'viː] *(das)* **Fernsehen** watching TV **im Fernsehen** on TV
Fernsehsendung programme ['prəʊgræm]
fertig *(bereit)* ready ['redi] **Auf die Plätze, fertig, los!** Get ready. Steady. Go! [get redi stedi 'gəʊ]
Fest festival ['festɪvl]
Feuer fire ['faɪə]; *(Freudenfeuer)* bonfire ['bɒnfaɪə]
Feuerwehrmann/-frau firefighter ['faɪəfaɪtə]
Feuerwerk fireworks
Feuerwerkskörper firework ['faɪewɜːk]
Fieber temperature ['temprətʃə] **Ich habe Fieber.** I have a temperature.
fies mean [miːn]
Film film [fɪlm]
Filmstar film star ['fɪlm stɑː]
finden find [faɪnd] **Freunde finden** make friends [meɪk]
Finger finger ['fɪŋgə]
Fisch fish, *(pl)* fish [fɪʃ]
fit fit [fɪt]
Flachbildfernseher flat-screen TV ['flæt skriːn tiː viː]
Flagge flag [flæg]
Flasche bottle ['bɒtl]
Fleisch meat [miːt]
fliegen fly [flaɪ]
Flughafen airport ['eəpɔːt]
Flugzeug plane [pleɪn]
Fluss river ['rɪvə]
Föhn hairdryer ['heədraɪə]
fort away [ə'weɪ]
fortbewegen: sich fortbewegen travel ['trævl]
Foto photo ['fəʊtəʊ] **ein Foto machen** take a photo
Fotoapparat camera ['kæmərə]
Frage question ['kwestʃən]
Fragebogen questionnaire [kwestʃə'neə]
fragen ask [ɑːsk] **jn. nach dem Weg fragen** ask sb. the way
Frankreich France [frɑːns]
Französisch; französisch French [frentʃ]
Frau
1. woman, *(pl)* women ['wʊmən], ['wɪmɪn]
2. *(allgemeine Anrede f. Frauen)* Ms … [mɪz], [məz]
3. *(Anrede f. unverheiratete Frauen)* Miss … [mɪs]
4. *(Anrede f. verheiratete Frauen)* Mrs … ['mɪsɪz]
frei free [friː]
Freitag Friday ['fraɪdeɪ], ['fraɪdi]
fressen eat [iːt]
Freund/in friend [frend]; *(feste Freundin)* girlfriend ['gɜːlfrend]; *(fester Freund)* boyfriend ['bɔɪfrend]
freundlich friendly ['frendli]; kind [kaɪnd] **Mit freundlichen Grüßen** *(Briefschluss)* Yours sincerely [jɔːz sɪn'sɪəli]
Frisör/in hairdresser ['heədresə]
froh happy ['hæpi] **ich bin froh** I'm glad [glæd]
Frucht, Früchte fruit [fruːt]
früh early ['ɜːli]
Frühstück breakfast ['brekfəst]
Frühstückspension bed and breakfast (B&B)
Fuchs fox [fɒks]
fühlen; sich fühlen feel [fiːl]
Führerschein driving licence ['draɪvɪŋ laɪsns]
füllen fill [fɪl]
Füller pen [pen]
fünf five [faɪv]
funktionieren work [wɜːk]
für for [fɔː], [fə]
Fußball football ['fʊtbɔːl]
Fußballspielen playing football
Fußballspieler/in footballer ['fʊtbɔːlə]
Fußballverein football club (FC)
Fußgänger/in walker ['wɔːkə]
Futter food [fuːd]
füttern feed [fiːd]

G

ganz: den ganzen Tag (lang) all day [ɔːl 'deɪ]
Garage garage ['gærɑːʒ]

Garagenflohmarkt *(privater Flohmarkt)* garage sale ['gærɑ:ʒ seɪl]
Garten garden ['gɑ:dn]
Gast guest [gest]; visitor ['vɪzɪtə]
Gebäude building ['bɪldɪŋ]
geben give [gɪv] **es gibt** there are ... ['ðeər ɑ:]; there's [ðeəz] **es gibt keine Bäume** there aren't any trees ['eni]
geboren born [bɔ:n]
gebrochen *(kaputt)* broken ['brəʊkən]
Geburtstag birthday ['bɜ:θdeɪ] **Herzlichen Glückwunsch zum Geburtstag!** Happy birthday! **Sie hat Geburtstag.** It's her birthday. **Wann hast du Geburtstag?** When's (= when is) your birthday?
Gedicht poem ['pəʊɪm]
gefährlich dangerous ['deɪndʒərəs]
gegen against [ə'genst]
Gegend neighbourhood ['neɪbəhʊd]
gehen go [gəʊ] **Wie geht's? / Wie geht es dir/euch?** How are you? **(zu Fuß) gehen** walk [wɔ:k]
geizig mean [mi:n]
gelangweilt sein be bored [bɔ:d]
gelb yellow ['jeləʊ]
Geld money ['mʌni] **Geld verdienen** make money
gemein mean [mi:n]
Gemüse vegetables, *infml auch* veg ['vedʒtəblz], [vedʒ]
gemütlich comfortable ['kʌmftəbl] **es sich gemütlich machen** make yourself comfortable
genau: genau jetzt right now [raɪt 'naʊ] **genau wie Berry** just like Berry [laɪk]
genervt sein feel fed up [fed 'ʌp]
genießen enjoy [ɪn'dʒɔɪ]
genug enough [ɪ'nʌf]
geöffnet open ['əʊpən]
Geografie geography [dʒi'ɒgrəfi]
gerade jetzt right now [raɪt 'naʊ]
geradeaus: Geh geradeaus (weiter). Go straight on. [streɪt]
Gerät *(Maschine)* machine [mə'ʃi:n]
Geräusch noise [nɔɪz]
gern: ich hätte gern I'd like (= I would like) [laɪk] **ich würde gern mitmachen** I'd like to (= I would like to) join **Ich würde sehr gern kommen.** I'd love to come. [lʌv]
Gesamtbetrag total ['təʊtl]
Gesamtschule *(GB)* high school ['haɪ sku:l]
Geschäft
1. shop [ʃɒp]; *(verkauft gespendete Waren für wohltätige Zwecke)* charity shop ['tʃærəti ʃɒp]
2. *(Betrieb)* business ['bɪznəs] **ein Geschäft aufmachen** start a business
3. *(Vereinbarung)* deal [di:l] **ein Geschäft abschließen, vereinbaren** make a deal
Geschäftsführer/in manager ['mænɪdʒə]
geschehen happen ['hæpən] **Bitte, gern geschehen.** You're welcome. ['welkʌm]
Geschenk present ['preznt]
Geschichte *(Erzählung)* story ['stɔ:ri]; *(vergangene Zeiten)* history ['hɪstri]
Geschirrspülmaschine dishwasher ['dɪʃwɒʃə]
geschlossen sein be closed [kləʊzd]
Gesicht face [feɪs]
gespannt excited [ɪk'saɪtɪd]
Gespenst ghost [gəʊst]
Gespräch talk [tɔ:k]; *(Unterhaltung)* chat [tʃæt]
gestern yesterday ['jestədeɪ]
gesund healthy ['helθi]
Getränk drink [drɪŋk]
gewaltsam violent ['vaɪələnt]
gewalttätig violent ['vaɪələnt]
Gewinn *(Profit)* profit ['prɒfɪt]
gewinnen win [wɪn]
Gewinner/in winner ['wɪnə]
Gitarre guitar [gɪ'tɑ:]
glauben believe [bɪ'li:v]; think [θɪŋk] **Du wirst es kaum glauben!** Wait for this. *(infml)* ['weɪt] **ich glaube** I guess [ges]
gleich, das gleiche the same [seɪm]
Glocke bell [bel]
Glück: du hast Glück you're lucky ['lʌki] **Viel Glück!** Good luck. [lʌk]
glücklich happy ['hæpi] **Du Glückliche/r!** Lucky you! ['lʌki]
glücklicherweise luckily ['lʌkɪli]
Glückwunsch: Herzlichen Glückwunsch (zu ...)! Congratulations (on ...)! [kəngrætʃu'leɪʃnz] **Herzlichen Glückwunsch zum Geburtstag!** Happy birthday! [hæpi 'bɜ:θdeɪ]
GPS GPS [dʒi: pi: 'es]
Gras grass [grɑ:s]
grau grey [greɪ]
Grieche/Griechin Greek [gri:k]
griechisch; Griechisch Greek [gri:k]
groß big [bɪg]; *(Person)* tall [tɔ:l] **ich mache mir große Sorgen** I worry a lot [ə 'lɒt]
großartig great [greɪt]
Großbritannien (Great) Britain ['brɪtn]
Großstadt city ['sɪti]
Großvater grandfather ['grænfɑ:ðə]
grün green [gri:n]
Grund *(Begründung)* reason ['ri:zn] **aus vielen Gründen** for lots of reasons
Gruppe group [gru:p]
Gruppenarbeit group work ['gru:p wɜ:k]
gruselig scary ['skeəri]
Grüße: Mit freundlichen Grüßen *(Briefschluss)* Yours sincerely [jɔ:z sɪn'sɪəli] **Viele Grüße, ...** Best wishes ['wɪʃɪz]
gut good [gʊd]; fine [faɪn]; *(Adverb)* well [wel] **gut abschneiden** do well **Guten Morgen.** Good morning. **Gut gemacht!** Well done. **gut sein in etwas** be good at sth. **Es geht mir gut.** I'm fine.; I'm OK. **es gut machen** do well **Hört sich gut an.** Sounds fun.
Guy-Fawkes-Puppe guy [gaɪ]
Gymnastik gymnastics [dʒɪm'næstɪks]

H

Haar, Haare hair [heə]
Haartrockner hairdryer ['heədraɪə]
haben have [hæv]
Hafen harbour ['hɑ:bə]
Hähnchen chicken ['tʃɪkɪn]
Hallo. Hello. [hə'ləʊ]; Hi! [haɪ]
Halloween *(Abend des 31. 10.)* Halloween [hæləʊ'i:n]
Hals throat [θrəʊt] **Mir tut der Hals weh.** I have a sore throat. [sɔ: 'θrəʊt]
Halsschmerzen a sore throat [sɔ: 'θrəʊt]
halten: halten von think of/about [θɪŋk] **Halt den Mund!** Shut up! [ʃʌt 'ʌp]
Hamburger *(Frikadelle)* burger ['bɜ:gə]
Hamster hamster ['hæmstə]
Hand hand [hænd]

Handschuh glove [glʌv]
Handtuch towel ['taʊəl]
Handy mobile (phone) [məʊbaɪl 'fəʊn]
Happy End *(glückliches Ende)* happy ending [hæpi 'endɪŋ]
hart hard [hɑːd] **hart arbeiten** work hard
Hauptstadt capital ['kæpɪtl]
Hauptstraße high street ['haɪ striːt]
Haus house [haʊs] **nach Hause** home [həʊm]
Hausarbeiten erledigen *(Haushalt)* do chores [tʃɔːz]
Hausaufgabe/n homework ['həʊmwɜːk] **ich mache (meine) Hausaufgaben** I do my homework
Häuschen cottage ['kɒtɪdʒ]
Haustier pet [pet]
Heftseite page [peɪdʒ]
Heim *(Zuhause)* home [həʊm]
heiß hot [hɒt]
heißen: Wie heißt du? What's your name?
helfen help [help]
Helfer/in helper ['helpə]
Hemd shirt [ʃɜːt]
heraus out [aʊt]
herausfinden find out [faɪnd 'aʊt]
Herr Smith Mr Smith ['mɪstə]
herrisch bossy ['bɒsi]
herstellen make [meɪk]
herzlich: Herzlichen Glückwunsch (zu …)! Congratulations (on …)! [kəngrætʃu'leɪʃnz] **Herzlichen Glückwunsch zum Geburtstag!** Happy birthday! [hæpi 'bɜːθdeɪ]
heute today [tə'deɪ] **heute Morgen/Nachmittag/Abend** this morning/afternoon/evening
hier here [hɪə] **Hier, bitte.** Here you are. **Hier spricht Rob Blake.** *(am Telefon)* This is Rob Blake.
hierher here [hɪə]
Hilfe help [help]
Himmel sky [skaɪ]
hinauf up [ʌp]
hinaus out [aʊt]
hinausgehen go out [gəʊ 'aʊt]
hinfallen fall [fɔːl]
hinsetzen: sich hinsetzen sit [sɪt]; sit down
hinter behind [bɪ'haɪnd]
Hintergrund background ['bækgraʊnd]
hinüber: da hinüber over there [əʊvə 'ðeə]
hinunter down [daʊn]
Hip-Hop hip hop ['hɪp hɒp]
Hit hit [hɪt]
Hobby hobby ['hɒbi] **einem Hobby nachgehen** do a hobby
hoch high [haɪ]; *(nach oben)* up [ʌp]; *(z.B. große Gebäude)* tall [tɔːl]
Hockey hockey ['hɒki]
hoffen hope [həʊp]
Holz wood [wʊd]
horchen auf listen for ['lɪsn fə]
hören hear [hɪə]
Hose trousers *(pl)* ['traʊzəz]
Hot Dog *(heißes Würstchen in einem Brötchen)* hot dog ['hɒt dɒg]
Hotel hotel [həʊ'tel]
Hügel hill [hɪl]
hügelig hilly ['hɪli]
Huhn chicken ['tʃɪkɪn]
Hund dog [dɒg]
Hundeheim dogs' home
hundert a hundred, one hundred ['hʌndrəd]
Hunger haben be hungry ['hʌŋgri]
hungrig hungry ['hʌŋgri]
hupen hoot [huːt]
hurra yippee [jɪ'piː]
Hut hat [hæt]
Hütte cottage ['kɒtɪdʒ]

I

ich I [aɪ] **Ich bin's.** It's me. **ich selbst** myself [maɪ'self]
ideal ideal [aɪ'dɪəl]
Idee idea [aɪ'dɪə]
Idiot/in idiot ['ɪdiət]
ihm him [hɪm]
ihn him [hɪm]
ihnen them [ðem], [ðəm]
Ihnen *(höfliche Anrede)* you [juː]
ihr: mit ihr with her [hɜː]
ihr *(Plural von „du")* you [juː] **ihr selbst** yourselves [jɔː'selvz]
Ihr/e *(vor Nomen; besitzanzeigend) (zu höflichen Anrede „you")* your [jɔː]
ihr/e *(vor Nomen; besitzanzeigend)* **1.** *(zu „she")* her [hɜː] **2.** *(zu „it")* its [ɪts] **3.** *(zu „they")* their [deə]
im: im Bus on the bus **im Fernsehen** on TV **im Kino** at the cinema
Imbissstube diner *(AE)* ['daɪnə]
immer always ['ɔːlweɪz] **immer noch** still [stɪl]
in in [ɪn] **in den Klassenraum (hinein)** into the classroom ['ɪntu], ['ɪntə] **in der Schule** at school **in der Stadt** in town **in einem Restaurant** at a restaurant **in England** in England **in Papas Wohnung gehen** go to dad's flat **Warst du schon mal in London?** Have you ever been to London?
Information fact [fækt] **Information(en) (über)** information (about) *(no pl)* [ɪnfə'meɪʃn]
Informations- und Kommunikationstechnologie ICT (information and communication technology) [aɪ siː 'tiː], [ɪnfəmeɪʃn ənd kəmjuːnɪkeɪʃn tek'nɒlədʒi]
Informationsblatt newsletter ['njuːzletə]
Ingwer ginger ['dʒɪndʒə]
insbesondere especially [ɪ'speʃəli]
Instrument instrument ['ɪnstrəmənt]
interessant interesting ['ɪntrəstɪŋ]
interessieren: sich interessieren für be interested in ['ɪntrəstɪd]
interessiert sein an be interested in ['ɪntrəstɪd]
Internet internet ['ɪntənet]
Interview interview ['ɪntəvjuː]
irisch, aus Irland Irish ['aɪrɪʃ]
Irrenhaus madhouse ['mædhaʊs]

J

ja yes [jes]; yeah *(infml)* [jeə]
Jacke coat [kəʊt]; jacket ['dʒækɪt]
Jackett jacket ['dʒækɪt]
Jahr(gang) year [jɪə]
Januar January ['dʒænjuəri]
Jeans jeans [dʒiːnz]
jeder everybody ['evribɒdi]; everyone ['evriwʌn]
jede(r, s) every ['evri]
je(mals) ever ['evə]
jemand somebody ['sʌmbədi]; someone ['sʌmwʌn]
jene (CDs) those (CDs) [ðəʊz]
jetzt now [naʊ] **gerade/genau jetzt** right now [raɪt 'naʊ]
Job job [dʒɒb]
Jogging jogging ['dʒɒgɪŋ]
Joghurt yogurt ['jɒgət]
Judo judo ['dʒuːdəʊ]
Jugendliche/r kid [kɪd]
Juli July [dʒu'laɪ]
jung young [jʌŋ]
Junge boy [bɔɪ]
Juni June [dʒuːn]
Junkfood *(ungesundes Essen)* junk food ['dʒʌŋk fuːd]

K

Kaffee coffee ['kɒfi]
Kalender calendar ['kælɪndə]
kalt cold [kəʊld]
Kamera camera ['kæmərə]
kämpfen fight [faɪt]
Kanada: aus Kanada Canadian [kə'neɪdiən]
Kanadier/in Canadian [kə'neɪdiən]
kanadisch Canadian [kə'neɪdiən]
Kaninchen rabbit ['ræbɪt]
Kantine canteen [kæn'tiːn]
kaputt broken ['brəʊkən]
Kapuzenpullover hoodie ['hʊdi]
Karate karate [kə'rɑːti]
Karotte carrot ['kærət]
Karte card [kɑːd]
Kartoffel potato, *(pl)* potatoes [pə'teɪtəʊ]
Kartoffelchips crisps *(pl)* [krɪsps]
Käse cheese [tʃiːz]
Kasten box [bɒks]
Katastrophe disaster [dɪ'zɑːstə]
Kätzchen kitten ['kɪtn]
Katze cat [kæt] **junge Katze** kitten ['kɪtn]
kaufen buy [baɪ]; shop [ʃɒp]
Kaufpreis price [praɪs]
Kehrseite downside ['daʊnsaɪd]
kein/e no [nəʊ] **es gibt keine Bäume** there aren't any trees ['eni] **Ich bin kein Junge.** I'm not a boy.
Keks biscuit ['bɪskɪt]
Kellner waiter ['weɪtə]
Kellnerin waitress ['weɪtrəs]
kennen know [nəʊ]
kennenlernen meet [miːt]
Kilometer kilometre (km) ['kɪləmiːtə]
Kilt *(Schottenrock)* kilt [kɪlt]
Kind child, *(pl)* children [tʃaɪld], ['tʃɪldrən]; kid [kɪd]
Kino cinema ['sɪnəmə]
Kirche church [tʃɜːtʃ]
Kissen cushion ['kʊʃn]
klar clear [klɪə]
Klasse class [klɑːs]
Klassenarbeit test [test]
Klassenlehrer/in class teacher ['klɑːs tiːtʃə]
Klassenraum classroom ['klɑːsruːm]
Klavier piano [pi'ænəʊ]
Kleid dress [dres]
Kleiderschrank wardrobe ['wɔːdrəʊb]
Kleidung(sstücke) clothes *(pl)* [kləʊðz]
klein little ['lɪtl]; small [smɔːl]; *(Person)* short [ʃɔːt]
klettern (auf) climb [klaɪm] Klettern *(Sport)* climbing
Klingel bell [bel]
klingeln ring [rɪŋ]
Klingelton *(Handy)* ringtone ['rɪŋtəʊn]
klingen sound [saʊnd] **Klingt, als ob es Spaß macht.** Sounds fun.
Klub club [klʌb]
klug clever ['klevə]
Kneipe pub [pʌb]
kochen cook [kʊk]
Kochrezept recipe ['resəpi]
kommen come [kʌm] **Ich würde sehr gern kommen.** I'd love to come. **Komm(t) (schon)! / Ach komm!** Come on!
Kommentar comment ['kɒment]
Komödie comedy ['kɒmədi]
König king [kɪŋ]
Königin queen [kwiːn]
können can [kæn], [kən] **nicht können** can't (= cannot) **etwas gut können** be good at sth. **du könntest** you could [kʊd] **sie konnte** she could
kontrollieren check [tʃek]
Konzert concert ['kɒnsət]
Kopfschmerzen haben have a headache ['hedeɪk]
Kopfsprung: einen Kopfsprung machen dive [daɪv]
korrigieren correct [kə'rekt]
Kosten cost [kɒst]
kosten cost [kɒst] **Der Taschenrechner kostet 1 Pfund.** The calculator is £ 1. **Die Handys kosten 10 Pfund.** The mobiles are £ 10.
kostenlos free [friː]
Kram *(Zeug)* stuff [stʌf]
krank ill [ɪl]
Krankenhaus hospital ['hɒspɪtl]
Krawatte tie [taɪ]
Krebs crab [kræb]
Kreuzung *(Straßenkreuzung)* crossroads, *(pl)* crossroads ['krɒsrəʊdz]
kriegen get [get]
Krimiserie crime series, *(pl)* crime series ['kraɪm sɪəriːz]
Krokodil crocodile ['krɒkədaɪl]
Küche kitchen ['kɪtʃɪn]
Kuchen cake [keɪk]
Kugelschreiber pen [pen]
Kuh cow [kaʊ]
Kultur culture ['kʌltʃə]
kümmern: sich kümmern um look after [lʊk 'ɑːftə]
Kunde, Kundin customer ['kʌstəmə]
Kunst art [ɑːt]
Kunststoff plastic ['plæstɪk]
Kunststück trick [trɪk]
kurz short [ʃɔːt]
Kuscheltier toy animal [tɔɪ 'ænɪml]
Kuss kiss [kɪs]

L

lächeln; *(das)* **Lächeln** smile [smaɪl]
lachen laugh [lɑːf]
Laden shop [ʃɒp]
Lampe lamp [læmp]; light [laɪt]
Land country ['kʌntri] **auf dem Land** in the country **aufs Land** to the country
landen land [lænd]
Landkarte map [mæp]
Landwirt/in farmer ['fɑːmə]
lang long [lɒŋ]
Langeweile haben be bored [bɔːd]
langsam slow [sləʊ]
langweilig boring ['bɔːrɪŋ]
Laptop laptop ['læptɒp]
Lärm noise [nɔɪz]
Lasagne lasagne [lə'zænjə]
lassen let [let] **lass(t) uns** let's (= let us) **Lass(t) uns (mal) sehen.** Let's see.
Laterne lantern ['læntən]
Läufer/in runner ['rʌnə]
laut loud [laʊd]; noisy ['nɔɪzi]
läuten ring [rɪŋ]
Leben life, *(pl)* lives [laɪf], [laɪvz]
leben live [lɪv]
Lebensmittel food [fuːd]
Lebensstil lifestyle ['laɪfstaɪl]
lecker! yum! [jʌm]
leer empty ['empti]
leeren empty ['empti]
legen put [pʊt] **Er legt sie zu den anderen Dingen.** He puts it with the other things.
lehren teach [tiːtʃ]
Lehrer/in teacher ['tiːtʃə]
leicht *(einfach)* easy ['iːzi]
leidtun: Tut mir leid. Sorry. / I'm sorry. ['sɒri]
leihen hire ['haɪə] **sich etwas (aus)leihen** borrow sth. ['bɒrəʊ]
leise quiet ['kwaɪət]
Leiter/in leader ['liːdə]
lernen learn [lɜːn]
lesen read [riːd]; *(das)* **Lesen** reading ['riːdɪŋ]
Leser/in reader ['riːdə]

Letterbox *(Behälter, der beim Letterboxing versteckt wird)* letterbox ['letəbɒks]
Letterboxing *(Spiel, eine Art Schnitzeljagd)* letterboxing ['letəbɒksɪŋ]
letzte(r, s) last [lɑ:st]
Leute people ['pi:pl]; *(als Anrede verwendet)* guys [gaɪz]
Licht light [laɪt]
Liebe/r … Dear … [dɪə]
lieben love [lʌv]
lieber: etwas lieber mögen like sth. better ['betə] **etwas lieber mögen als etwas** prefer sth. to sth. [prɪ'fɜ:]
Lieblings- favourite ['feɪvərɪt] **Lieblingssache** favourite thing
Lied song [sɒŋ]
Lieferwagen van [væn]
Limonade lemonade [lemə'neɪd]
Lineal ruler ['ru:lə]
links left [left] **auf der linken Seite** on the left **nach links** left
locker: Bleib mal locker. Take it easy!
Lokal diner *(AE)* ['daɪnə]
Londoner/in Londoner ['lʌndənə]
los: Auf die Plätze, fertig, los! Get ready. Steady. Go! [get redi stedi 'gəʊ]
lustig funny ['fʌni]

M

machen do [du:]; make, [meɪk] **Gut gemacht!** Well done. [wel 'dʌn] **ich mache (meine) Hausaufgaben** I do my homework ['həʊmwɜ:k]
Mädchen girl [gɜ:l]
mähen *(Rasen)* cut [kʌt]
Mahlzeit meal [mi:l] **kleine Mahlzeit** snack [snæk]
Mai May [meɪ]
Make-up make-up ['meɪkʌp]
Mal time [taɪm] **nächstes Mal** next time **zum letzten Mal** for the last time
Mama mum [mʌm]
man you
Manager/in manager ['mænɪdʒə]
manchmal sometimes ['sʌmtaɪmz]
Mann man, *(pl)* men [mæn], [men]
Mannschaft team [ti:m]
Mantel coat [kəʊt]
Markt market ['mɑ:kɪt]
Marmelade jam [dʒæm]
März March [mɑ:tʃ]
Maschine machine [mə'ʃi:n]
Maske mask [mɑ:sk]
Mathematik maths [mæθs]
Matsch mud [mʌd]
Mauer wall [wɔ:l]
Mechaniker/in mechanic [mɪ'kænɪk]
Meer sea [si:] **am Meer** at the seaside ['si:saɪd]
Mehl flour ['flaʊə]
mehr more [mɔ:] **immer mehr** more and more
Mehrfamilienhaus block of flats [blɒk əv 'flæts]
Meile *(ca. 1,6 km)* mile [maɪl]
mein/e *(vor Nomen)* my [maɪ]
meine/r; meins mine [maɪn]
meinen *(denken, glauben)* think [θɪŋk]; *(sagen wollen)* mean [mi:n]
Meinung opinion [ə'pɪnjən] **meiner Meinung nach** in my opinion
meistens usually ['ju:ʒʊəli]
meiste(r, s): das meiste Geld, am meisten Geld the most money [məʊst]
Meister/in *(Sport)* champion ['tʃæmpiən]
Mensa canteen [kæn'ti:n]
Menschen people ['pi:pl]
Messer knife, *(pl)* knives [naɪf]
Meter metre ['mi:tə]
mich me [mi] **mich selbst** myself [maɪ'self]
mieten hire ['haɪə]
Milch milk [mɪlk]
Milchshake milkshake ['mɪlkʃeɪk]
Million million ['mɪljən]
Minute minute ['mɪnɪt]
mir me [mi] **Mir ist nicht danach.** I don't feel like it. **mir selbst** myself [maɪ'self]
Mist: Es ist Mist! It sucks! [sʌks] **So ein Mist!** What a pain! [peɪn]
mit with [wɪð] **mit 16** at 16 **mit dem Bus fahren** go by bus
mitbringen bring [brɪŋ]
mitkommen come [kʌm]
Mitleid mit jm. haben be/feel sorry for sb. ['sɒri]
mitmachen: bei etwas mitmachen take part in sth. [teɪk 'pɑ:t]
mitmachen (bei) join [dʒɔɪn]
Mittag: (zu) Mittag essen have lunch [lʌntʃ]
Mittagessen lunch [lʌntʃ]
mittags at lunchtime ['lʌntʃtaɪm]
Mittagszeit: zur Mittagszeit at lunchtime ['lʌntʃtaɪm]
Mitte centre ['sentə]; middle ['mɪdl] **in der Mitte** in the middle
Mitteilung message ['mesɪdʒ]
Mitteilungsblatt newsletter ['nju:zletə]
Mittwoch Wednesday ['wenzdeɪ], ['wenzdi]
möchten: ich möchte (…) haben I'd like (= I would like) [laɪk] **ich möchte gern mitmachen** I'd like to (= I would like to) join
Modell model ['mɒdl] **Modellauto** model car [mɒdl 'kɑ:]
modern modern ['mɒdn]
Mode(trend) fashion ['fæʃn]
mögen like [laɪk] **etwas am liebsten mögen** like sth. best **etwas lieber mögen** like sth. better **etwas lieber mögen als etwas** prefer sth. to sth. [prɪ'fɜ:] **sehr mögen** love [lʌv]
möglich possible ['pɒsəbl]
Möhre carrot ['kærət]
Monat month [mʌnθ]
Monitor monitor ['mɒnɪtə]
Monster monster ['mɒnstə]
Montag Monday ['mʌndeɪ], ['mʌndi]
morgen tomorrow [tə'mɒrəʊ]
Morgen morning ['mɔ:nɪŋ]
müde tired ['taɪəd]; sleepy ['sli:pi]
Muffin muffin ['mʌfɪn]
Müll rubbish ['rʌbɪʃ]
Mülleimer rubbish bin ['rʌbɪʃ bɪn]
Mund mouth [maʊθ] **Halt den Mund!** Shut up! [ʃʌt 'ʌp]
Museum museum [mju'zi:əm]
Musik music ['mju:zɪk]
Musik- musical ['mju:zɪkl]
musikalisch musical ['mju:zɪkl]
Musikgruppe band [bænd]
Müsliriegel cereal bar ['sɪəriəl bɑ:]
müssen must [mʌst] **etwas tun müssen** have to do sth. ['hæv tə] **etwas nicht tun müssen** not have to do sth.
mutig brave [breɪv]
Mutter mother ['mʌðə]
Mutti mum [mʌm]
Mütze hat [hæt]

N

nach *(örtlich)* to [tu], [tə]; *(zeitlich)* after ['ɑ:ftə] **nach Hause** home [həʊm]
Nachbar/in neighbour ['neɪbə]
Nachbarschaft neighbourhood ['neɪbəhʊd]
nachgehen: einem Hobby nachgehen do a hobby

Nachmittag afternoon [ɑːftə'nuːn]
Nachricht *(Botschaft)* message ['mesɪdʒ]
Nachrichten news [njuːz]
nächste(r, s), als Nächstes next
Nacht night [naɪt] **in der Nacht** at night
Nachteil downside ['daʊnsaɪd]
nachts at night [ət 'naɪt]
Nähe: in der Nähe von near [nɪə]
nahe (bei) near [nɪə]
Name name [neɪm]
Nase nose [nəʊz] **die Nase voll haben** feel fed up [fed 'ʌp]
nass wet [wet]
national national ['næʃnəl]
Nationalpark national park [næʃnəl 'pɑːk]
Natur- natural ['nætʃrəl]
Naturkunde natural history [nætʃrəl 'hɪstri]
natürlich natural ['nætʃrəl]; of course [əv 'kɔːs]
Naturwissenschaft science ['saɪəns]
Nebel fog [fɒg]
nebelig foggy ['fɒgi]
neben next to ['nekst tə]
negativ negative ['negətɪv]
nehmen take [teɪk] **den Bus nehmen** get the bus **einen Salat nehmen** have a salad
nein no [nəʊ]
nennen call [kɔːl] **Wie nennt man ...?** What do you call ...?
nerven: Es nervt! It sucks! [sʌks]; What a pain! [peɪn]
nervös nervous ['nɜːvəs]
nett nice [naɪs]; *(freundlich)* friendly ['frendli]; kind [kaɪnd]
Netz network ['netwɜːk]
neu new [njuː]
neun nine [naɪn]
Neunzigerjahre 90s ['naɪntiz]
nicht not [nɒt] **auch nicht** not ... either ['eɪðə] **noch nicht** not ... yet [jet]
nichts not (...) anything ['eniθɪŋ]; nothing ['nʌθɪŋ]
niedlich cute [kjuːt]
nie(mals) never ['nevə]
niemand nobody ['nəʊbədi]
Nistkasten birdhouse ['bɜːdhaʊs]
noch still [stɪl] **noch ein/e** another [ə'nʌðə] **noch einmal** again [ə'gen] **noch nicht** not ... yet [jet]
Norden, Nord- north [nɔːθ]
nördlich north [nɔːθ]
Nordosten, nordöstlich north-east [nɔːθ'iːst]
Nordwesten, nordwestlich north-west [nɔːθ'west]
normal normal ['nɔːml]; usual ['juːʒʊəl]
normalerweise usually ['juːʒʊəli]
November November [nəʊ'vembə]
Null *(im gesprochenen Englisch)* oh [əʊ]
Nummer number ['nʌmbə]
nun now [naʊ]
nur just [dʒʌst]; only ['əʊnli]
nützlich useful ['juːsfl]

O

oben upstairs [ʌp'steəz]; *(am oberen Ende)* at the top [tɒp] **nach oben** upstairs
Obst fruit [fruːt]
oder or [ɔː]
offen open ['əʊpən]
öffnen, sich öffnen open ['əʊpən]
oft often ['ɒfn], ['ɒftən]
ohne without [wɪ'ðaʊt]
Ohr ear [ɪə]
oje! Oh dear! [dɪə]
Oktober October [ɒk'təʊbə]
olympisch Olympic [ə'lɪmpɪk] **Olympische Spiele** Olympic Games
Oma grandma ['grænmɑː]
Onkel uncle ['ʌŋkl]
online, Online- online [ɒn'laɪn]
Opa grandad ['grændæd]; grandpa ['grænpɑː]
Orange orange ['ɒrɪndʒ]
orange(farben) orange ['ɒrɪndʒ]
ordentlich tidy ['taɪdi]
Ort place [pleɪs]
Osten, Ost- east [iːst]
östlich east [iːst]

P

paar: ein paar some [sʌm], [səm]
Päckchen packet (of) ['pækɪt]
packen pack [pæk]
Packung packet (of) ['pækɪt]
Palast palace ['pæləs]
Papa dad [dæd]
Park park [pɑːk]
parken park (a car) [pɑːk]
Parkplatz car park ['kɑː pɑːk]
Parlament parliament ['pɑːləmənt]
Partner/in partner ['pɑːtnə]
Partnerarbeit partner work ['pɑːtnə wɜːk]
Party party ['pɑːti] **eine Party feiern** have a party
passieren *(geschehen)* happen ['hæpən]
Pastete *(mit Fleisch-/Gemüse-füllung)* pasty ['pæsti]
Pause break [breɪk]
Pence pence [pens] **50 Pence** 50p [piː]
Penny *(kleinste britische Münze)* penny ['peni]
perfekt perfect ['pɜːfɪkt]
Person person ['pɜːsn]
Pfad track [træk]
Pfeife *(Trillerpfeife)* whistle ['wɪsl]
Pferd horse [hɔːs]
Pflanze plant [plɑːnt]
Pfund *(britische Währung)* pound (£) [paʊnd]
Pickel spot [spɒt]
Picknick picnic ['pɪknɪk] **ein Picknick machen** have a picnic
Plan plan [plæn]
planen plan [plæn]
Plastik plastic ['plæstɪk]
Plastiktüte plastic bag [plæstɪk 'bæg]
Platz *(Stelle, Ort)* place [pleɪs]; *(freier Raum)* space [speɪs] **Auf die Plätze, fertig, los!** Get ready. Steady. Go! [get redi stedi 'gəʊ]
Plätzchen *(Keks)* biscuit ['bɪskɪt]
plaudern (mit) chat (with) [tʃæt]
plötzlich suddenly ['sʌdənli]
Polizei police *(pl)* [pə'liːs]
Polizeibeamter/-beamtin police officer [pə'liːs ɒfɪsə]
Pommes frites chips *(pl)* [tʃɪps]
Pony pony ['pəʊni]
populär popular ['pɒpjələ]
Post *(Briefe etc.)* post [pəʊst]
Post(amt) post office ['pəʊst ɒfɪs]
Poster poster ['pəʊstə]
Postkarte postcard ['pəʊstkɑːd]
Praline chocolate ['tʃɒklət]
Präsident/in president ['prezɪdənt]
Preis
1. *(Kaufpreis)* price [praɪs]
2. *(Kosten)* cost [kɒst]
3. *(Gewinn)* prize [praɪz]

preiswert cheap [tʃiːp]
Prinz prince [prɪns]
pro: pro Ballon per balloon [pɜː], [pə] **10 Pfund pro Woche** £10 a week
probieren try [traɪ]
Problem problem ['prɒbləm]
Profit profit ['prɒfɪt]
Prospekt brochure ['brəʊʃə]
prüfen check [tʃek]

Pullover pullover ['pʊləʊvə]
pünktlich on time [ɒn 'taɪm]
Puzzle jigsaw ['dʒɪgsɔ:]

Q

Quiz quiz [kwɪz]

R

Rad *(Fahrrad)* bike [baɪk] **Rad fahren** cycle ['saɪkl]; ride a bike
Radiergummi rubber ['rʌbə]
Rap rap [ræp]
rappen rap [ræp]
Ratte rat [ræt]
Raum *(Zimmer)* room [ru:m]; *(freier Raum)* space [speɪs]
Realität reality [ri'ælɪti]
Recht haben be right [raɪt]
rechte(r, s): auf der rechten Seite on the right
rechts right [raɪt]; on the right
Rede talk [tɔ:k]
Redewendung phrase [freɪz]
Redner/in talker ['tɔ:kə]
Regel rule [ru:l]
Regen rain [reɪn]
Regenhose rain trousers *(pl)* ['reɪn traʊzəz]
Regenjacke rain jacket
Region region ['ri:dʒən]
regnen rain [reɪn]
regnerisch rainy ['reɪni]
reichen: 50 Pence reichen (auch) 50 p will do
Reise trip [trɪp] **eine Reise machen** do a trip
reisekrank travel-sick ['trævlsɪk]
reisen travel ['trævl]
reiten ride [raɪd] **auf einem Pony/ein Pony reiten** ride a pony *(das)* **Reiten** riding
relaxen chill [tʃɪl]
rennen run [rʌn]
Reporter/in reporter [rɪ'pɔ:tə]
repräsentieren represent [reprɪ'zent]
reservieren book [bʊk]
Reservierung reservation [rezə'veɪʃn]
Restaurant restaurant ['restrɒnt]
retten save [seɪv]
Rezept *(Kochrezept)* recipe ['resəpi]
richtig right [raɪt] **das ist richtig** that's right
Rock skirt [skɜ:t]
Rock(musik) rock (music) ['rɒk mju:zɪk]
Rollstuhl wheelchair ['wi:ltʃeə]
Rolltreppe escalator ['eskəleɪtə]
rosa pink [pɪŋk]
rot red [red]
rotblond ginger ['dʒɪndʒə]
Rücken back [bæk]
Rucksack rucksack ['rʌksæk]
Rückseite back [bæk]
rufen shout [ʃaʊt]; call [kɔ:l]
Rugby *(Ballsportart)* rugby ['rʌgbi]
ruhig calm [kɑ:m]; quiet ['kwaɪət]
Ruine ruin *(oft auch pl:* ruins*)* ['ru:ɪn]
Rundfahrt tour [tʊə]
Rundgang (durch) tour (of) [tʊə]
runter down [daʊn]

S

Sache thing [θɪŋ]
Saft juice [dʒu:s]
sagen say [seɪ] sagen wollen *(meinen)* mean [mi:n]
Sahne cream [kri:m]
Salat *(Gericht/Beilage)* salad ['sæləd]
Salz salt [sɔ:lt]
sammeln collect [kə'lekt]
Samstag Saturday ['sætədeɪ], ['sætədi]
Sandwich sandwich ['sænwɪtʃ]
Sänger/in singer ['sɪŋə]
Satz sentence ['sentəns]
sauer sein feel fed up [fed 'ʌp]
Schachtel packet (of) ['pækɪt]
Schaf sheep, *(pl)* sheep [ʃi:p]
schauen look [lʊk]
Schauer shower ['ʃaʊə]
Schauspiel drama ['drɑ:mə]
schauspielern act [ækt]
Scherz joke [dʒəʊk]
scherzen joke [dʒəʊk]
schicken send [send]
schießen *(mit dem Fuß)* kick [kɪk]
Schiff ship [ʃɪp]; boat [bəʊt]
Schild sign [saɪn]
Schlaf sleep [sli:p]
schlafen sleep [sli:p]
Schlafparty sleepover ['sli:pəʊvə]
Schlafsack sleeping bag ['sli:pɪŋ bæg]
Schlafzimmer bedroom ['bedru:m]
Schlagzeug drums [drʌmz]
Schlamm mud [mʌd]
Schlange snake [sneɪk]
schlau clever ['klevə]
schlecht bad [bæd]
schließen close [kləʊz]
schließlich at last [ət 'lɑ:st]; in the end [ɪn ði 'end]
schlimm bad [bæd]
Schlittschuhlaufen ice skating ['aɪs skeɪtɪŋ]
Schluss end [end] **zum Schluss** in the end
Schlussverkauf sale [seɪl]
schmal narrow ['nærəʊ]
schmerzhaft sore [sɔ:]
Schnauze *(Tier)* mouth [maʊθ]
schneiden cut [kʌt]
schnell quick [kwɪk]
Schokolade chocolate ['tʃɒklət]
Schokoriegel chocolate bar ['tʃɒklət bɑ:]
schon: Warst du schon mal ...? Have you ever been ...? ['evə]
schön beautiful ['bju:tɪfl]; fine [faɪn]; nice [naɪs] **Schön, wieder zusammenzusein.** Nice to be together again. **Ich wünsche dir einen schönen Tag. / Schönen Tag noch.** Have a good day.
schottisch, aus Schottland Scottish ['skɒtɪʃ]
Schottland Scotland ['skɒtlənd]
schrecklich terrible ['terəbl]
schreiben write [raɪt] **schreiben an** write to
Schreibtisch desk [desk]
schreien scream [skri:m]
Schuh shoe [ʃu:]
Schuld: jm. die Schuld geben (an) blame sb. (for) [bleɪm]
Schule school [sku:l]
Schüler/in student ['stju:dnt]
Schulheft exercise book ['eksəsaɪz bʊk]
Schulklasse class [klɑ:s]
Schulleiter/in principal ['prɪnsəpl]
Schulmensa canteen [kæn'ti:n]
Schulsport PE (physical education) [pi: 'i:], [fɪzɪkl edʒu'keɪʃn]
Schulter shoulder ['ʃəʊldə]
Schuluniform uniform ['ju:nɪfɔ:m]
Schwanz tail [teɪl]
schwänzen *(Schule)* skive [skaɪv]
Schwänzer/in *(Schule)* skiver ['skaɪvə]
schwarz black [blæk]
Schwein pig [pɪg]
schwer
1. *(Gewicht; Regen)* heavy ['hevi]
2. *(schwierig)* difficult ['dɪfɪkəlt]; hard [hɑ:d]
Schwester sister ['sɪstə]
schwierig difficult ['dɪfɪkəlt]; hard [hɑ:d]
Schwierigkeiten trouble ['trʌbl]
Schwimmbad swimming pool ['swɪmɪŋ pu:l]

schwimmen: schwimmen gehen go swimming ['swɪmɪŋ] *(das)* **Schwimmen** swimming
sechs six [sɪks]
Second-Hand-Laden second-hand shop [sekənd 'hænd]
See *(Binnensee)* lake [leɪk]; *(die See, das Meer)* sea [siː]
sehen look [lʊk]; see [siː]
Lass(t) uns (mal) sehen. Let's see.
Sieh mal, Adam. Look, Adam.
sehr very ['veri] **ich bin sehr besorgt** I worry a lot [ə 'lɒt] **jn. so sehr vermissen/mögen/lieben** miss/like/love sb. so much [səʊ 'mʌtʃ]
Seife soap [səʊp]
Seifenoper soap [səʊp]
Seilrutsche zip wire ['zɪp waɪə]
sein be [biː]
sein/e *(besitzanzeigend)*
1. *(zu „he")* his [hɪz]
2. *(bei Dingen und Tieren)* its [ɪts]
Seite page [peɪdʒ]
selbst *(sogar)* even ['iːvn]
selbstverständlich of course [əv 'kɔːs]
senden send [send]
Sendung programme ['prəʊgræm]
September September [sep'tembə]
setzen: sich setzen sit [sɪt]; sit down
Show show [ʃəʊ]
sich *(Reflexivpronomen)*
1. *(zu „he")* himself [hɪm'self]
2. *(zu „she")* herself [hɜː'self]
3. *(zu „it")* itself [ɪt'self]
4. *(zu „them")* themselves [ðəm'selvz]
sicher sure [ʃʊə]; *(gefahrlos)* safe [seɪf]
Sicherheit security [sɪ'kjʊərəti]
in Sicherheit safe [seɪf]
sie
1. *(weibliche Person)* she **für sie** for her [hɜː] **sie/sich selbst** herself [hɜː'self]
2. *(bei Dingen und Tieren)* it [ɪt] **sie/sich selbst** itself [ɪt'self]
3. *(Plural)* they [ðeɪ] **für sie** for them [ðem], [ðəm] **sie/sich selbst** themselves [ðəm'selvz]
Sie *(höfliche Anrede)* you [juː]
Sie/sich selbst *(Singular)* yourself [jɔː'self] *(Plural)* yourselves [jɔː'selvz]
sieben seven ['sevn]
singen sing [sɪŋ]
sitzen sit [sɪt]
Skateboard skateboard ['skeɪtbɔːd]
Skateboardfahren skateboarding ['skeɪtbɔːdɪŋ]
Skilaufen *(Sport)* skiing [skiːɪŋ]
Sklave, Sklavin slave [sleɪv]
SMS text (message) ['tekst mesɪdʒ]
eine SMS schicken text [tekst]
Snack snack [snæk]
so so [səʊ] **So viel kostet das nicht.** It's cheaper than that.
so viel wie as much as
Socke sock [sɒk]
Sofa sofa ['səʊfə]
sogar even ['iːvn]
Sohn son [sʌn]
sollen: du solltest you should [ʃʊd]
Sommer summer ['sʌmə]
Sonne sun [sʌn]
Sonnenbrille sunglasses *(pl)* ['sʌnglɑːsɪz]
sonnig sunny ['sʌni]
Sonntag Sunday ['sʌndeɪ], ['sʌndi]
Sonst noch etwas? Anything else? ['eniθɪŋ]
Sorgen: sich Sorgen machen (wegen, um) worry (about) ['wʌri]
sorgfältig careful ['keəfl]
Sorte: Welche Sorte (von) ...? What sort of ...? [sɔːt]
Spanien Spain [speɪn]
Spaß: es macht Spaß, mit ihnen zusammenzusein they're fun [fʌn] **Klingt, als ob es Spaß macht.** Sounds fun. **Viel Spaß!** Enjoy yourself/yourselves. [ɪn'dʒɔɪ]
spät late [leɪt] **Wie spät ist es?** What's the time?
später later ['leɪtə]
Speiseeis ice cream [aɪs 'kriːm]
Speisekarte menu ['menjuː]
Spiegel mirror ['mɪrə]
Spiel game [geɪm] **Spiele spielen** playing games [pleɪɪŋ 'geɪmz]
spielen play [pleɪ]
Spielzeug toy [tɔɪ]
Spitze: an der Spitze (von) at the top (of) [tɒp]
Sport sport [spɔːt]; *(in der Schule)* PE (physical education) [piː 'iː], [fɪzɪkl edʒu'keɪʃn]
Sportart sport [spɔːt]
Sportgeschäft sports shop ['spɔːts ʃɒp]
sportlich sporty ['spɔːti]
Sportschuh trainer ['treɪnə]
Sprache language ['læŋgwɪdʒ]
sprechen speak [spiːk] **sprechen mit** speak to **sprechen über** talk about [tɔːk] **Wer spricht (da)?** *(am Telefon)* Who's speaking?
springen jump [dʒʌmp]
Stadion stadium ['steɪdiəm]
Stadt *(Großstadt)* city ['sɪti]; *(Kleinstadt)* town [taʊn]
Stadtmitte centre ['sentə]
Stadtplan map [mæp]
Stammbaum *(der Familie)* family tree
Star star [stɑː]
stark strong [strɒŋ]
staubsaugen hoover ['huːvə]
stehen stand [stænd] **stehen bleiben** stop [stɒp]
Stelle place [pleɪs]
stellen put [pʊt]
sterben die [daɪ]
Stiefbruder stepbrother ['stepbrʌðə]
Stiefel boot [buːt]
Stiefmutter stepmum ['stepmʌm]
Stiefschwester stepsister ['stepsɪstə]
Stiefvater stepdad ['stepdæd]
Stift pen [pen]
still calm [kɑːm]; quiet ['kwaɪət]
stimmen: das stimmt that's right
das stimmt nicht that's wrong
Was stimmt nicht mit ...? What's wrong with ...?
stimmen für jn. vote for sb. [vəʊt]
Stolz pride [praɪd]
stolz (auf) proud (of) [praʊd]
Strand beach [biːtʃ]
Straße *(in Ortschaften)* street [striːt]; *(Landstraße zwischen Orten / Straße in Orten)* road [rəʊd]
Strauch bush [bʊʃ]
Streichelzoo pets corner ['kɔːnə]
Streifenhörnchen chipmunk ['tʃɪpmʌŋk]
streng strict [strɪkt]
strikt strict [strɪkt]
Student/in student ['stjuːdnt]
Stuhl chair [tʃeə]
Stunde hour [aʊə]; lesson ['lesn]
Stundenplan timetable ['taɪmteɪbl]
suchen look for ['lʊk fə]
Süden, Süd- south [saʊθ]
südlich south [saʊθ]
Südosten, südöstlich south-east [saʊθ'iːst]
Südwesten, südwestlich south-west [saʊθ'west]
Summe total ['təʊtl]

Supermarkt supermarket ['su:pəmɑ:kɪt]
Suppe soup [su:p]
süß cute [kju:t]
Süßigkeiten sweets [swi:ts]
Szene scene [si:n]

T

Taekwondo tae kwon do [taɪ kwɒn 'dəʊ]
Tag day [deɪ]
Tag Rugby *(kontaktlose Rugby-Variante)* tag rugby ['tæg rʌgbi]
Tagesausflug day out [deɪ 'aʊt]
Tageszeitung newspaper ['nju:zpeɪpə]
Talkshow talk show ['tɔ:k ʃəʊ]
Tante aunt [ɑ:nt]
tanzen dance [dɑ:ns] *(das)* **Tanzen** dancing
Tänzer/in dancer ['dɑ:nsə]
Tasche bag [bæg]; *(an Kleidungsstücken)* pocket ['pɒkɪt]
Taschendieb/in pickpocket ['pɪkpɒkɪt]
Taschengeld pocket money ['pɒkɪt mʌni]
Taschenrechner calculator ['kælkjuleɪtə]
Tasse cup [kʌp] **eine Tasse Tee** a cup of tea
Tatsache fact [fækt]
Tauchen *(Sport)* diving ['daɪvɪŋ]
Taxi taxi ['tæksi]
Team team [ti:m]
Technik technology [tek'nɒlədʒi]
Technologie technology [tek'nɒlədʒi]
Tee tea [ti:]
Teenager teenager ['ti:neɪdʒə]; teen [ti:n]
Teenageralter: Kinder im Teenageralter teenage kids ['ti:neɪdʒ]
Teil part [pɑ:t]
teilnehmen: an etwas teilnehmen take part in sth. [teɪk 'pɑ:t]
Telefon telephone ['telɪfəʊn]; phone [fəʊn]
Telefonanruf (phone) call ['fəʊn kɔ:l]
Telefonnummer phone number ['fəʊn nʌmbə]
Temperatur temperature ['temprətʃə]
Tennis tennis ['tenɪs]
Test test [test]
teuer expensive [ɪk'spensɪv]
Theater theatre ['θɪətə] **Theater spielen** act [ækt]
Theaterstück play [pleɪ]
tief deep [di:p]
Tier animal ['ænɪml]
Tiger tiger ['taɪgə]
Tisch table ['teɪbl]
Tischtennis table tennis ['teɪbl tenɪs]
Toast(brot) toast [təʊst]
Tochter daughter ['dɔ:tə]
Toilette toilet ['tɔɪlət]
Toilettenpapier: Rolle Toilettenpapier toilet roll ['tɔɪlət rəʊl]
toll great [greɪt]
Tor gate [geɪt]
Tour tour [tʊə]
Tourist/in tourist ['tʊərɪst]
tragen *(Kleidung)* wear [weə]
Trampolin trampoline ['træmpəli:n]
Transporter *(Lieferwagen)* van [væn]
Transport(wesen) transport ['trænspɔ:t]
Traum dream [dri:m]
traurig sad [sæd]
treffen; sich treffen meet [mi:t]
treten kick [kɪk]
Trick trick [trɪk]
Trimester term [tɜ:m]
trinken drink [drɪŋk]
trocknen dry [draɪ]
Trommeln drums [drʌmz]
trotzdem still [stɪl]
Tschüs. Bye. [baɪ]; See you.
T-Shirt T-shirt ['ti:ʃɜ:t]
tun do [du:] *(etwas wohin)* **tun** put [pʊt] **(viel) zu tun haben** be busy ['bɪzi]
Tupfen *(Leopard)* spot [spɒt]
Tür door [dɔ:]
Türkei Turkey ['tɜ:ki]
Turm tower ['taʊə]
Turnen gymnastics [dʒɪm'næstɪks]

U

U-Bahn underground ['ʌndəgraʊnd]; *(in London)* the Tube [tju:b]
üben practise ['præktɪs]
über
1. about [ə'baʊt] **schreiben über** write about
2. *(quer über)* across [ə'krɒs]
überall(hin) everywhere ['evriweə]
überfliegen *(Text)* skim [skɪm]
überprüfen check [tʃek]
überqueren cross [krɒs]
überrascht surprised [sə'praɪzd]
Überraschung surprise [sə'praɪz]
Überwachungskamera(s) CCTV [si: si: ti: 'vi:]
Überwachungssystem CCTV [si: si: ti: 'vi:]
üblich usual ['ju:ʒʊəl]
Übung exercise ['eksəsaɪz] **Übungen machen** do exercises
Übungsheft exercise book ['eksəsaɪz bʊk]
Uhr clock [klɒk] **5 Uhr morgens/vormittags** 5 am [eɪ'em] **5 Uhr nachmittags/abends / 17 Uhr** 5 pm [pi:'em] **um 1 Uhr / um 13 Uhr** at one o'clock [ə'klɒk]
Uhrzeit time [taɪm]
um: um 1 Uhr at 1 o'clock
umschauen: sich umschauen (in) look around [ə'raʊnd]
umziehen *(an einen neuen Wohnort)* move house [mu:v] **umziehen nach** move to
uncool uncool [ʌn'ku:l]
und and [ænd], [ənd] **Und du?** What about you?
Unfall accident ['æksɪdənt]
unfreundlich unfriendly [ʌn'frendli]
ungefähr about [ə'baʊt]
ungesund unhealthy [ʌn'helθi]
Unglück *(Katastrophe)* disaster [dɪ'zɑ:stə]
unglücklich unhappy [ʌn'hæpi]
unheimlich *(beängstigend)* scary ['skeəri]
Uniform uniform ['ju:nɪfɔ:m]
uninteressant uninteresting [ʌn'ɪntrəstɪŋ]
Unit unit ['ju:nɪt]
unordentlich messy ['mesi]
Unrecht haben be wrong
unrichtig false [fɔ:ls]
uns us [ʌs], [əs] **uns selbst** ourselves [aʊə'selvz]
unser/e our ['aʊə], [ɑ:]
unsicher unsure [ʌn'ʃʊə]
Unsinn rubbish ['rʌbɪʃ]
unten: nach unten down [daʊn]
unter under ['ʌndə]
Unterführung subway ['sʌbweɪ]
Unterhaltung *(Gespräch)* chat [tʃæt]
unterrichten teach [ti:tʃ]
Unterrichtsstunde lesson ['lesn]
Unterschied difference ['dɪfrəns]
unterschiedlich different ['dɪfrənt]
unterstreichen underline [ʌndə'laɪn]
Urlaub holiday ['hɒlədeɪ]
USA (= Vereinigte Staaten von Amerika) US (= the United

States) [juː 'es], [junaɪtɪd 'steɪts]; USA [juː es 'eɪ]
usw. (und so weiter) etc. [et'setərə]

V

Vater father ['fɑːðə]
Vati dad [dæd]
verändern; sich verändern change [tʃeɪndʒ]
Veränderung change [tʃeɪndʒ]
Verbandkasten first-aid kit [fɜːst 'eɪd kɪt]
verbringen: Zeit verbringen (mit) spend time (on) [spend]
verdienen: : Geld verdienen make money
Verein club [klʌb]
Vereinbarung deal [diːl]
Vereinigte Staaten US (United States) [juː 'es], [junaɪtɪd 'steɪts]
Verfasser/in writer ['raɪtə]
vergessen forget [fə'get] **Ich habe meine Hausaufgaben vergessen.** I forgot my homework. [fə'gɒt] **nicht vergessen** remember [rɪ'membə]
Vergnügen: Viel Vergnügen! Enjoy yourself/yourselves. [ɪn'dʒɔɪ]
verhalten: sich verhalten behave [bɪ'heɪv]
Verkauf sale [seɪl]
verkaufen sell [sel]
Verkäufer/in salesperson, *(pl)* salespeople ['seɪlzpɜːsn], ['seɪlzpiːpl]
Verkehrsampel traffic lights *(pl)* ['træfɪk laɪts]
Verkehrsmittel transport ['trænspɔːt]
verkehrsreich busy ['bɪzi]
verlassen: jn. verlassen leave sb. [liːv]
verlieren lose [luːz]
vermissen miss [mɪs]
vermisst missing ['mɪsɪŋ]
verschieden different ['dɪfrənt]
verschlafen *(müde)* sleepy ['sliːpi]
verschwenden waste [weɪst]
Verschwendung waste [weɪst]
Verspätung: mein Bus hat Verspätung my bus is late [leɪt]
verstehen understand [ʌndə'stænd]
versuchen try [traɪ]
vertreten *(repräsentieren)* represent [reprɪ'zent]
verwundert amazed [ə'meɪzd]
Video video ['vɪdiəʊ]
Videochat video chat ['vɪdiəʊ tʃæt]
viel(e) a lot of [lɒt]; lots of ['lɒts əv] **viel** much [mʌtʃ] **So viel kostet das nicht.** It's cheaper than that. **Viele Grüße, ...** *(Briefschluss)* Best wishes ['wɪʃɪz] **Viel Glück!** Good luck. [lʌk] **Wie viele ...?** How many ...? ['mæni]
vielleicht maybe ['meɪbiː]; perhaps [pə'hæps]
vier four [fɔː]
Viertel *(Nachbarschaft)* neighbourhood ['neɪbəhʊd]
Vogel bird [bɜːd]
voll full [fʊl] **voller ...** full of ...
Volleyball volleyball ['vɒlibɔːl]
von
1. from [frɒm] **eine SMS von Mama** a text from mum **von Montag bis Freitag** from Monday to Friday
2. of [ɒv], [əv] **von den Ferien** of the holidays
3. by [baɪ] **(geschrieben) von Sam Holmes** by Sam Holmes

vor *(räumlich)* in front of [ɪn 'frʌnt əv]; *(zeitlich)* before [bɪ'fɔː] **vor zwei Jahren** two years ago [ə'gəʊ]
vorbei: am Geschäft vorbei past the shop [pɑːst]
Vorbild role model ['rəʊl mɒdl]
Vordergrund foreground ['fɔːgraʊnd]
Vorführung show [ʃəʊ]
vorige Woche last week [lɑːst 'wiːk]
Vorschrift rule [ruːl]
vorsichtig careful ['keəfl] **vorsichtig fahren** drive carefully ['keəfəli]
vorstellen: Stell dir nur vor! Wait for this. *(infml)* ['weɪt]
Vortrag talk [tɔːk] **einen Vortrag halten** give a talk
Vorwurf: jm. Vorwürfe machen (wegen) blame sb. (for) [bleɪm]
vorziehen: etwas einer Sache vorziehen prefer sth. to sth. [prɪ'fɜː]

W

wählen pick [pɪk]
wahr true [truː]
Wald wood [wʊd]
Wand wall [wɔːl]
Wanderer/Wanderin walker ['wɔːkə]
wandern walk [wɔːk] *(das)* **Wandern** hiking ['haɪkɪŋ]
wann? when? [wen] **Wann hast du Geburtstag?** When's your birthday?
warm warm [wɔːm]; hot [hɒt]
warten (auf) wait (for) [weɪt]
warum? why? [waɪ]
was? what? [wɒt] **Was ist mit dir?** What about you?
Wasser water ['wɔːtə]
Wasserkocher *(elektrisch)* kettle ['ketl]
Waveboarden street surfing ['striːt sɜːfɪŋ]
Website website ['websaɪt]
Wechsel change [tʃeɪndʒ]
wecken wake [weɪk]
Weg way [weɪ]; *(Feldweg)* track [træk] **jm. den Weg beschreiben** tell sb. the way **jn. nach dem Weg fragen** ask sb. the way
weg away [ə'weɪ]
Wegbeschreibung(en) directions *(pl)* [də'rekʃnz]
weggehen go away [gəʊ ə'weɪ]; leave [liːv]
wehtun: Ihr Bein tat weh. Her leg was sore. [sɔː] **Mir tut der Hals weh.** I have a sore throat. [sɔː 'θrəʊt]
Weide field [fiːld]
weil because [bɪ'kɒz]
weinen cry [kraɪ]
weiß white [waɪt]
weit far [fɑː] **100 Meter weit** for 100 metres
weitere more [mɔː]
welche(r, s)? which? [wɪtʃ]; what? [wɒt] **welcher See?** which lake? **Welche(s) sind ...?** What are ...?
Welt world [wɜːld]
wem? who? [huː]
wen? who? [huː]
weniger less [les] **immer weniger** less and less
wenn *(falls)* if [ɪf]; *(zeitlich)* when [wen] **erst, wenn sie 13 sind** not (...) until they're 13 [ən'tɪl]
wer? who? [huː]
Werbung advert ['ædvɜːt]
werden
1. **kalt werden** get cold
2. *(Zukunft)* will [wɪl] **das Wetter wird gut sein** the weather will be good **es wird nicht** it won't (= will not) [wəʊnt]
3. *(Plan, Vorhaben)* be going to ['gəʊɪŋ tə] **ich werde fragen** I'm going to ask

werfen throw [θrəʊ]
Werktag weekday ['wi:kdeɪ]
Westen, West- west [west]
westlich west [west]
Wettbewerb competition [kɒmpə'tɪʃn]
Wetter weather ['weðə] **Wie ist das Wetter?** What's the weather like?
Wettstreit *(im Rap)* battle ['bætl]
wichtig important [ɪm'pɔ:tənt]
wie like [laɪk] **genau wie Berry** just like Berry **so viel wie** as much as
wie? how? [haʊ] **Wie geht's?** How are you? **Wie ist das Wetter?** What's the weather like? **Wie nennt man ...?** What do you call ...? **Wie spät ist es?** What's the time?
wieder again [ə'gen]
Wiedersehen: Auf Wiedersehen. Goodbye. [gʊd'baɪ]
wild (lebend) wild [waɪld]
Willkommen in Plymouth! Welcome to Plymouth. ['welkʌm]
Wind wind [wɪnd]
windig windy ['wɪndi]
winken wave [weɪv]
Winter winter ['wɪntə]
wir we [wi:] **wir selbst** ourselves [aʊə'selvz]
wirklich real [rɪəl] **wirklich nett** really nice ['rɪəli]
Wirklichkeit reality [ri'æləti]
wissen know [nəʊ]
Witz joke [dʒəʊk]
Witze machen joke [dʒəʊk] **Du machst wohl Witze! / Spitzenwitz!** You're joking!
WLAN *(kabellose Datenübertragung)* Wi-fi ['waɪ faɪ]
Woche week [wi:k] **eine Woche / sechs Wochen Urlaub** a week's/six weeks' holiday
Wochenende weekend [wi:k'end]
Wochentag weekday ['wi:kdeɪ]
wo(hin)? where? [weə]
wohltätige Organisation charity ['tʃærəti]
Wohnblock block of flats [blɒk əv 'flæts]
wohnen live [lɪv]
Wohnung flat [flæt]
Wohnzimmer living room ['lɪvɪŋ ru:m]
Wolke cloud [klaʊd]
wolkig cloudy ['klaʊdi]
wollen want [wɒnt] **kaufen wollen** want to buy
Wort word [wɜ:d]
Wörterbuch dictionary ['dɪkʃənri]
Wörterverzeichnis: alphabetisches Wörterverzeichnis dictionary ['dɪkʃənri]
Wortnetz network ['netwɜ:k]
wunderschön beautiful ['bju:tɪfl]
Wurst sausage ['sɒsɪdʒ]
Würstchen sausage ['sɒsɪdʒ]
wütend angry ['æŋgri]

Z

zahlen pay [peɪ]
zehn ten [ten]
Zeichen sign [saɪn]
Zeichentrickfilm cartoon [kɑ:'tu:n]
zeigen show [ʃəʊ]
Zeile line [laɪn]
Zeit time [taɪm] **Hast du um ein Uhr Zeit?** Are you free at one o'clock? [fri:]
Zeitschrift magazine [mægə'zi:n]
Zeitung newspaper ['nju:zpeɪpə]; paper ['peɪpə] **Zeitungen austragen** do a paper round
Zelt tent [tent]
Zentrum centre ['sentə]
zerbrechen break [breɪk]
zerbrochen broken ['brəʊkən]
Zeug *(Kram)* stuff [stʌf] **dummes Zeug** *(Unsinn)* rubbish ['rʌbɪʃ]
ziehen nach *(umziehen)* move to [mu:v]
Zimmer room [ru:m] **Zimmer mit Frühstück** bed and breakfast (B&B)
Zirkus circus ['sɜ:kəs]
Zoo zoo [zu:]
zu
1. *(örtlich)* to [tu], [tə] **zu Hause** at home **bei Ellie zu Hause** at Ellie's house **Er legt sie zu den anderen Dingen.** He puts it with the other things. **zum Beispiel** for example
2. zu klein too small **zu spät** late [leɪt]
3. Zeit zu essen time to eat
4. *(geschlossen)* closed [kləʊzd] **zu sein** be closed
Zucker sugar ['ʃʊgə]
zuerst first [fɜ:st]
Zug train [treɪn]
zugreifen: Greift zu! *(z.B. beim Essen)* Help yourselves.
Zuhause home [həʊm]
zuhören listen ['lɪsn]
Zuhörer/in listener ['lɪsənə]
Zukunft future ['fju:tʃə]
zumachen close [kləʊz]
zurück back [bæk]
zurücklassen leave [li:v]
zusammen together [tə'geðə] **Schön, wieder zusammenzusein.** Nice to be together again.
zusammenzucken *(vor Schreck)* jump [dʒʌmp]
zustimmen agree with [ə'gri:]
zwei two [tu:]
Zweibettzimmer twin room [twɪn 'ru:m]
zweimal twice [twaɪs]
zweite(r, s) second ['sekənd]
zwischen between [bɪ'twi:n]
zwölf twelve [twelv]

First names (Vornamen)
Abigail ['æbɪgeɪl]
Alec ['ælɪk]
Alex ['ælɪks]
Alexander ['ælɪkzɑːndə]
Alfie ['ælfi]
Ali ['ɑːli]
Alice ['ælɪs]
Amy ['eɪmi]
Andy ['ændi]
Angelo ['ændʒələʊ]
Arif ['ɑːrɪf]
Becky ['beki]
Burak ['bjʊrək]
Cal [kæl]
Ciara ['kɪərə]
Dan [dæn]
Dara ['dɑːrə]
Darren ['dærən]
Dave [deɪv]
Duncan ['dʌŋkən]
Edward ['edwəd]
Evie ['iːvi]
Habib [ha'biːb]
Hamish ['heɪmɪʃ]
Hannah ['hænə]
Jamie ['dʒeɪmi]
John ['dʒɒn]
Josh ['dʒɒʃ]
Jodie ['dʒəʊdi]
Jordan ['dʒɔːdn]
Julia ['dʒuːliə]
Kara ['kɑːrə]
Karan [kɑː'ræn]
Kate [keɪt]
Liam ['liːəm]
Livvy ['lɪvi]
Luigi [lu'iːdʒi]
Luke [luːk]
Marcus ['mɑːkəs]
Marty ['mɑːti]
Mehdy ['medi]
Molly ['mɒli]
Natasha [nə'tæʃə]
Noah ['nəʊə]
Pinar ['pɪnə]
Rob [rɒb]
Robert [rɒbət]
Roger ['rɒdʒə]
Ruby ['ruːbi]
Sammy ['sæmi]
Sandra ['sɑːndrə]
Sarah ['seərə]
Serena [sə'riːnə]
Simon ['saɪmən]
Talia ['tɑːliə]
Tally ['tæli]
Tarik [tɑːrɪk]
Tasha ['tæʃə]

Family names / Surnames (Familiennamen)
Atkinson ['ætkɪnsən]
Blake [bleɪk]
Bantam ['bæntəm]
Bell [bel]
Burns [bɜːnz]
Butler ['bʌtlə]
Chung [tʃʌŋ]
Dolby ['dɒlbi]
Fitzwarren [fɪts'wɒrən]
Grant [grɑːnt]
Hall [ɔːl]
Harper ['hɑːpə]
Henson ['hensn]
Johnson ['dʒɒnsn]
Jonas ['dʒəʊnəs]
Jones [dʒəʊns]
Keating ['kiːtɪŋ]
Macdonald [mək'dɒnəld]
Malone [mə'ləʊn]
O'Brien [əʊ'braɪən]
O'Connor [əʊ'kɒnə]
Smith [smɪθ]
Taylor ['teɪlə]
Webster ['webstə]
Whittington ['wɪtɪŋtən]

Place names (Ortsnamen)
Aberdeen [æbə'diːn]
Albert Dock [ælbət 'dɒk]
Battersea Park [bætəsi 'pɑːk]
Baker Street ['beɪkə striːt]
Brick Tower [brɪk 'taʊə]
Britannia Vaults [brɪ'tænjə 'vɔːlts]
Buckingham Palace [bʌkɪŋəm 'pæləs]
Cairngorms [keən'gɔːmz]
Cam River [kæm 'rɪvə]
Camden Market [kæmdən 'mɑːkɪt]
Catbrook ['kætbrʊk]
the Cavern Club ['kævn]
Chelsea ['tʃelsi]
Chipping Campden [tʃɪpɪŋ 'kæmdən]
Clava Cairns [klɑːvə 'keənz]
the Cotswolds ['kɒtswəʊldz]
Covent Garden [kɒvənt 'gɑːdn]
Culloden [kə'lɒdn]
Dores [dɔːz]
Dublin ['dʌblɪn]
Dyers Lane [daɪəz 'leɪn]
Edinburgh ['edɪnbərə]
Fulham Broadway [fʊləm 'brɔːdweɪ]
Glasgow ['glɑːzgəʊ]
Glenfinnan [glen'fɪnən]
Grafton Street ['grɑːftən striːt]
Hammersmith ['hæməsmɪθ]
Ha'penny Bridge [heɪpəni 'brɪdʒ]
Heathrow Airport [hiːθrəʊ 'eəpɔːt]
Hogwarts ['hɒgwɔːts]
Hyde Park [haɪd 'pɑːk]
Inverness [ɪnvə'nes]
Kingcomb Lane [kɪŋkəʊm 'leɪn]
Knightsbridge ['naɪtsbrɪdʒ]
Laggan ['lægən]
Leadenhall ['lednhɔːl]
Leaky Cauldron [liːki 'kɔːldrən]
Leeds [liːdz]
Liverpool ['lɪvəpuːl]
Loch Ness [lɒx 'nes]
Mallaig ['mæleɪg]
Manchester ['mæntʃɪstə]
Mersey ['mɜːzi]
Mickleton ['mɪkltən]
the Millennium Bridge [mɪ'leniəm]
Moore Street ['mʊə striːt]
O'Connell Street [əʊ'kɒnl striːt]
Odeon ['əʊdiən]
Oxford Street ['ɒksfəd striːt]
the River Liffey ['lɪfi]
the River Tay [teɪ]
Slains Castle [sleɪnz 'kɑːsl]
Stamford Bridge [stæmfəd 'brɪdʒ]
Stephen's Green [stiːvnz 'griːn]
St James's Park [sənt dʒeɪmzɪz 'pɑːk]
St Paul's Cathedral [sənt pɔːlz kə'θiːdrəl]
the Strand [strænd]
Stratford-upon-Avon [strætfəd əpɒn 'eɪvn]
Temple Bar [templ 'bɑː]
the Thames [temz]
Toxteth ['tɒkstəθ]
Trafalgar Square [trəfælgə 'skweə]
Waterloo Station [wɔːtəluː 'steɪʃn]
Wembley ['wembli]
Westminster ['westmɪnstə]
Wimbledon ['wɪmbldən]
Woodlands ['wʊdləndz]

Other names (Andere Namen)
Arsenal ['ɑːsnəl]
Arthur Conan Doyle ['ɑːθə 'kɒnən dɔɪl]
The Beatles ['biːtlz]
Billy Eliot [bɪli 'eliət]
Braveheart ['breɪvhɑːt]
Cavern Club ['kævən klʌb]
George Harrison [dʒɔːdʒ 'hærɪsən]
Harrods ['hærədz]
the Jacobite Steam Train [dʒækəbaɪt 'stiːm treɪn]
the Jeanie Johnston [dʒiːni 'dʒɒnstən]
John Lennon [dʒɒn 'lenən]
Kenny Dalglish [keni dæl'gliːʃ]
Leo Burdock's [liːəʊ 'bɜːdɒks]
Lochside B&B ['lɒxsaɪd biːənd'biː]
MacBean's [mək'biːnz]
Madame Tussaud's [mə'dɑːm tu'səʊdz]
Maggie's Lodge [mægiz 'lɒdʒ]
Milo ['maɪləʊ]
Paul McCartney [pɔːl mək'kɑːtni]
Queen Elizabeth II [kwiːn i'lɪzəbəθ ðə 'sekənd]
Ringo Star [rɪŋgəʊ 'stɑːr]
Sean Connery [ʃɔːn 'kɒnəri]
Shamrock Rovers [ʃæmrɒk 'rəʊvəz]
Shannon Rovers [ʃænən 'rəʊvəz]
the Titanic [taɪ'tænɪk]
Urquhart Castle [ɜːkət 'kɑːsl]
Wally ['wɒli]

Illustrationen

Beehive Illustration, Cirencester (**Pete Smith**: S. 71; S. 73; S. 74; S. 75; S. 88); **Roland Beier**, Berlin (Umschlaginnenseite 2 Ireland castle icon (M)); **Carlos Borrell**, Berlin (Umschlagseite 2 British Isles (M); **Jeongsook Lee**, Heidelberg (Umschlagseite 2 icons außer Irleand castle (M); S. 124; S. 135; S. 149; S. 150; S. 151; S. 153; S. 154; S. 155; S. 156; S. 157 no parking, unten; S. 159; S. 160; S. 162; S. 164 two girls; S. 165); **David Norman**, Meerbusch (S. 31; S. 32; S. 34; S. 35; S. 40; S. 44; S. 50 (u. 103); S. 54; S. 55; S. 58 unten; S. 60; S. 82 oben; S. 100 unten); **Dorina Tessmann**, Berlin (S. 9; S. 12 Bild G; S. 1415; S. 20 Bild A-C; S. 28; S. 29; S. 30; S. 36; S. 41 (u. 102); S. 42 (u. 90); S. 53 table; S. 58 oben; S. 61 (u. 109); S. 63; S. 81 (u. 114); S. 82 Bild 1–8 (u. 115); S. 92; S. 93; S. 102; S. 114; S. 126; S. 129; S. 131; S. 133; S. 134; S. 136; S. 137)

Titelbild

Shutterstock.com/Bernhard Richter

Bildquellen

Susan Abbey & Frank Donoghue, Nenagh (S. 29 farm (M)); **Alamy**, Abingdon (S. 4 Mitte re.: Cultura Creative (RF)/Monty Rakusen; S. 6 unten li.: Incamerastock/ICP-UK; S. 8 Bild 5: Mattia Bicchi; S. 11 unten: Greg Balfour Evans; S. 12 Bild A: Jack Sullivan. "Billy Elliot the Musical logo courtesy of Billy London Limited"; S. 12 Bild C: Stuart Kelly. Used by courtesy of Transport of London and National Rail, Bild D: Travelshots. com/Peter Phipp; S. 13 unten re.: Alex Segre; S. 17 Bild B: London Entertainment. The image shown depicts wax figures created and owned by Madame Tussauds; S. 19 oben (M) (u. 39 u. 59 u. 79): Steve Cavlier; S. 25 oben: Hugh Threlfall; S. 28 unten: Graham Toney; S. 29 oben: PetStockBoys/The Art Of Animals.co.uk, girl holding lamb (M): Cultura Creative (RF)/ Monty Rakusen; S. 32 girl holding lamb (M) (u. 99): Cultura Creative (RF)/Monty Rakusen, river (u. 99): Robert Read Thames Portfolio; S. 43 oben: Peter Titmuss; S. 48 Bild C: Howard Harrison; S. 49 Bild H oben: Paul Thompson Images/ Chris Ballentine; S. 66 oben: Image Source7/Gary John Norman; S. 69 Bild F: Elizabeth Leyden, Bild G: newsphoto; S. 72 RockNess: Ross Gilmore, Lochside B&B: Senarb Commercial; S. 78 Bild 2 sports: Sam Strickler; S. 80 oben: PhotoAlto/James Hardy; S. 84 Bild A: South West Images Scotland; S. 85 oben li.: Nifro UK, re.: Simon Price; S. 86 Mitte: Radharc/Images/JoeFox; S. 87 Mitte li.: Image Source Plus/IS773; S. 88: Radharc Images/JoeFoxDublin; S. 89 Grafton Street: B.O'Kane, O'Connell Street: plpix, The Jeanie Johnston: Ruth Grimes, Moore Street: Barry Mason, Temple Bar: Radharc Images/JoeFoxDublin, Molly Malone: World Pictures, Stephen's Green: Barry Mason, The Ha'penny Bridge: incamerastock, Dublin Bay: Adrian Muttitt; S. 107 unten li.: PhotoAlto/Laurence Mouton; S. 110 Bild G: Oote Boe Ph; S. 118 oben u. unten: theatrepix, Mitte: UpperCutImages/Image Studios, S. 119 oben li. u. Mitte: theatrepix; S. 146 fast food stand: Peter Erik Forsberg/ Lifestyle; S. 147 tractor (M): Juice Images, unten: Alvey & Towers Picture Library); **avenue images**, Hamburg (S. 28 Mitte: agefotostock/Olaf Protze); **Chelsea Football Club** (S. 12 Bild B logo, football player. Used by permission of Chelsea Football Club); **Corbis**, Düsseldorf (S. 24 oben li.: Simon Marcus, unten: Maurizio Rellini/Grand Tour/Grand Tour; S. 49 Bild G: Terra/Paul Thompson; S. 56: Paul Cunningham; S. 64 oben li.: Bettmann; S. 121 unten: The Mariners' Museum); **Cornelsen Schulverlage** (S. 4 oben re.; S. 10 Sam, Ruby, Tally; S. 11 oben; S. 19 Bild A-F; S. 29 crossroads, church, market, high street, gate, wood, pub, hill, farm; S. 30 oben re.; S. 37 oben; S. 39 scene 1–6; S. 59 a competition Bild A-D, who said what? Bild A-C; S. 79 Bild A-D); **Fotolia.de** (S. 52 unten Mrs Fox (M): Farina3000; S. 117 unten re.: OSCAR; S. 146 baker's: contrastwerkstatt); **Getty Images**, München (S. 8 Bild 1: AWL Images/Julian Love; S. 17 Bild C: Getty Images Entertainment/Fred Duval. The image shown depicts wax figures created and owned by Madame Tussauds; S. 77 unten: Taxi/Photo and Co); **Glow Images**, München (S. 24 oben Mitte, re.; S. 123 oben re.; S. 128 oben re.: Image Source); **International Slavery Museum** (S. 49 Bild E: © Redman Design); **Picture Alliance**, Frankfurt/Main (S. 95: EMPICS Sport; S. 113 re.: Costa/Leemage); **iStockphoto.com** (S. 4 Mitte li. (u. 28): Matthew Dixon; S. 6 unten re.: lubilub; S. 21 Bild A, B: hohl; S. 48 Bild B: hmproudlove; S. 53 oben li.: mbrowe; S. 66 unten: mauro grigollo; S. 70 unten: tbradford; S. 78 Bild 2 Nessie: ARTPUPPY; S. 83 unten: Claudiad; S. 84 Bild E mountain biking: pale62; S. 86 oben: lubilub; S. 97: ozgurdonmaz; S. 106: wdstock; S. 110 Bild A: Creativeye99, Bild C: atiatiati, Bild D: lucentius; S. 119 unten: Mimadeo; S. 120 unten: theatrepix; S. 123 kilt: jeangill; S. 137 tourists: erlucho; S. 138: ARTPUPPY; S. 139: AdobeDweller; S. 141: mammothis; S. 142: Pickledjo; S. 143 oben: IgorZakowski; S. 144: Peter Bajohr; S. 145 unten: Shannon Toth; S. 146 tram station: onfilm, chemist's: sjlocke, newsagent's: Giorgio Fochesato, ice rink: CEFutcher, skate park: Brad Ralph; S. 157 oben: bobash); **Liverpool One** (S. 4 unten li u. S. 91 li.: Used by courtesy of Liverpool One); **Madame Tussauds**, London (S. 17 Bild D. The image shown depicts wax figures created and owned by Madame Tussauds); **Mauritius**, Mittenwald (S. 146 youth centre: Maskot); **Mersey Ferries** (S. 64 oben re.: Used by courtesy of Mersey Ferries); **National Museums Liverpool** (S. 48 Bild A u. S. 91 re.: Used by permission); **O2 Arena London** (S. 12 Bild E: used by courtesy of The O2); **Picture Alliance**, Frankfurt/Main (S. 8 Bild 3: Jan Haas; S. 9 Bild 7: dpa; S. 21 Bild D: Robert Haas; S. 49 Bild H unten: empics; S. 69 Bild E: Adina Tovy/Robert Harding World Imagery, S. 77 oben: APA/picturedesk.com/Karl Schöndorfer; S. 84 Bild D: Arco Images/F.Scholz; S. 95: EMPICS Sport; S. 121 oben li.: landov, oben Mitte: Illustrated London News Ltd/Mary Evans Picture Library; S. 123 unten: United Archives/TopFoto); **Thomas Schulz**, Teupitz (S. 13 oben girl (M), step 2–3; S. 23 unten; 33 unten; S. 41 unten; S. 98; S. 105); **Transport for London** (S. 136 tube map © Transport for London – map used by permission of Pulse Creative Limited); **Shutterstock.com** (S. 4 oben li.(u. 8 Bild 3): S. Borisov, unten re.: East; S. 6 oben li.: Rob van Esch, oben re. (u. 70): Jorg Hackemann; S. 8 Bild 2: Mypokcik/London Uderground Roundel ® Transport for London. Reproduced by kind permission of Transport for London; S. 9 Bild 6: QQ7; S. 12 Bild F: pcruciatti; S. 13 oben London Eye (M): cycreation, unten li.: Ovchynnikov Oleksii; S. 17 Bild A: Jaguar PS. The image shown depicts wax figures created and owned by Madame Tussauds; S. 18 li. (u. 96): Horst Petzold, re. (u. 96): SergeBertasiusPhotography; S. 21 Bild C: Joerg Beuge; S. 22: Lance Bellers; S. 23 Bild A: Kamira, Bild B: Bikeworldtravel, Bild C: Paul Cowan; S. 25 unten unhappy emoticon (u. 45 u. 65 u. 85): Dawn Hudson, happy emoticon (u. 45 u. 65 u. 85): In-Finity; S. 26 oben: HENX, unten: CREATISTA; S. 27 Bild 2: Mark William Richardson, unten footsteps: Helga Chirk; S. 28/29 Hintergrund: carstests; S. 29 block of flats: David Hughes; S. 30 oben li.: Yuri Arcurs, dog: Mat Hayward, van: Sally Wallis; S. 33 oben: auremar, Mitte (M): Dobroslawa Szulc; S. 37 unten: Yuri Arcurs; S. 38 Bild A: Linn Currie, Bild C (u. 43): Nuno Andre; S. 41 oben: Yanik Chauvin; S. 46 unten li.: Vera F, unten re.: Fotokostic; S. 47 oben icons: Ziven, unten: egd; S. 48/49 skyline: YurkaImmortal; S. 50 Ben: East; S. 51 Bild A: Nattika, Bild B: Nata-Lia, Bild C: Oleksiy Mark, Bild D: Dudarev Mikhail, Bild E: margouillat photo, Bild F: Madlen, Bild G: Ian 2010, Bild H: Kesu; S. 52 oben u. unten Ben (M) : East, oben u. unten classroom (M): Tanchic; S. 61 Ben (u. 109): East; S. 62 Bild 1: gualtiero boffi, Bild 2–6, 8: Sarunyu_foto, Bild 7: Carsten Reisinger; S. 65 Kelly: Pressmaster, Jordan: Nolte Lourens, Evie: Alan Bailey; S. 68/69 Hintergrund tartan: Brandon Bourdages; S. 68 Welcome to Scotland button thistle (M): armvector, Scotland map: AndOcean, Bild A: Rob van Esch, Bild B: Grant Glendinning, Bild C: Zdenek Krchak, monster sign: Jeff Morin, Bild D: Pinon Road; S. 69 Bild H clouds (M): Archipoch, flag of Wales, Scotland, England (M): Maxx-Studio; S. 70 Bild A: Stuart Monk, Bild B: Mat Hayward, Bild

C: Tracy Whiteside, Bild D: Jorg Hackemann, Dores sign: Ryan Carter; S. 71: Gail Johnson; S. 72 Urquhart Castle: Lian Deng, twin room: hxdbzxy, monster: Ralf Juergen Kraft; S. 77 drums: 3drenderings, guitar and bass guitar: tele52, piano: zzveillust; S. 78 Bild 1: Serg Zastavkin, Bild 2 rooms: Nikolay Dimitrov – ecobo; S. 80 Bild A: CandyBox Images, Bild B: kurhan, Bild C: runzelkorn, Bild D: krsmanovic, Bild E: terekhov igor, Bild F: Africa Studio; S. 83 oben: iralu; S. 84 Bild B quad: Adrian Chinery, canyoning: Paulo Resende, white-water rafting: bokononist, Bild C: Heartland, Bild E: pale62; S. 86 unten: alexmillos; S. 87 oben re.: Ulga, unten: Eskymaks; S. 100 oben: Toonstyle.com; S. 107 happy smiley, unhappy smiley: Memo Angeles, unten Mitte: Alexandra Lande, unten re.: oliveromg; S. 110 Bild B: chungking, Bild E: grekoff, Bild F: Africa Studio, Bild H: arka38; S. 111 LHF Graphics; S. 112 Bild 1: Markus Mainka, Bild 2: Pincasso, Bild 3: Yuri Arcurs, Bild 4: Diego Cervo, Bild 5: MANDY GODBEHEAR, Bild 6: Andrey Shadrin; S. 116–117 Hintergrund London icons: Iveta Angelova; S. 116 oben li.: Philip Lange, oben Mitte: rSnapshotPhotos, oben re.: Bikeworldtravel, unten li.: Rob Wilson, unten re.: Sverlova Mariya; S. 117 oben re.: 1000 Words, Mitte hat: Zinchuk_ Oksana, unten li.: myfavoritescene; S. 120 oben: Luba V Nel; S. 121 Hintergrund iceberg: XYZ; S. 122 oben: leigh, oil rig: Yvan, Mitte re.: Maaster, unten: Maxx-Studio; S. 123 oben li.: Nathan Holland, haggis: Norman Pogson, bagpipes: Dieter H; S. 124: Jacek Chabraszewski; S. 125 screwdriver: Snap2Art, screws, nails: Z-art, Mitte typical: Blend Images, Mitte Hotelzimmer: Ermolaev Alexander, unten: gpointstudio; S. 127: M.Stasy; S. 128 oben li.: graphixmania, unten: Yayayoyo; S. 130 li.: Shaiith, re. shinty ball (M): The Cute Design Studio, shinty stick (M): Tribalium; S. 131: Javier Brosch; S. 137 radio: Nenov Brothers Images, unten sign (M): Vitezslav Valka; S. 143 unten: Igor Zakowski; S. 145 oben: Jonathan Cooke; S. 146 garage: Dmitry Kalinovsky, petrol station: Avesun, butcher's: Arturo Limon, bikeriderlondon, inline skate track: Alexey Fursov, tennis court: dotshock, children's playground: Againstar; S. 147 countryside (M): Kevin Eaves, horses (M): Eric Isselee; S. 148 egg: Karramba Production, chocolate spread: O.Bellini, cereals: mikute, jam: Rafa Irusta, honey: Neirfy, ham: Viktor1, gherkins: Andrey Starostin, trail mix: Andre Bonn, rice: showice, pasta: Aaron Amat; S. 151 underground: Patrik Mezirka./London Uderground Roundel ® Transport for London. Reproduced by kind permission of Transport for London, 151 bell li.: Andy.M, bell re.: Verdateo; S. 152: Linda Bucklin; S. 154 oben: Tiplyashin Anatoly, woman: redstone; S. 156: Yeko Photo Studio; S. 158 oben: Federico Rostagno, Mitte: Aerostato, unten: Sergieiev; S. 160 Gandolfo Cannatella; S. 161 vita khorzhevska; S. 162 oben: MagSpace, unten: Brykaylo Yuriy; S. 163 oben li.: Robert Adrian Hillman, oben re.: Elnur, unten: Matthew Cole; S. 164 oben street sign: Thorsten Rust); **ullstein bild**, Berlin (S. 49 Bild F: imagebroker.net/Stephan Goerlich; S. 113 li.: The Granger Collection; S. 117 oben li.: EUROLUFTBILD.DE; S. 121 oben re.: Imagestate Collection/ National Geographic Society); **vario images**, Bonn (S. 51 Ben's father)

Liedquelle

Pride. Text, OT: MacDonald, Amy Elizabeth. Copyright: Warner Chappell Music Ltd, Neue Welt Musikverlag GmbH, Hamburg.

IRREGULAR VERBS

infinitive	simple past	past participle	
be	**was/were**	**been**	sein
begin	**began**	**begun**	beginnen, anfangen
break	**broke**	**broken**	brechen, zerbrechen
bring	**brought**	**brought**	bringen, mitbringen
buy	**bought**	**bought**	kaufen
catch	**caught**	**caught**	fangen, erwischen
come	**came**	**come**	kommen
cost	**cost**	**cost**	kosten
cut	**cut**	**cut**	schneiden; *(Rasen)* mähen
do	**did**	**done** [ʌ]	tun, machen
drink	**drank**	**drunk**	trinken
drive [aɪ]	**drove**	**driven** [ɪ]	*(mit dem Auto)* fahren; (an)treiben
eat	**ate** [et, eɪt]	**eaten**	essen
fall	**fell**	**fallen**	fallen, hinfallen
feel	**felt**	**felt**	fühlen; sich fühlen
fight	**fought**	**fought**	kämpfen
find	**found**	**found**	finden
fly	**flew**	**flown**	fliegen
forget	**forgot**	**forgotten**	vergessen
get	**got**	**got**	bekommen; holen, werden; (hin)kommen
give	**gave**	**given**	geben
go	**went**	**gone** [ɒ]	gehen
have	**had**	**had**	haben
hear [ɪə]	**heard** [ɜː]	**heard** [ɜː]	hören
hurt	**hurt**	**hurt**	verletzen; wehtun
keep	**kept**	**kept**	behalten
know [nəʊ]	**knew** [njuː]	**known** [nəʊn]	wissen; kennen
leave	**left**	**left**	abfahren; (weg)gehen; zurücklassen
lose [uː]	**lost** [ɒ]	**lost** [ɒ]	verlieren
make	**made**	**made**	machen
mean [iː]	**meant** [e]	**meant** [e]	bedeuten; meinen, sagen wollen
meet	**met**	**met**	treffen; sich treffen; kennenlernen
pay	**paid**	**paid**	bezahlen
put	**put**	**put**	*(etwas wohin)* tun, legen, stellen
read [iː]	**read** [e]	**read** [e]	lesen
ride [aɪ]	**rode**	**ridden** [ɪ]	reiten; *(Rad)* fahren
ring	**rang**	**rung**	läuten, klingeln; anrufen
run	**ran**	**run**	rennen, laufen
say [eɪ]	**said** [e]	**said** [e]	sagen
see	**saw**	**seen**	sehen
sell	**sold**	**sold**	verkaufen
send	**sent**	**sent**	schicken, senden
sing	**sang**	**sung**	singen
sit	**sat**	**sat**	sitzen
sleep	**slept**	**slept**	schlafen
speak	**spoke**	**spoken**	sprechen
spend	**spent**	**spent**	ausgeben *(Geld)*; verbringen *(Zeit)*
stand	**stood**	**stood**	stehen; sich (hin)stellen
take	**took**	**taken**	nehmen; mitnehmen; dauern, *(Zeit)* brauchen
teach	**taught**	**taught**	unterrichten, lehren
tell	**told**	**told**	erzählen, berichten
think	**thought**	**thought**	denken
throw	**threw**	**thrown**	werfen
understand	**understood**	**understood**	verstehen
wear [eə]	**wore** [ɔː]	**worn** [ɔː]	tragen, anhaben *(Kleidung)*
win	**won** [ʌ]	**won** [ʌ]	gewinnen
write	**wrote**	**written**	schreiben